PSYCHOLOGY
OF WOMEN

PSYCHOLOGY OF WOMEN

A STUDY OF BIO-CULTURAL CONFLICTS

JUDITH M. BARDWICK

HARPER & ROW, PUBLISHERS
New York   Evanston
San Francisco   London

PSYCHOLOGY OF WOMEN:
A Study of Bio-Cultural Conflicts

To John, Jan, and Ed—with many thanks.

CONTENTS

Introduction, 1

1 Psychoanalytic Theory, 5
2 The Effect of Body States on the Psyche, 21
3 Psychology and the Sexual Body, 47
4 Psychosomatic Dysfunctions of the Female Reproductive System, 70
5 Differences Between Male and Female Brains, 83
6 Sex Differences in Personality and Learning Ability, 99
7 Dependence, Passivity, and Aggression, 114
8 Identification, 135
9 The Ego and Self-Esteem, 154
10 The Motive to Achieve, 167
11 Changes in Motives and Roles During Different Stages in Life, 188
12 A Summing Up and Some Concluding Remarks, 206

References, 219
Index, 239

INTRODUCTION

Almost every woman alive is aware that she is part of some huge problem. Almost every magazine published has devoted large amounts of space to it. Alternate solutions, offered with great passion, range from salvation in the marketplace to fulfillment in the supermarket. Yet hardly a sound is heard from the professional literature of psychologists; here the problem of the psychology of women has never become a widespread issue.

Years ago, when I was a graduate student in psychology and the mother of two tiny children, I found myself finished with courses and obliged to write a major review of the literature as a preliminary to the doctoral dissertation. Unfortunately, I found myself without a topic—at least without a topic to which I could devote the next two years. It also happened about this time that my college friends, now married and the mothers of toddlers, were sending me letters extolling my uniqueness in going back to school. I wrote back (at length) that there was nothing to it, that the world was full of women doing the same thing (in the microcosm of the university that seemed true), and that if they wanted to, they could do at least as much as I.

Still without a topic, with deadlines approaching, I decided to do a paper on role conflict in women—stimulated mostly, I think, by the unhappy letters from my friends. My interest was not in role conflict per se but in the personality characteristics of women and their probable success in the marketplace, in whether there really were any generalized personality differences between men and women, and in the origins of any differences.

When I began to read I found that the most important theorists were psychoanalytic or neoanalytic. I also found that I could not believe what I was reading. To a woman who had spent most of the preceding three years with an obstetrician, and who was spending most of a 28-hour day nurturing two small children, the idea that pregnancy and infant-nurturance were motivated largely by an unresolved search for male genitals was nonsense beyond belief. That this particular view was widely promulgated, repeated, and enlarged bordered on professional lunacy. It seemed to me then, and still does, that psychological sex differences might have as *one* origin differences in the reproductive systems. I suggest that it is not the absence of male genitals but the presence of a female reproductive system that might be important. (Can you believe that this is a professionally controversial statement?)

This was the mainspring for my interest in the subject of women, and I started to teach a graduate seminar called "The Psychology of Women." In that class we talked about, criticized, and tried to integrate very disparate experiments and theoretical articles. Over the years we gradually came to see that the personality qualities of passivity, dependence, and, most of all, lack of self-esteem were the variables that repeatedly differentiated women from men. This, then, is also a book about self-esteem and the lack of it— and the resultant effects on behavior.

Most of the voices on this subject are strident, raised loudly in order to right wrongs or justify custom. I do not wish to shout, nor am I offering advice, at least not directly. My purpose in this book is to examine the information that is now available to see whether we can understand the reasons for motives, behaviors, and conflicts. We are limited by the data available, and today's accepted information is often proved false tomorrow. And while I try to review much of the data, some selection unavoidably occurs. It is inevitable that this book will be perceived as controversial because many people will search in it for a justification of their views. With understanding, but without apology, I anticipate that many will be disappointed.

Data suggest that constitutional differences between male and female infants lead to their perceiving and experiencing the world around them differently—but this does not mean, as Freud's "anatomy-is-destiny" partisans suppose, that anatomical differences simplistically result in unalterable personality differences. It is also true that even children become aware of the values and mores of the culture and internalize those values; they mold their behaviors and learn to evaluate themselves in terms of their culture —but this does not mean, as the partisans of cultural determinism suppose, that biological differences have little effect. I think that differences between men and women originate interactively: in genetic temperamental differences, in differences in the adult reproductive system, and in sex-linked values specific to each culture. What are the bases for differences between the sexes, and how do they develop? From infant differences in gross activity levels and sensitivity to stimuli (temperament), from parental responses which are sex-linked, from pressures to identify with appropriate models of the same sex, from the ramifications of the physiology of the mature reproductive system, from an internalized concept of masculine and feminine that is a source of self-evaluation. This position is more complicated than either the classically psychoanalytic view or the culturally oriented view—but it is, perhaps, closer to the truth.

Important difficulties confront us as soon as we set out to explore such a complicated content as the psychology of women. We will be emphasizing sex differences, but we must keep in mind that in many ways men and women are alike. Ignoring similarities results in a somewhat distorted perspective—talking about differences as though they are absolute makes one forget that there is always a distribution of traits. We are also oversimplifying in another way. We sometimes talk as though the specific culture has only *one* set of values, as though there are no internal contradictions, as though we are not exposed to different models within the culture. But if we did not oversimplify in this way, our discussion would become so complex as to be unproductive. Another great difficulty is that the scientific method forces us to analyze one or a very few characteristics at a time, separating out one factor in order to see it more clearly. As a result I sometimes have the feeling that the psychological data on human beings bear little resemblance to people we know. Perhaps the gifted novelist can capture the complexity of a human being; in this respect, I am limited. In this book we are largely restricted to data from middle-class American whites, and especially the available and cooperative college undergraduate. Many of the ideas and conclusions are derived from this population, and we do not know how much can be applied to other populations.

Despite the difficulties of generalizing, it seems to me that psychologically men and women are very different in some basic ways: in their life styles, in the organization of their egos, in their personality qualities, in their motives, and in their goals. While it is true that values do not *have* to be linked to these differences, it is rather pollyannish to deny that they are. Since this culture values achievement, particularly individual achievement in work, honors attach to those who achieve and who have the personal qualities that allow them to achieve. The role conflict of women over achievement is not an automatic result of growing up in this culture, and the majority of women experience relatively little of it. But the role conflict that does exist is the result of the differential values of the culture, which have been internalized by both the men and the women. In this book we shall examine the reasons why women are motivated to achieve the traditional feminine goals, why some women are motivated to achieve in work, why many are not so motivated although they too have internalized the general values, and why the needs of women change over the life span.

The areas to which men and women devote their major efforts derive not only from tradition but from personality qualities that are basic. We will find that in the competitive world of work, men have a distinct advantage not simply because there is sex-linked prejudice but because their personality qualities of independence and aggression give them an advantage in that particular kind of achieving. The personality qualities of women, especially their empathy with other people, their sensitivity and nurturance, give them an advantage in noncompetitive kinds of achieving. *But*—in our culture both men and women apply masculine criteria to their performance. The greatest esteem is awarded to women who distinguish themselves professionally, yet simultaneously these women run the risk of alienation, of the suspicion of being failures as women. Traditionally, American women who bring qualities of ambition, aggression, and organization to nonprofessional or volunteer activities can gratify some "masculine" achievement aspirations without incurring the slurs of nonfemininity. Working women experience the outrage of prejudice because of their sex; at the same time, many of them use the idea of male prejudice to explain away occupational failure.

Briefly, then, what are we going to discuss? After describing the traditional psychoanalytic ideas and my disagreement with them, we are going to discuss the contribution of the body to sex differences in the infant and in the sexually mature adult. Then we will explore differences in the personality qualities and in the skills of the sexes and discuss the origin and development of these differences. We will present the data on differences in the ego development and the self-esteem of the sexes and trace the evolution of the motive to achieve through the life span. We will describe sex differences and similarities in goals and motives, in productivity and creativity, in traditional roles and work roles. We will not be concerned with psychopathology, with recipes for happiness, nor with the reality of sex prejudice—we will have our hands full trying to understand the psychological dynamics of the middle-class American woman. Much of this book represents only my opinions; I hope that these opinions will stimulate a search for more data.

chapter 1
PSYCHOANALYTIC
THEORY

The most influential formulations of personality development in the United States have been, and still are, derived from the psychoanalytic theory of Freud. While there have been neoanalytic revisions of the classic theory and diverse nonpsychoanalytic theories, no one has captured the imagination and loyalty of both the public and the profession as Freud did. His genius is unassailable; but his formulations about women reflect values that emerged during the Victorian era.

Historically, ideas about the psychology of women have reflected political sentiments as much as scientific investigation. For Freud, the world was clearly dominated by men and he took the phallocentric viewpoint, emphasizing the penis as the source of power. Opposition to this idea originated with a few female psychoanalysts, notably Karen Horney. She was unable to rid herself of Freud's view of life as phallocentric, but she ascribed the origin of phallocentrism to male envy of the creativity of the female uterus. Since all creativity must pale in comparison with the act of creating another human being, men, out of profound envy for women's procreative function, have seized cultural power and as a result are envied by women. I tend to

5

call this the reaction-formation idea. The third set of theories takes the very popular position that there are no basic differences between the sexes, only those imposed by a masculine society, and that noticing differences between the sexes must inevitably lead to evaluations of the differences, with women (noticeably) coming in second. Thus, there are three basic schools of theory on the personality development of women. In the course of this book we are going to reject all three of them. I cannot believe that normal women are primarily motivated by their lack of male genitals; nor can I believe that men are searching for a substitute uterus. In agreement with most laymen, I do think that there are fundamental psychological differences between the sexes that are, at least in part, related to the differences in their bodies.

THE BASIC FREUDIAN THEORY

In psychoanalytic theory, both sexes are assumed to go through identical stages of oral and anal development until about the age of 5, when they enter the phallic stage. Children of 5 are seen as extremely curious about their genitals and the genitals of the opposite sex (this is obvious to any parent who has suddenly discovered his child busily exhibiting his genitals or peering and giggling at the genitals of a friend). While a girl might have been previously aware of her lack of a penis, it now becomes a focal issue. Inadequately endowed for sexual gratification, she suffers from "penis envy." In the depths of her sexual self she envies, covets, feels mutilated, cheated, disappointed, and angry. Unlike the boy, she doesn't really suffer from a traumatic fear of castration because, so far as she is concerned, she is already castrated. She envies the boy his "superior endowment," and in anger and disappointment she blames and rejects her mother for cheating her of a penis and turns to her father for a penis or a child. This is one origin of the female Oedipus complex. For the little boy the Oedipus complex stimulates the castration complex. His sexual desire to possess his mother and kill his father arouses deep fears that his all-powerful father will angrily retaliate for these forbidden wishes and punish him in the most terrible and relevant way—by castrating him. For the girl the order is reversed; observation of anatomical difference induces feelings, identified as the female castration complex, which will stimulate the Oedipus complex.

In this theory the girl's penis envy, based on observation of anatomical differences, will persist unresolved as feelings of inferiority and a predisposition to jealousy. She will loosen her ties to her mother, give up active penis envy, clitoral masturbation, and masculine competitive kinds of striving and will convert the wish for a penis to a wish for a child from the father. Because she is doomed to unending frustration in the search for a penis, she substitutes baby for penis; thus the intensity of her maternal desire will be proportionate to her unresolved wish for a penis.

To psychoanalysts, penis envy resulting from the discovery of "castration" is never entirely sublimated and retains a considerable amount of unconscious energy throughout life. It is the major motivating factor throughout feminine development. When the wish for a penis, conceived of as activity, is replaced by the wish for a child, conceived of as passivity (all of the female reproductive sexual functions are considered to be passive), the "female situation" is achieved. Thus the woman's greatest fulfillment is achieved when she has a child, especially if the child is a son who "brings the longed-for penis with him" (Freud, 1933).

Psychoanalysis sees normal female sexuality as based upon passivity and masochism, which is not self-destructive because the female is also narcissistic. In the pre-Oedipal period, both boys and girls are seen as transforming passive experiences into active ones. But with the weakening of the girl's attachment to her mother and a simultaneous new attachment to her father, passive fantasies become dominant and active ones atrophy. This can be accounted for both by the wish to be passively impregnated by the father to attain the substitute penis in the form of a child and by a culturally reinforced idea of proper feminine behavior in which active aggression must be given up. Her changing behavior is likely to evoke more real affection from the father. In analytic theory it makes sense for the girl to be active and penetrating while she is still tied to the mother and can have fantasies in which she possesses a penis. But the transference of her primary affection and longing to the father signifies, more or less, her renunciation of her penis "delusion"; it is a consequence of her penis envy and leads to an emphasis on more receptive and passive ways of relating.

Actually Freud himself felt that the conventional distinction of masculine-active and feminine-passive (referring especially to aggression) was important primarily in reference to the genitals but was not necessarily a constitutional "given" or a generalized personality characteristic. He was quick to warn that social conventions also force women into passive attitudes. He said that psychological femininity probably means a preference for passive aims but that it often requires a good deal of activity to achieve a passive aim. "It may be that the part played by women in the sexual function leads them to incline toward passive behavior and passive aims, and that this inclination extends into their ordinary life to a greater or less degree, according to whether the influence of their sexual life as a model is limited or far reaching" (1933). Certainly "feminine" and "passive" are everywhere equated in the psychoanalytic literature, almost as though they were synonymous—but we also know that motherhood, which is the essence of femininity, is active and not passive.

Masochism, or the acceptance of pain, is seen as truly feminine. Thus we find Bonaparte saying that coitus is "the only one of the reproductive functions of women which should really be free of suffering" (1962). Because of their sexual constitution and because of societal pressure, women repress their aggressiveness and turn their aggression inward to the self. The healthy development is to bind these destructive impulses with erotic impulses. We see this as masochism, in this context necessary for the sublimation of a potentially destructive force into pleasure associated with the pain of reproduction (or, more parsimoniously, the acceptance of a certain inevitable amount of pain in the reproductive system).

In psychoanalytic theory, the girl has an additional and difficult task if she is going to become a mature and healthy woman. Girls have to give up clitoral sexuality and masturbation and develop vaginal sexuality. The psychologically healthy woman must be able to change from a clitoral orgasm to a vaginal orgasm. At the beginning of the phallic phase the little girl is still acting like a little boy, obtaining pleasure from manipulation of the clitoris and beginning to associate it with ideas of intercourse. Under the impact of penis envy, when she renounces her mother, she renounces clitoral masturbation and becomes more passive. The analysts equate the clitoris with the penis and see it as an active rather than a passive organ. At this time the vagina remains undiscovered as an important organ or a primary source of pleasure. Feminine identification demands the renunciation of clitoral sexuality. The girl must become less of a male and more of a female; this is achieved in part through the change in the investment of libidinal energy from clitoris to vagina; aggression, envy, and competition must be sublimated.

The superego is the psychoanalytic name for a part of the psychic apparatus that has within itself two components. One part of the superego is the familiar conscience, or the awareness of guilt when we have done something that we define as wrong. The other part of the superego is the "idealized ego," or an internal and idealized image of one's parents which serves as the internal criteria for our evaluation of self. The person with a mature superego has an internal set of personal standards, knows himself, and evaluates himself independently of others' assessments. The person with a weak superego continues to evaluate himself as a child does, in terms of others' reactions to him, and he governs his behavior by the reactions he anticipates.

Freud observed that the superego of women is never as impersonal or independent as that of men. He felt that this difference was due to the difference in the Oedipal complexes of the two sexes. Because of the boy's immense castration fear he abandons his Oedipal longings decisively and dramatically, and in most normal boys a superego is the sublimated result. But the girl, who cannot fear castration because in her mind it has already occurred, never has a decisive crisis; the Oedipal situation remains viable much longer and she may never abandon it completely. The result is a less well-developed superego, one that remains dependent upon its sources in the external world—that is, the punishing and rewarding parents or some other important person. The fully internalized superego, which is much more characteristic of the male, is independent of these external sources of reward and punishment. (This is a very important idea. We shall disagree with the source of the difference in the two superegos, but the observable dependence of the female upon others as a source of self-esteem is a principal difference that we shall come upon throughout this book. No matter how described, the mature person can be seen as less dependent upon reflected appraisals of his self.)

Freud felt that because women remain in the Oedipal complex indefinitely, abandoning it only later in life and then incompletely, their superego formation suffers; therefore he concluded that generalizations about the character weaknesses of women are not simply the disparagement of prejudiced men. "Women show less sense of justice, are less willing to submit to the great necessities of life, and are more often influenced in their judgments by feelings of affection and hostility" (1927). We can see this as separation anxiety, or the fear of losing love. We can also see it as the fear of losing a person one wants to love, an indication of an active as well as passive disposition. Compared with men, women remain more dependent on the love and appreciation of others to determine their self-worth.

Freud wrote that the psychology of women was still a problem and an unresolved riddle, and he wondered how much the "feminine characteristics" were rooted in biology, anatomy, or social conventions.

We have only described women in so far as their natures are determined by their sexual function. The influence of this factor is of course very far reaching but we must remember that an individual woman may be a human being apart from this.[!] [1933]

On the other hand he also interpreted any effort that a woman made to participate in the real world as a desire to make up for her lack of a penis, the organ of "power and creativeness" (Riesman, 1953). How strong were his convictions? "Anatomy is destiny" (1927); the "anatomical tragedy" of woman who is a "castrated," "maimed," "mutilated creature" (1927); "a little creature without a penis" (1932), who lacks "the only proper genital organ" and who comes to acknowledge the "fact of her own castration [and] the consequent superiority of the male and her own inferiority but rebels against these unpleasant facts" (1932).

IN OPPOSITION TO THE FREUDIAN THEORY

How could this perverted point of view have evolved? Stated baldly, the psychoanalytic position is that the primary motives of women derive from a poor attempt at sublimating impulses that emanate from a lack of male genitals. I shake my head in disbelief at the perpetuation of this mythology. The brilliant Erik Erikson (1964) is kinder than I am when he writes that the psychoanalytic psychology of women is

. . . largely reconstructed from women patients necessarily at odds with their womanhood and with the permanent inequality to which it seemed to doom them. [This view] has been strongly influenced by the fact that the first and basic observations were made by clinicians whose task it was to understand suffering and to offer a remedy; and that they by necessity had to understand the female psyche with male means of empathy, and to offer what the ethos of enlightenment dictated, namely, the "acceptance of reality." They saw, in the reconstructed lives of little girls, primarily an attempt to observe what could be seen and grasped (namely, what was there in boys and hardly there in girls) and to base on this observation "infantile sexual theories" of vast consequence. It does not seem reasonable to assume that observation and empathy, except in moments of acute or transitory disturbance, would so exclusively focus on what is *not* there.[1]

I do not doubt that the phenomena described in the psychoanalytic literature exist, but this seems to be the classic illustration of the danger of generalizing to a normal population from an abnormal population seeking relief from its terrors. Complex theories have arisen on the strongest of theoretical assumptions from the weakest clinical data. The fundamental assumptions of the psychoanalytic point of view seem ludicrous when they are divorced from the clinical situation.

The insistence that femininity evolves from necessarily frustrated masculinity makes femininity a sort of "normal" pathology. Erikson writes,

Again, such envy exists and is aggravated in some cultures; but the explanation of it in male terms or the suggestion that it be borne with fatalism and compensated for by a redoubled enjoyment of the feminine equipment (duly certified and accepted as second rate) has not helped women to find their places in the modern world. For it made of womanhood an ubiquitous compensation neurosis marked by a repetitive insistence on being restored.

The question is not so much whether penis envy exists—it does—but whether it is an important factor for the large group of normal females.

It seems that psychoanalysis, without being explicit, makes the enormous assumption that the genital (phallic) sexual drives of boys and girls are the same and equal. In young children we would see this behaviorally as equal masturbatory activity by boys and girls. In psychoanalytic theory the girl is at a disadvantage because the clitoris is perceived as inadequate, in comparison with the penis, to discharge sexual energy or to gratify sexual impulses. Thus we really have two assumptions: one is that these genital impulses are of enormous importance to both sexes, and the other is that the clitoris can generate more excitement than it can discharge. There is the additional derived assumption that it is possible to imagine and therefore

[1]This and subsequent quotations reprinted by permission from *Daedalus*, Journal of the American Academy of Arts and Sciences, volume 93, number 2.

envy physical experiences that one is structurally incapable of having.

It seems impossible or at least improbable that the most powerful motive of the female is the result of envy of an experience which she is structurally incapable of knowing. The smaller amount of neural innervations in the vagina tend to make it an unimportant organ, so far as sexual excitation is concerned, until coitus. The clitoris, in contrast, is basically an erotic organ, but it is smaller and less accessible than the penis. Psychoanalytic theory is not based on the desire for the privileges of the boy but on the girl's jealousy of actual penile sensations. I think it is more logical to stop insisting that female and male sexuality are equal in childhood. The availability to the boy of an external, sensitive, erotic organ makes genital sex more important to him at an earlier stage.

I think that the girl will not envy what she is incapable of experiencing; the clitoris is not a penis. Masturbatory activity through clitoral stimulation in the girl is less frequent than penile stimulation in the boy, because the clitoris is smaller and less accessible and the physical sensations are not as intense.[2] It seems probable that the differences in the external genitals result in less intense and less significant sexual impulses for the girl. Stated very simply, I believe that in children the genital sexuality of the boy is stronger.

Bosselman (1960) has pointed out that in psychiatric studies the penis-envy motif is not nearly as consistent a finding for women as castration anxiety is for men. That's highly logical. The sensitive and pleasurable, easily accessible genitals of the male are charged with sexual energy early, are valued early, and are conceived of as a very special part of the self. Simultaneously, proportionate to its value, the penis is conceived of as accessible and vulnerable. For girls, the genitals are a relatively silent force until puberty when there is an enormous change in the erogenous potential of the body. In truth, one ought not to insist that boys and girls develop in an identical or even parallel fashion, and one should not permit the importance of the genitals to be uniquely exaggerated in a theory of normal development. The ego is a body ego, but the genitals are not the only area of the body. We ought to explore the effect on the ego of the difference in body erogeneity.

The psychoanalytic goal of a vaginal orgasm as the *sine qua non* of normal healthy sexuality has been pursued by countless women.[3] It is illuminating to see how this originated: Because psychoanalysis conceives of

---

[2] "I have the impression that with the passing of the anal phase, vaginal excitations become an important, at times discernible, source of tension. *This could not be deduced from direct observation of young children* [Italics mine]. . . . Since the vagina hardly ever is cathected as an organ or libidinous zone before the experience of intercourse, it cannot function as a dominant zone of the body scheme earlier than that. It is not surprising that reports of vaginal sensations in childhood are rare" (Kestenberg, 1956).

[3] Female sexuality will be discussed at length in the next chapter, but for now let me point out that Masters and Johnson (1966) laid this myth to rest when they found that an orgasm is a reaction of the *entire* pelvic area.

sex as man's major motivation, it seemed necessary to ascribe the same kind of importance to the vagina as the boy feels toward the penis. This, in spite of the differences in accessibility and sensitivity of the two organs.

How is the clitoris perceived in traditional psychoanalytic theory? As a male organ misplaced in a female body, because it is actively sexual—as a homologue to the penis, although clearly inferior. The active, "male" clitoris is described as being in conflict with the passive, female vagina, and the genital sensations emanating from the two organs are seen as competing. Where the two sets of sensations balance out, the female's sense of identity will be confused. Thus the theory assumes a self-identity coming directly from genital sensations and also assumes the extraordinary physical event of hermaphroditism in the normal female. Insisting on female passivity, psychoanalysis made the clitoris an alien object.

The idea of the renunciation of clitoral sexuality is a myth. I think that what is important is the complex change in female sexuality in adolescence, when girls develop a new body, a new body image, and a slowly emerging sensitization of the vagina. This is much more complex than the relatively simple and linear sexual development of the boy.

Some of the neoanalysts, notably Horney (1924) and Thompson (1961) conceive of penis envy as a cry of outrage from women, the second-class citizens. Thompson wrote, "It seems to me that when such a wish is expressed the woman is but demanding in this symbolic way some form of equality with men" (1942). Horney felt that the phallocentric viewpoint of classical analysis inevitably led to the conclusion that the female half of the human race is discontented with its sex and can overcome this discontent only in favorable circumstances. This picture is "decidedly unsatisfying, not only to feminine narcissism but also to biological science." Since this is a man's world, women have been evaluated in terms of masculine standards. Indeed, the "motives for flight into male roles are later reinforced socially by the actual subordination of women" (Horney, 1926).

We will return to the idea of the generalized masculine standards for self-evaluation and of masculine-occupational goals as sources for self-esteem in Chapter 9. Here I should like to point out the error in this kind of neoanalytic theory. In the main, these theoreticians have seen that society as a whole, and the individual in particular, has internalized masculine standards of achievement, thereby denying the value of feminine qualities, goals, and achievements. This is, I think, an easily observed datum, worthy of examination and not subject to denial. But the next assumption is debatable; that is, that qualities of masculinity or femininity are lightly donned, attributable only to cultural reward and punishment. It will be my thesis that differences between the sexes have early genetic origins and that these constitutional dispositions are responded to differentially by a particular culture according to the values of that culture.

Those of us who have children are quite familiar with the little girl's verbalized envy of a boy's genitals, especially a brother's. But for normal girls this is an envy without intense affect, except insofar as a girl might be jealous of a boy for some real reason. If a little girl perceives a boy as receiving preferential treatment, especially from the parents, she may grasp the idea that the origin of this difference in privilege comes from the only perceptible physical difference between them. I believe that this allows her to make her jealousy concrete, allows her to rationalize a more general envy, and that it is less threatening to her self-esteem than questioning whether his greater privileges come because he may be more loved, or nicer, or smarter. The extent and intensity of verbalized penis envy will depend upon the entire perceived relationship of the girl to her brother or other boys.

When a little girl asks her parents why her brother has a penis and she has none, she is usually told that when she is grown she will have both breasts and babies and the boy will not. This is usually sufficient reassurance of the equality of physical equipment simply because the real time lag involved is beyond the comprehension of small children. Also, and of prime importance, the little girl who is normal is not profoundly involved in this envy in the first place. Because of the less intense sexual impulses in the girl, I think it probable that penis envy in neurotic girls is less a function of sexual impulses than of aggressive impulses, with a concomitant desire for castration of the boy.

PASSIVITY, MASOCHISM, AND NARCISSISM

We have noted that psychoanalytic theory sees the psychologically mature woman as characterized by the qualities of passivity, masochism, and narcissism. Let us look at this assumption more closely.

Passivity has several meanings but most frequently it is used in two senses: to describe low levels of externally directed activity or low levels of externally directed aggression. Girls and women are more passive in that they are less motorically active than boys and men. And if we define passivity as the absence of externalized physical aggression, we find that girls and women are less motorically aggressive. Female passivity is observable in nursery school; it continues throughout life. This seems to support the psychoanalytic position. Not quite. Who is lucky enough not to know a shrew (always conceived of as female), a harpy (another female), a gossip (again), or a "Jewish Mother" (not necessarily Jewish)?

Aggression in women is more often subtle, less easily recognized for what it is, than the obvious, overt, immediate aggression of the male. Women show anger in words and in interpersonal manipulation of other people. Sometimes we see what I call the tyranny of the weak—that is, the use by a woman of her weakness in order to get others to do for her what she would otherwise have to do herself. In the next chapter we are going to talk about the relationship between the woman and her body, but for now let me note that the internal reproductive system in women is highly active. Female activity, like female aggression, takes its own feminine forms.

It seems to me that the analytic error was in generalizing from the obvious, overt differences in activity of the genitals to an entire personality syndrome. The genitals do not make a personality, the female reproductive system is internally active, and female aggression simply takes nonmasculine forms. Actually, we have found in our research that the woman who is very passive in the sense of being unable and unwilling to directly express aggression at any time to anyone who is important to her is so lacking in self-esteem as to be clearly neurotic. When persons remain terribly dependent for their feelings of esteem upon others' reactions to them, they never run the risk of alienating others. Such persons are overtly passive and subtly aggressive. Again, psychoanalysis has generalized from a severely neurotic population to the norm, using masculine behavior as a definition of activity and aggression. We should add here that there is a healthy kind of passivity in which the woman responds to frustration and aggression with an elaboration of compromise solutions in thought and fantasy instead of in activity directed outward. This healthy response probably has its origins in the woman's special relationship to her body interior, in her weaker musculature, and in her highly developed verbal skills.

As to masochism as a feminine quality, we know that many female biological functions involve some physical discomfort and sometimes significant levels of pain. Before anesthesias and pain-reducing drugs were available, masochism would have been a very functional part of the woman's psychic equipment. In the face of inevitable pain, a little enjoyment would have gone a long way. Actually, I have mixed feelings about this idea. When pain is liable to be very severe, as in childbirth, most American women opt for anesthesia. But I also find that many women do not seek relief from the less extreme discomforts they experience when they menstruate, and occasionally I am told that they are glad to experience the symptoms as a monthly affirmation of their womanhood. It is also possible that during coitus women find moderate amounts of pain erotic, perhaps because the vagina is not very sensitive. In that case pain would heighten the physical sensation of genital fusion. In any event, normal healthy women accept, if they don't enjoy, the necessary physical discomforts of pregnancy and childbirth; acceptance of extreme pain may be a sign of pathology.

The third element of the triad, after passivity and masochism, is narcissism. In analytic terms, narcissism is an investment of psychological energy in the self, which functions to prevent the self-destruction that might result from masochism. I think that healthy women, like healthy men, are narcissistic. By that I mean that healthy people have enough integrity and self-esteem not to permit (much less enjoy) their destruction by other people. In the analytic model, the female is more narcissistic because the sexual, reproductive, and personal demands made upon her are greater than those made upon men, and narcissism serves as a kind of defense in which integrity of the self does not dissolve in the face of agreeing to other people's demands. This view assumes that female sex and reproduction, in the service of the species, are of great cost to the individual woman. I suggest that sex, but especially pregnancy and maternity, is the source of the greatest narcissistic gratifications for women. I have led into an idea which I will return to in the next chapter—the idea that maternity and not sex is the crucial source of gratification for women. Generalizing from the male body and reflecting the sexual frustration of a Victorian and puritanical era, our culture has viewed maternity, which is the most basic pleasure for women, as second-rate and merely a spin-off from sexual pleasure.

I think that it is not the absence of the penis but the presence of creative inner space that is important for girls. It is not a grieving renunciation of a "lost" penis but an anticipatory pleasure and rehearsal of future maternity that looms large. This is not subtle but observable. Indeed, we take for granted the universal activities of little girls' dollplay and preadolescent babysitting. We take for granted the joys of handling babies, which can be observed even in quite young children.

Erikson (1964) has observed that this awareness of a dynamic inner space has early body origins.

Kate Franck, a student of Erikson's, devised a test to measure feminine awareness of internal body space, closed and protected, and masculine feelings of activity, protrusion, vitality. I have been using this test with grown women and had begun to wonder about its validity. Quite by accident my 9-year-old son found a copy of the test, which is composed of 36 incomplete drawings that the subject is asked to complete. He asked if he could take one, and then gave copies to his 5-year-old sister and his 11-year-old sister. Each of them went to a different room to complete the test "in secret." The results were startling to me: the two girls, although clearly different in age and sophistication, completed the drawings according to adult female criteria. My son completed the drawings according to adult masculine norms. Indeed, seven of the girls' drawings were identical. They drew houses, faces, and enclosed, quiet, protected spaces. Peter drew exuberant cartoons, rockets, and sharks— active, aggressive, outward.

It is clear that parents and the general culture reinforce behaviors appropriate to one sex or the other. But Erikson suggests that there is a body contribution to sexual identity which is normal and independent of pressure and reward. This is another idea that I will return to—the speculation that the body itself makes a contribution to one's sexual identity. That is, in addition to societal reinforcement of sex-role behavior, physical states directly affect psychological states, and there are different physical states in the two sexes.

THE OEDIPAL CONFLICT

Within the traditional theory the Oedipal conflict is seen as crucial in the development of the personality; successful resolution of the conflict is absolutely necessary for the development of the healthy psyche. I think this is probably true for boys. The impetus for a boy's Oedipal conflict lies in the strength of his sexual impulses and his pleasure in genital masturbation—and in his fear of the loss of the source of this pleasure. In addition to unconscious, deeply rooted anxieties, the fear of castration comes from living in a world in which every child's pleasures and privileges are at the mercy of unpredictable parents. The basis for castration anxiety is the fear of parental anger against sexual impulse and pleasure. For boys, the greater sexual impulses and ensuing masturbation require greater control of both impulses and anxiety. The result, usually described as the Oedipal conflict resolution, is that male ego defenses and superego structures are formed earlier and are more sharply defined. Girls' impulses are weaker, masturbation is less frequent, parental prohibitions for sexual behaviors are rarer, anxiety is lower. Psychoanalytic theory describes the Oedipal conflict in girls as being more complex, vaguer, and very slowly resolved. I suggest that no comparable Oedipal situation exists for girls because the precipitating factors are absent.

THE DEVELOPMENT OF SEX DIFFERENCES IN CHILDREN

I agree that the psychological differences between the sexes are based in part on the genital differences. The important difference is that boys have a visible, sensitive, and accessible organ whereas girls have an inaccessible clitoris and an insensitive vagina. Other physical differences contribute to the tendency of little girls to be less motorically impulsive, less physically aggressive, and less sexually active than little boys. That they tend not to get into trouble in general and into fights in particular, and that they tend not to masturbate, means that they are less likely to perceive their parents as people who thwart their impulses. To the extent that girls are not alienated from their parents, they are not *forced* to develop internal controls and an independent sense of self.

The girl does not have to earn her sex designation as early as the boy. The dependency, passivity, tears and affection-seeking normal to both sexes in younger children are defined as feminine in older children, and girls can remain dependent and infantile longer. Thus, by virtue of her own lower level of impulses and by the parents' definition of appropriate behavior, the girl is not pressured as early as the boy to become independent. A boy becomes alienated from his parents to some significant extent because his aggressiveness, impulsiveness, and sexuality are responded to with parental prohibitions. He can no longer depend upon his parents for uncritical support and nurturance. As the boy grows older and loses the external source of self-esteem, he is pushed to develop internal, independent sources. If he is successful, pushed by his own personality dispositions and parental reactions to them, he will have his own criteria for self-esteem and will achieve an independent sense of self. He may not be successful. The ratio of boys to girls brought into psychiatric clinics and hospitals runs as high as five to one.

We see then that cultural norms and specific parental behavior reinforce the tendency derived from physiology; girls tend to continue in the affectional dependent relationships of all young children. More than boys, they will continue for an extended period of their lives to value the self as a function of reflected self-appraisal. This has a very pervasive and significant effect: unless something intervenes, the girl will continue to have throughout womanhood a great need for approval from others. Her behavior will be guided by the fear of rejection or loss of love. An independent sense of self with a resulting sense of self-esteem can only evolve when the individual, alone, sets out to attain goals and, with reasonable frequency, achieves them. For many reasons, and that is a core idea of this book, the American girl rarely achieves an independent sense of self and self-esteem.

An independent sense of self can only occur when one has many experiences in which he is responsible while he cannot completely depend upon his original sources of love and support. Let me hasten to add that I am not advocating a total alienation by any child from his parents or peers. A complete alienation between parent and child results in terrible pathology. I am describing an ambivalent relationship, which is the norm, especially for a boy. He is loved and he knows it—but he is also punished and he anticipates it.

In my view, the absence of an Oedipal crisis in girls results in less mature defenses against sexual and aggressive impulses, the absence of an internalized ego-ideal, a greater dependence upon others for feelings of self-esteem, and less of a drive for independence. In analytic terms, less energy is bound up with impulse control; therefore more energy is available for the conflict-free cognitive and perceptual spheres of the ego. In the early school years the girl is better able to give all of her efforts to the impulse-free world of learning because she is less preoccupied with the control and expression of prohibited impulses. This enables girls to learn more swiftly than boys in the early grades, especially when the emphasis is on memorized skills that do not require abstract, independent conceptualization and when schoolwork can be largely conforming to adult directions. Girls usually learn to read and write much earlier than boys, and tend not to be class behavior problems. This is usually described as indicating the generally greater maturity of girls. It can as readily be described as a period of striving for the development of self-control by boys, which will result in *their* greater maturity.

Because the girl continues to depend upon the appraisal of others, she will tend to be largely oriented toward people and she will be more susceptible to the influence of the general culture as she sees it in her parents and teachers. The significantly influential persons in her life will change over time, generalizing from parents to peers to teachers, but dependence upon their esteem will make her conform to their expectations. In general, this will produce, at least in middle-class girls, a standard kind of scholastic achievement and a general acceptance by parents, peers, and teachers, which will result in the continuation of conforming "good" behavior. Her dominant anxiety will be a concern about her acceptability, about her being loved.

ACHIEVEMENT, AMBITION, AND CASTRATION ANXIETY

If the normal girl has not experienced parental rejection because of her sex, if she has a positive sense of self as a girl, and if she is not neurotically fixated at pregenital levels, she will learn techniques of achievement without rejecting her sex. If her experiences and psychosexual development have, on the other hand, precluded acceptance of herself as a girl, she can maximize the competitive techniques of success; each "A" can assure her that she can do what a boy can do and therefore "has a penis" or that her success has castrated everyone else in class.

The increase in ovarian hormone production in early adolescence will reinforce the girl's self-perception as a female. Because menstruation and the development of secondary sex characteristics will indicate that she is now capable of reproduction, she will increasingly value her femininity. But the neurotic who has rejected her sex will find the physiological changes of puberty traumatic because they challenge her repudiation of her sex. She may deny her femininity, ignore menstruation, or even become amenorrheic. Fleeing femininity, she may increase her efforts to gain a penis or castrate a male. At least symbolically.

Our culture strongly emphasizes goals and behaviors that have been traditionally masculine, and self perceptions dependent upon achievement in the marketplace. There is an essential difference, however, between a wish for masculinity arising from penis envy, reinforced by cultural values and buttressed by the availability of traditionally masculine activities for defensive purposes, and a self-percept that, along with acceptance of oneself as feminine, desires the activities and successes that men achieve. A neurotic flight from womanhood implies penis envy in the adult woman; in the normal woman, pursuit of activities in the marketplace does not carry the same implication. Successful scholastic or occupational competition is a general cultural goal. It need not threaten one's feminine identity unless one is punished for striving or punished for succeeding.

Normal women express a most fundamental need for and give value-priority to those role activities we call feminine. Their sex-role identification is feminine and they are most strongly involved in the welfare of their families, in creating a home, in nurturing their children, and in maintaining their own lovability. But since the culture rewards occupational-role activities, to the extent that women have achieved success in these activities a second perception of the self is as one who is able successfully to pursue these achieving activities. Achievement in traditionally "masculine" roles may form a strong secondary component of self-identity and a basis for self-evaluation. We shall find, incidentally, that the percentage of American women for whom this is true has traditionally been small.

It is to the credit of the psychoanalysts that they have elaborated upon the idea that the body is a direct contributor to one's self-percept and ego development. But preoccupied with genital sex, the traditional theory has overemphasized the idea that the sexual body equals the self, thus denying the relative importance of other factors. Insisting on the equality of the sexual impulse in men and women, they have stressed the absence of a penis rather than the presence of a uterus. Even among the analysts who are unique in their understanding that the ego is a body ego, there is a scarcity of papers dealing with physical phenomena unique to women—such as menstruation, pregnancy, birth, and lactation—except insofar as these processes are seen as sublimations of an unresolved penis envy, separation from the original mother's nipple, and so on. Thus the reproductive activities and the body of the female have not been examined as making definite and positive contributions to the psychology of the woman.

I think that the dominance of the masculine cultural values results in the disparagement of specifically female activities and specifically feminine personality characteristics. Female emotional demands are either tolerated or resented, but not understood. Dependency, passivity, conformity, and emotional lability—assumed to be characteristic of normal women—are seen as negative qualities. Simultaneously, women are suspect when they are independent, active, aggressive, competitive, nonconformist, or impersonal. Designated inferior because they are not occupied with the "important" things of life, women internalize a low self-concept. Simultaneously, efforts to participate in professional roles, in the "significant" activities of society, are likely to evoke their anxiety about their femininity. This is especially true if a woman actually is successful—because then she is likely to be competitive, independent, active, and initiating.

Society rewards individual competitive achievement—and just about any female can have a child. Thus, even the ultimate woman's role of motherhood is not a source of status (but the negative, infertility, incurs a loss of status and a mixture of contempt and pity). Females are likely to internalize the masculine values as well as rebel against them. I suspect that the current liberation movement among women is a response to their having accepted and internalized masculine standards. Women learn in a very general way to despise their femaleness and simultaneously to value it. Classical psychoanalysis errs in overemphasizing the importance of the genitals per se, yet is valid in insisting that one's self-esteem depends upon one's human qualities and upon one's success as a male or female.

The ascription of genital inferiority to females, with a resulting assumption of the general inferiority of the entire sex, has not led to valid theory. When we look for the psychological effects of the female body we ought to be investigating the effects of menstruation, the secondary sex characteristics, pregnancy, lactation, parturition, and menopause. If we are going to understand women we ought to explore needs that derive from the female reproductive system, and we must understand that personal attitudes towards these functions reflect both body demands and cultural attitudes.

chapter 2
THE EFFECT
OF BODY STATES
ON THE PSYCHE

We know astonishingly little about how physical states influence psychological states; we know equally little about the relationships between particular sex hormones and specific male and female behaviors. This ignorance or uncertainty reflects methodological problems in both psychology and endocrinology. In psychology it also reflects what has been a fairly pervasive disinterest in nonenvironmental factors. The nature-nurture controversy is so old and so cliché-ridden that only introductory psychology classes spend much time discussing it, and they always conclude that it is a specious question; psychologists and psychiatrists have long emphasized the overwhelming importance of the environment. I have, nonetheless, taken the apparently eccentric position that the body makes direct contributions to the psyche of the individual. I am going to have to make conceptual leaps from the data but I shall try to demonstrate that differences in the behavioral responses of males and females exist even before parents differentiate the sexes in their handling of infants; the differences in personality characteristics begin to develop *before birth*, and they are responded to differentially by the parents.

My interest in the physiological basis of behavior and the effect of the sex hormones derives from my assumption that the reproductive system in women has some important effects upon their psyche. We are all aware that *attitudes* about the body or sex or pregnancy are important. I am posing a different set of questions: Does the reproductive system *directly* influence psychological states? Are some differences between the sexes *directly* related to the physiology of these systems rather than to attitudes about the systems? To explore these questions, we will briefly review the endocrine system and then look at the possible psychological effects of its changes during the menstrual cycle, pregnancy, menopause, and during the use of oral contraceptives. We will also discuss the role hormones play in sexual arousability.

THE SEX HORMONES

All aspects of reproduction, in all animals, are basically dependent upon the presence of the appropriate sex hormones. Hormones are powerful chemical substances that are produced in the endocrine glands and secreted into the bloodstream to affect other parts of the body. The known endocrine glands are the pituitary, the thyroid, the pancreatic islets, and the gonads (ovary, testis). Complex hormonal mechanisms regulate the development and the maintenance of primary and secondary sex characteristics. In the male, the main hormone involved in developing and maintaining the sex characteristics is testosterone, one of the group known as androgens. This single hormone supplies the chemical basis for male sexual behavior. In the female the hormonal interrelationships are more complicated. We will use as simplified a description as possible.

The flow of hormones among the endocrine glands is controlled by a negative feedback system. The pituitary gland controls endocrine levels but is itself under the command of the hypothalamus, a portion of the upper brain stem known as the "seat of emotion." The hypothalamus regulates the back-and-forth passage between psychological states and physiological states. When the pituitary gland sends out a "chemical message" in the form of a stimulating hormone, the signal enters the bloodstream and is picked up by a receptive gland, which then manufactures an appropriate hormone and secretes it in turn into the bloodstream. As the optimum hormone level is reached, the pituitary responds by sending out new messages to inhibit further production.

The cycle of menstruation is regulated by a complex series of hormonal feedbacks between the pituitary and the ovary (see Figure 1). The pituitary gland initiates the cycle by sending out a follicle-stimulating hormone (FSH), which signals the ovary to bring several follicles to maturity by producing a hormone called estrogen. As the level of estrogen in the ovary

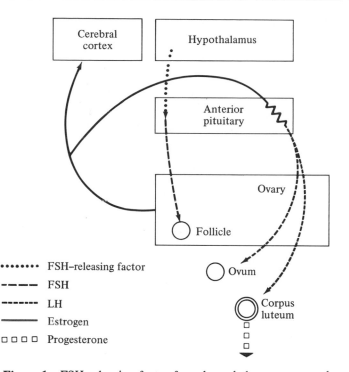

Figure 1 FSH-releasing factor from hypothalamus acts on the anterior pituitary, which secretes FSH, causing follicle to ripen. Estrogen from the ovary feeds back to the brain, to create a "feminine environment," and to the anterior pituitary, where it transiently inhibits FSH to permit LH elaboration. Under the influence of LH, the corpus luteum is stimulated to secrete progesterone. (Adapted from Behrman, 1969, p. 34.)

increases, the follicular growth reaches its peak and a critical level of estrogen is secreted into the bloodstream. This high level of estrogen signals the pituitary to decrease production of FSH and to release luteinizing hormone (LH). The primary function of LH is to induce ovulation, that is, to get one follicle to release the egg within it. For a while FSH and LH act together to produce a further surge of estrogen production, and this increase in estrogen serves to further inhibit the production of FSH. Now the LH becomes dominant and ovulation can take place: a single follicle reaches maturity, and two days later it ruptures and releases the egg (see Figure 2).

After the egg, or ovum, has been ejected from the ovary, the wall of the follicle collapses and reddish-yellow cells, called the corpus luteum, mass at the place of the rupture. At this point the pituitary releases a third hormone, luteotropic hormone (LTH), which directs the corpus luteum to manufacture progesterone, next to estrogen the most sig-

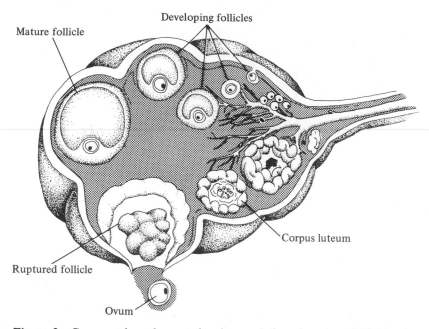

Figure 2 Cross-section of ovary showing ovulation. A mature follicle ruptures and releases its egg. (From K. L. Jones, L. W. Shainberg, and C. O. Byer, *Sex,* Harper & Row, 1969, fig. 4.3.)

nificant female hormone. When progesterone reaches a specific level it will inhibit the production of LH, the ovulation-stimulating hormone, and will simultaneously stimulate the pituitary to release FSH, the hormone that tells the ovary to begin maturing new follicles for the next menstrual cycle. Menstruation is the sloughing off of the inner lining of the uterus, and it occurs when estrogen and progesterone are both at their lowest levels (see Figure 3).

Estrogen is responsible for building up the inner lining of the uterus, for the development of the uterus, cervix, vagina, and the skin immediately adjacent to the vagina, for the development of ducts in the breasts, for support of the vaginal epithelium, and for regulation of pituitary action. Estrogen is also responsible for development of the secondary sex characteristics.

Progesterone causes secretory changes in the uterus, stimulates the end portions of ducts in the breasts, and regulates the maintenance of pregnancy. Under the influence of progesterone the secretory phase of the menstrual cycle begins.

At the start of the menstrual cycle estrogen is at a low level.[1] It rises

[1]For our purposes it seems sufficient to refer to "levels" of estrogen. Actually, at least three forms of estrogen are secreted by women: estradiol, estrone, and estriol. Estradiol is the most

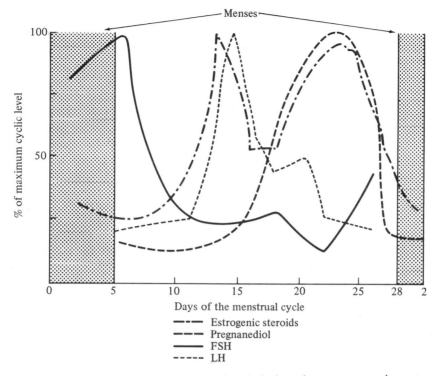

Figure 3 Variations in urinary gonadal and pituitary hormone secretion rates during the menstrual cycle. Hormone secretion rates are expressed as a percentage of the maximal cyclic level. Pregnanedial is a metabolite derived in part from progesterone and is assayed in order to estimate progesterone levels. (Adapted from Schwartz, 1968, fig. 3.2.)

to a high peak at midcycle, or ovulation, dips, and then once again rises to a peak, falling sharply before the onset of menstruation. The progesterone level is extremely low before ovulation. It rises swiftly, and, like estrogen, falls sharply before menstruation. Although other endocrine gland secretions may be important, the data suggest that the levels of the sex hormones estrogen, progesterone, and androgen are of critical importance in their effect upon psychological states.

Testosterone is the most potent hormone in the androgen group associated with male activity. It has important effects upon genital development and is involved with sexual arousability. Until fairly recently it was believed that only the male testis was capable of producing testosterone.

active estrogenic steroid, estrone next, and estriol least. Similarly, in addition to progesterone, two metabolites are elaborated by the ovary during pregnancy. We refer to testosterone levels, but there are at least two important androgens elaborated by the ovaries, testosterone and one of the "delta" hormones, Δ^4-androstenedione (Jaffe et al., 1969).

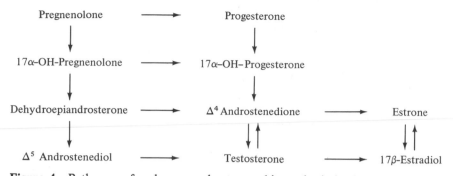

Figure 4 Pathways of androgen and estrogen biosynthesis in the human ovary (Adapted from Jaffe et al., 1969, fig. 3.)

Although estimates of exact quantities differ, it is now established that women do produce testosterone (see Figure 4) and it is likely to have an effect on the responsiveness of the clitoris. Jaffe et al. (1969) report that testosterone and Δ⁴-androstenedione, another androgen, are elaborated by the ovary. Current data suggest that ovaries produce estrogen, progesterone, and testosterone, but testosterone is not secreted in large amounts in adult women (Gold, 1968). Salhanick and Margulis (1968) report that isolation of testosterone from the normal ovary has not been achieved consistently. There are few data on levels of testosterone in ovarian veins but there are many assays of levels in peripheral blood. "Most investigators report concentrations of testosterone of less than 0.1 μg per ml plasma with little cyclic variation in normal women. Men have about five times that quantity" (Salhanick and Margulis, 1968). We will deal with the implications of this research later in this chapter, in the section on androgens and eroticism.

CYCLE PHASE AND PERSONALITY CHANGE

Human behavior is clearly very variable, and this variability originates in the reaction of the hypothalamus and central nervous system to internal stimuli within the individual and to the environmental stimuli that affect the internal stimuli. When we look at *specific* behavior, women seem very different from other female primates and mammals, whose sexual arousability, for example, is stimulated solely by high estrogen levels. But if we take a closer look at *general* mood shifts, feelings of self-esteem and self-deprecation, depression and well-being, we begin to discern the physiologically linked affect cycle which underlies the specific behavior.

Regular, predictable changes occur in the personality of the sexually mature woman, and these changes correlate with changes in the menstrual cycle. The personality changes occur in spite of individual personality differences and may even be extreme; they are a consequence of endocrine and related physical changes. The *content* of the emotional state is a function of the psyche and the real world of the individual—the *direction* of the change is a function of the physical state. This idea is supported by the experimental data; in this section we will review some of the studies that have demonstrated a direct causal relationship between endocrine levels (or other physical change) and emotional shifts.

Most studies correlate emotional changes with the estrogen and progesterone levels of the different phases of the menstrual cycle. Let us briefly review these hormonal changes. Estrogen is at a low level during menstruation and immediately following menstruation. It rises to a peak at about the time of ovulation, decreases for several days, and again reaches a high level on about the twenty-second day. This second high level of estrogen production is maintained until a few days before menstruation, when it rapidly declines. Progesterone is secreted in very small amounts until midcycle. After ovulation, progesterone production steadily increases until the twenty-first or twenty-second day, after which, a few days before menstruation, it also rapidly declines.

In 1931, Frank labeled the emotional changes that occur after about the twenty-second day "premenstrual tension," and this served to focus medical attention on the syndrome. Depression, irritability, anxiety, and feelings of low self-esteem have been reported to affect from 24 to 100 percent of the population studied, the variation in frequency depending upon definition and type of measurement. Sutherland and Stewart (1965) studied 150 women and found that premenstrual depression and irritability were associated with a wide range of unpleasant physical symptoms. Premenstrual irritability was found in 69 percent of their sample, depression in 63 percent, and both affects together in 45 percent. Coppen and Kessel (1963) found in a study of 465 women that depression and irritability were generally more severe before menstruation than during menstruation. They believe that the severity of the premenstrual change is related to general neuroticism. It is possible that neurotic women react more severely to menstruation and to the cyclic emotional changes, but I think that the emotional variations are found with approximately equal frequency in normal women. Sample populations of normal, neurotic, and psychotic women show similar affect cycles. But the severity of the symptom or its "meaning" to the woman may well vary according to psychological pathology.

Gottschalk et al. (1962) and Ivey and Bardwick (1968) found transient decreases in levels of anxiety and hostility during ovulation or midcycle. During the estrogen phase of ovulation, the women studied were characterized by low levels of negative affects and high levels of self-esteem; during the low-estrogen and low-progesterone premenstrual period, they were significantly anxious, hostile, and depressed. Shainess (1961) also found that the premenstrual phase was generally associated with feelings of helplessness, anxiety, and defensive hostility, and a yearning for love. Using a population of 39 institutionalized schizophrenic women, Housman (1955) found that during menstruation there was an increasing need for affection and approval, a greater sensitivity to interpersonal slights, and a higher anxiety level. Moos (1968) found that approximately 30 to 50 percent of responses by 839 normal young married women to a questionnaire indicated cyclic symptoms in irritability mood swings, tension, and depression.

Dalton (1964) found that a large proportion of women who commit suicide or engage in criminal acts of violence do so during the four premenstrual days and the four menstrual days of the cycle. Forty-five percent of the female industrial employees who report sick, 46 percent of the females who are admitted to psychiatric care, 49 percent of the females admitted for acute medical and surgical problems, 52 percent of female emergency-accident admissions, and 49 percent of females who commit a crime are in the premenstrual or menstrual phase of the cycle. In 1966 Dalton reported another interesting finding: 54 percent of the children who were brought to a clinic with minor colds were brought during their mothers' eight premenstrual and menstrual days. This behavior suggests an exaggeration of the mothers' normal anxiety levels. These statistics, in conjunction with the high frequency of symptoms in normal young women, suggest that the premenstrual-tension syndrome has more frequent and more important consequences than has been assumed.

An observation that I have always found very interesting was made by Levy in his study of maternal overprotection (1956). Levy studied a group of highly maternal mothers who had been consistently maternal all their lives. He also studied a group of nonmaternal mothers who had a consistent pattern of nonmaternal behavior all their lives. The same experiences that increased maternal behavior in maternal mothers increased maternal rejection in nonmaternal mothers. He also found a significant positive correlation between maternal behavior and the length of the menstrual flow. The majority of subjects who had a menstrual flow lasting four days or less were independently classified as low-maternal. The majority of mothers who had a flow lasting six days or longer were classified as high-maternal. As the length of the menstrual flow increased, the percentage of high-maternal mothers also increased. Like most of these studies, this is a correlational observation; we can make no claim to causation.

In 1942 Benedek and Rubenstein did an intensive study of 15 neurotic women who were in psychoanalytic therapy. They found striking effects of the physiological menstrual changes upon psychological states. There were consistent correlations between the hormonal phases of the menstrual cycle and the psychodynamic content of the therapeutic session. Passive-receptive tendencies and a feeling of well-being correlated with progesterone production, and active heterosexual striving correlated with estrogen production. In a later report Benedek (1959) described the premenstrual phase as being high in feelings of anxiety and depression, fears of mutilation and death, and sexual fantasies. During the high-estrogen phase of ovulation she found an almost total absence of anxiety-related themes.

Thus the independent and simultaneous measurement of hormone production, using the vaginal-smear[2] and basal body-temperature[3] techniques, correlated with the psychoanalytic interpretation of daily sessions to reveal that (1) there is a correlation between each hormonal variation in the menstrual cycle and the psychological manifestations of the sexual drive, and (2) an emotional cycle exists, and it correlates with the hormonal cycle. The endocrine and the emotional cycles together constitute the sexual cycle in women. "The gonadal cycle and the psychodynamic response pattern represent a psychosomatic unit" (Benedek, 1952).

According to Benedek and Rubenstein, when the production of estrogen gradually increases at the beginning of the menstrual cycle emotions are characteristically outward, active, object-directed, and heterosexual. This tendency, which has the biological aim of copulation, is usually accompanied by good feelings of well-being and alertness. These sexual aims can be seen in dreams, fantasies, conscious emotions, and behavior. For women who are not mature, or who are sexually fearful, one can see an increase in characteristic defenses against sexuality at this time. At the time of ovulation, Benedek and Rubenstein found that the active sexual tendency fuses with a passive-receptive tendency. This psychosexual fusion represents the biological and emotional preparation for conception. At this time the active sexual tendency is not as intense as it had been earlier in the cycle because it is modified by the receptive and passive predisposition. Dreams, fantasies, and behavior at ovulation reveal a wish to receive and retain. After ovulation, tension is relieved and there is a sense of relaxation and well-being. Estrogen levels are high, progesterone levels are rapidly increasing, and psychologically there is an intensification of the receptive-retentive tendencies that represent a psychological preparation for pregnancy. For the mature, nonneurotic woman, the psychological material during this high-progesterone phase reveals her wish to bear children and her pleasure in caring for her children.

When estrogen and progesterone levels swiftly decline during the pre-

---

[2] A cytologist can closely pinpoint the day of ovulation by staining daily vaginal smears on a glass slide, using the Papanicolaov technique. At ovulation the smear is characterized by a deeper stain, an almost complete absence of leukocytes, and a decrease in the clumping of the cells with the greatest degree of cellular cornification. (Behrman and Gosling, 1959)

[3] This is the most commonly used technique for detecting ovulation. A clearly biphasic shift in temperature means that ovulation has occurred. Ovulation most frequently occurs at, or shortly before, the low point in the temperature. It can also occur, the day after the low point, at the high point of the temperature change. The midcycle rise in temperature is probably due to the rise in progesterone levels. (Behrman and Gosling, 1959)

menstrual phase, Benedek and Rubenstein report, a regression occurs in psychosexual integration. There are individual variations in symptoms, but characteristically and frequently we can see anger, excitability, fatigue, crankiness, crying spells, and a fear of mutilation. Frustrations seem unbearable, gratification of needs seems imperative, and all emotions are less controlled than at any other time in the cycle. This regression to more infantile ways of responding and coping and the increased irritability of the sympathetic nervous system are seen as resulting from the low estrogen levels of the premenstrual phase. It is also true that sexual desire may be more imperative at this time than at any other; Masters and Johnson's data (1966) indicate that this may be due to the generalized swelling and retention of fluids (edema) frequently found at this time.

Benedek and Rubenstein found that the onset of menstruation is usually accompanied by a relaxation of the tension and irritability of the premenstrual phase, although physical symptoms often increase. Their subjects felt relief and sometimes also a mood of depression that continued for a few days until estrogen production began to increase in the next cycle. The increase in estrogen levels brought with it a return of feelings of well-being.

In an extension of the earlier work he did with Benedek, Rubenstein wondered whether one could produce psychological change by administering sex hormones. He gave androgens to a woman and found personality changes and behaviors which we usually call "more masculine." He gave estrogens to a woman with premenstrual tension; her morale improved and she felt better able to accept herself and her environment. He also administered long-acting progestational compounds and found that women were better able to accept their own passivity and narcissism. Rubenstein also found that the reactions to these hormones were mixed and were understandable only if one knew the multiple and often conflicting motives of each patient.

The *specific* reactions of an individual woman will reflect her motives, her maturity, her general psychological health. But the enormous *cyclic* changes in personality are not restricted to neurotic and psychotic women. In correlation with menstrual-cycle changes, normal women show the same general kinds of emotional variation, although intensity is variable.

I should like to give you some idea of the enormity of the psychological change even in normal subjects. Melville Ivey and I (1968) studied a group of 26 normal female college students over two menstrual cycles. Twice at ovulation or midcycle and twice at premenstruation we asked them to tell us about an experience they had had. Their replies were tape-recorded and were later scored, using Gottschalk's Verbal Anxiety Scale (Gottschalk et al., 1961). We scored themes related to death, mutilation, separation, guilt, shame, and diffuse anxiety.

When we combined the scores for all subjects we found that the premenstrual anxiety scores were significantly higher than the anxiety scores at ovulation.[4] This difference reached the 0.0005 level of significance (p), which means that there were less than 5 chances in 10,000 that this difference could have been due to chance factors alone. In other words, these are clearly significant results. This increase in premenstrual anxiety was apparent in 21 of the 26 subjects. One subject showed no significant difference between the two cycle phases, and three subjects had compelling problems in their lives at ovulation (in one instance, the attempted suicide of a friend). The Gottschalk measure is very sensitive to changes in current, real anxieties, so the real anxieties at ovulation precluded a significant difference for these three subjects between the two cycle phases.

When we combined the scores of all the subjects, we found that the premenstrual death-anxiety score was significantly higher than that at ovulation ($p < 0.02$) as was the diffuse anxiety score ($p < 0.01$). Separation anxiety, mutilation anxiety, and shame anxiety were also higher premenstrually (at approximately the 0.13 level), while guilt anxiety remained fairly constant.

This study was less depth-oriented than the Benedek and Rubenstein study, but the technique encourages less conscious or controlled responses than the more commonly used questionnaires. When we examined the tape recordings for consistent themes we found themes that were unique to a menstrual cycle phase. For example, a constantly recurring theme at ovulation was a feeling of self-satisfaction over success, or the ability to cope:

. . . so I was elected chairman. I had to establish with them the fact that I knew what I was doing. I remember one particularly problematic meeting, and afterwards, L. came up to me and said, "you really handled the meeting well." In the end it came out the sort of thing that really bolstered my confidence in myself.

This is a sample from the same girl, premenstrually:

They had to teach me how to water ski. I was so clumsy it was really embarrassing 'cause it was kind of like saying to yourself you can't do it and the people were about to lose patience with me.

Hostility was another theme that occurred often. The frequency of hostile themes was much greater premenstrually than at ovulation:

. . . talk about my brother and his wife. I hated her. I just couldn't stand her. I couldn't stand her mother. I used to do terrible things to separate them.

This hostile and incestuous verbal sample is in striking contrast to the sample from the ovulatory phase of the same cycle for the same girl:

Talk about my trip to Europe. It was just the greatest summer of my life. We met all kinds of terrific people everywhere we went and just the most terrific

---

[4]We may also note that no significant difference was found between the anxiety scores taken during two ovulation phases nor in scores taken during two premenstrual phases.

things happened.

At premenstruation, themes of death anxiety were common:

I'll tell you about the death of my poor dog M. . . . Oh, another memorable event, my grandparents died in a plane crash. That was my first contact with death and it was very traumatic for me. . . . Then my grandfather died.

In contrast, the sample at ovulation for the same girl:

Well, we just went to Jamaica and it was fantastic, the island is so lush and green and the water is so blue . . . the place is so fertile and the natives are just so friendly.

Premenstrual mutilation anxiety has been observed by many researchers. Here is one sample from our data:

. . . came around a curve and did a double flip and landed upside down. I remember the car coming down on my hand and slicing it right open and all this blood was all over the place. Later they thought it was broken because every time I touched the finger it felt like a nail was going through my hand.

The same girl, during the same cycle, at ovulation:

We took our skis and packed them on top of the car and then we took off for up north. We used to go for long walks in the snow and it was really just great, really quiet and peaceful.

When the effects of the menstrual cycle are under study, results may be confounded by the subject's awareness of the experimenter's interest in the cycle phase. We had one unexpected and accidental experimental control. One girl was interviewed on the fourteenth day of her menstrual cycle, the ovulation phase, and the recorded sample of her talk showed almost twice as much anxiety as the ovulation sample of the previous menstrual cycle. Thematically there were references to death, mutilation, and separation. The next day she began to menstruate, two weeks early.

We repeated our study with a larger sample of young married women, and the major hypotheses were substantiated. Again we found that general psychological mood-states correlated with menstrual cycle phases, and we found a high and normal incidence of premenstrual anxiety, depression, and hostility in this sample of normal women.

As psychologists we would expect to find strong individual differences in reactions during the menstrual cycle. Instead, in almost all of our subjects we found the consistent and significant mood swings characteristic of a particular menstrual phase. These physical changes, probably endocrine changes, so influence psychological behavior that in spite of individual personality differences, even in normal subjects, psychological behavior seems predictable on the basis of menstrual cycle phase alone. Women may cope or not cope, become anxious, hostile, or depressive, appear healthy or neu-

rotic, due as much to menstrual cycle phase as to core psychological characteristics.

Depression, anxiety, and irritability increase during the times when a woman is experiencing a tremendous drop in estrogen production—before menstruation, just after childbirth, and during menopause. These three physical states also correlate with an enormous drop in progesterone.[5] But generally speaking, the lowered level of estrogen is held to be responsible, and menopausal depression is commonly alleviated by administering estrogens. Some women are very severely affected, some hardly at all. Greenblatt (1955) has suggested that the symptoms may be due to the *rate* of decline in estrogen production—the swifter the decline, the more severe the symptoms.

Actually, correlational studies do not allow us to explain the physical causes, but the statement that psychological changes during the menstrual cycle are biochemically influenced is widely accepted among medical people. In a review article Southam and Gonzoga (1965) cite evidence for the physical causes that could be involved: sodium and water retention, an excessive production of the hormone aldosterone, excessive antidiuretic substances, low blood sugar, and an allergy to progesterone and its breakdown products. Other biochemical factors that have been suggested as causal include an increase in mineralocorticoids and glucocorticoids in relation to ovarian hormones (Dalton, 1964), a high estrogen-progesterone ratio (Green and Dalton, 1953), and the effect of adrenocortical hormones in general (Janowsky et al., 1966) and aldosterone in particular (Janowsky et al., 1967). Since the phenomenon does not seem limited to psychiatric patients it is to be hoped that psychosomatic effects of the reproductive system will become a more popular research area and we will be able to delineate the biochemical contributions more exactly.

PREGNANCY—WHEN PROGESTERONE AND ESTROGEN LEVELS ARE HIGH

Kestenberg (1956) has written that psychological preparation for pregnancy and nursing has a biological origin as well as psychological determinants. Like me, she is not certain what the biological factor might be but would expect to find a correlation between some biological variable and the specifically maternal and nurturant qualities.[6] I feel that there is a biological origin

[5]The end-of-pregnancy level of estrogen is roughly 10 times normal, and that of progesterone roughly 100 times normal. The levels of both return to normal within hours after childbirth.
[6]I sometimes wonder whether tendencies toward passivity and nurturance are normal in all mammals except that the critical early presence of androgens creates a tendency toward activity and aggression. Persky and his coauthors (1969) have reported significant correlations between externalized aggression and the production rate of testosterone in normal men. Persky

of maternal nurturance, especially of small and helpless infants. My reasons are intuitive, unscientific, and unsupported. A few years ago I watched an enormous colony of monkeys chasing one frantic female. The lone figure ran, terrorized, screaming and panicked, away from the chasing throng. In her arms she held the rigid corpse of a dead infant. In all the time I watched, the colony never succeeded in separating her from that body. I have been impressed with the exquisite tenderness older children, especially girls, show toward young children. My own daughters never played with dolls, never rehearsed maternal roles with toys. Their response to young children and animals is nurturant and gentle. I myself had never seen an infant before my eldest was born. Preoccupied with school and work, I had never given much thought to even my own imminent child. My response to my child was immediate, unrehearsed, and unexpected. In a second she was incredibly precious—to be loved and protected. My husband's response I remember better than my own: "No man will ever be good enough!" The anecdote is glib but my intent is serious. My reaction to my child was not comprehensible in terms of the differential reinforcements of learning theory. This was a primitive, gut-deep response, not amenable to easy verbalization, similar in kind and intensity to that of the monkey who could not give up the body of her dead infant. I have found that this feeling diminishes slowly as my children grow and successfully achieve their independence. But each new birth, each new child, brought forth the same immediate, profound surge of love and protectiveness.

The contentment of the pregnant woman and the "peace that shines forth from her eyes" are part of the tales of all cultures. Some supporting evidence for a physical basis does come from reports that, after inducing pseudopregnancy with hormones, patients who had been "feeling out of sorts" usually respond with feelings of well-being (Hamblen, 1962). Benedek (1959) found that the secretory half of the menstrual cycle, when progesterone production is high, is characterized by an intensification of receptive-retentive tendencies, which are the psychological preparation for pregnancy. Thus pregnancy can be understood as an enormous intensification of the progesterone phase of the menstrual cycle (both estrogen and progesterone levels increase immensely during pregnancy). Psychologically healthy pregnant women are characterized by an "increased integrative capacity of the ego." For Benedek the patience and the nurturance of the healthy, mature woman has its roots in high progesterone levels. Certainly, we would not expect a rejecting mother to become highly nurturant because we gave her progesterone; what Benedek is saying is that the rise in nurturance depends upon the hormone level as *well* as upon the personality characteristics that the ma-

---

suggests that although women may produce approximately 0.25 mg a day of testosterone, compared with 10 mg a day produced by men, the basic aggression–testosterone relationship may also be true for women. He is presently engaged in collecting this data (1971).

ture woman brings to the delivery room.[7] If Benedek is correct, perhaps the basic origin of the "biological factor" of maternal nurturance lies in progesterone. This would not, however, explain the nurturant behavior of sexually immature girls. If there is such a biological factor perhaps another variable is the sexually differentiated brain, an idea we will discuss in Chapter 5.

ORAL CONTRACEPTIVES—WHEN ESTROGEN
AND PROGESTERONE LEVELS ARE CHANGED

The oral progestogens are reported to be of value in treating psychological disorders associated with the female reproductive cycle. Pincus (1965) reported a decrease in the frequency of premenstrual depression in a large number of women taking oral contraceptives. Wiseman (1965) has also reported significant decreases in premenstrual depression, tiredness, and irritability in normal women using the oral contraceptives. Janowsky et al. (1966), Kane et al. (1966), and Swanson et al. (1964) have reported a reduction of severe cyclic psychiatric upsets in women on the pills. Lee (1965) writes that women receiving oral contraceptives show a lowered accident rate with an equal distribution through the cycle, in contrast to the premenstrual rise in accident rates of normally menstruating women. Kane (1965) has reported the successful use of Enovid in treating postpartum depression. There are several papers reporting the occurrence of psychic disorders after patients stopped using the oral contraceptives (Janowsky et al., 1966; Keeler et al., 1964; Idestrom, 1966). There are also reports that a certain percentage of women react to oral contraceptives with an increase in symptomatology (Moos, 1968), and it is likely that these women originally had higher symptom severity.

It would seem to be a reasonable hypothesis that the altered and elevated steroid hormone levels induced through the use of oral contraceptives would make for significant psychological change. That is, if the menstrual-cycle affect changes are due to changes in the levels of the sex steroids, if the psychological changes during pregnancy are due in part to elevated levels of progesterone or estrogen or both, if sexual behavior can be changed through endocrine changes—we have fair support for the idea that the sex hormones create psychological changes in mature organisms as well as in infants. As in most of this area, the critical studies have not been done, but I should like to report the results of a study conducted by Karen Paige (1969) while she was my student at the University of Michigan.

[7] I am currently beginning a study of pregnant women and hypothesize that since the menstrual endocrine cycle is eliminated during pregnancy, the monthly affect cycle will be eliminated. I also hypothesize that the stage of pregnancy (or the endocrine levels) may be more important than personality qualities in predicting phases of positive and negative affects and themes.

Paige compared cyclic mood changes of menstruating women with mood changes of women using oral contraceptives. Using the Gottschalk scales for anxiety and hostility, she analyzed the verbal samples of 102 married women (wives of graduate students at the university), collected at four different times in the cycle, in order to determine whether the mood fluctuations associated with the menstrual cycle also occurred in women who use oral contraceptives.

Three groups of subjects were formed: one group of 38 women who were not using oral contraceptives and never had; a second group of 52 women who were using the combination pill (20 consecutive days of pills containing both estrogen and progestin, followed by approximately 7 days off the pill); and a third group of 12 women using sequential pills (15 days of pills containing only estrogen followed by 5 days of pills containing both estrogen and progestin and then approximately 7 days off). All of the women were tested on the 4th day of menstruation, on the 10th day of the cycle, on the 16th day (midcycle), and two days before the next menstrual period. Various other data were collected at each interview to help disguise the nature of the study.

Paige thought that the magnitude of the anxiety and hostility expressed in the verbal samples would be related to the changes in the levels of estrogen and progesterone. For women using the combination pill, who take a constant amount of these hormones for 20 days, she hypothesized that the relatively constant level of these hormones over the pill cycle would eliminate the cyclic fluctuations in moods found in normal menstruating women. For women not using the pill, and for those using the sequential pills— where the hormone cycle simulates that of normally menstruating women —it was hypothesized that the level of anxiety and hostility would be lowest at ovulation and highest premenstrually, as was true in the first study described above (Ivey and Bardwick, 1968).

The results showed that the cycle phase had a very significant effect on the anxiety and hostility levels of women who were not using the pill (analysis of variance results were hostility $= p < .001$, anxiety $= p < 0.05$). As we had hypothesized, Paige found that the changes in the levels of anxiety for the women on sequential pills followed the same pattern as those for the menstruating women. For women on combination pills, there was no significant effect of the cycle phase on their level of hostility or anxiety (hostility $= p < 0.95$, anxiety $= p < 0.25$); in other words, these women showed no significant change in the amount of hostility and anxiety over the entire menstrual cycle. Women using the more common combination pill, who have constant high levels of estrogen and progestin, do not have wide swings in affects as do menstruating women or women whose contraceptive replicates the normal endocrine pattern.

When Paige looked at the mean levels of hostility for menstruating women, she found that the highest levels were reached premenstrually, after which there was a sharp decrease, with the lowest levels at ovulation. But the women on combination pills remained at a high level of hostility throughout the cycle, equal to menstruating women at menstruation. Hostility was relatively constant for women using combination oral contraceptives but fluctuated significantly for women not using those pills.

Both the Ivey-Bardwick study and the Paige study found that the lowest anxiety levels were at day 16 for both normally menstruating women and women using sequential pills. Women using combination pills had a very different pattern, with the highest level of anxiety at ovulation. The mean anxiety levels are not significantly different, but the *pattern* of anxiety has altered. Thus the nonpill group had a significant *decline* in anxiety level at day 16, while the combination pill group had a *rise* in anxiety that did not reach statistically significant levels. That is, within a flat affect pattern, there was some tendency to experience anxiety at a time when normally menstruating women experience their lowest levels of anxiety. Behaviorally we find that at ovulation these women express fears that they might be doing injury to their reproductive system that will result in infertility. This is a severe response by a group of women who are no longer experiencing the large mood swings characteristic of menstruating women.

Supporting the findings of the Ivey-Bardwick study, Paige's work revealed a relationship between emotions and the endocrine changes during the menstrual cycle. When the hormone levels are fairly constant during the cycle, as in the women on combination pills, anxiety and hostility levels are correspondingly constant. When the hormone levels fluctuate during the cycle, emotions correspondingly fluctuate. [8]

THE MENOPAUSE—WHEN ESTROGEN LEVELS DECLINE

Both somatic and psychological changes usually accompany the decrease in sex-hormone production during the climacteric. The climacteric refers to the involution or regression of the ovaries and includes menopause, the cessation of menstruation. Ovarian regression is the fundamental change, and it results in a significant decrease in estrogen output, a decline and cessation of menstruation, and an atrophy of tissues such as the external genitalia and the breasts, which are normally supported by estrogen.

The climacteric can bring on somatic symptoms such as hot flashes and breast pains; psychological symptoms such as irritability, crying spells, depression, confusion, and an inability to concentrate; and essentially psychosomatic symptoms such as headaches, dizzy spells, and poundings of the

[8]One should be aware that these are correlations using psychological tests; we cannot know from these data whether women on oral contraceptives differ significantly in their *behavior* from women who do not use the pills.

heart. Women may become intolerant, anxious, hypochondriacal, depressed. (Men experience nothing this drastic. The reduction in testosterone levels is far more gradual and less extreme and their secondary sex characteristics and genitals do not deteriorate swiftly.) There is a great deal of individual variability in symptoms during this time, although all women seem to have some symptoms to a greater or lesser extent. How many women actually experience symptoms is not known; estimates range from 50 to 85 percent.

In 1965 Neugarten and Kraines administered a symptom check-list to 460 women. The subjects were divided into six groups by age: 13–18, 20–29, 30–44, 45–54 (pre- or post-menopausal), 45–54 (menopausal), and 55–64. The two highest-symptom groups were the adolescent and the menopausal. Although psychological and social stresses are great for these groups, it is not certain that there is less stress for other age groups. But it is of interest that women in the 45–54 nonmenopausal group had lower symptom scores than those reporting themselves menopausal. Neugarten and Kraines feel that the more severe endocrine-related changes during any stress period seem to be the primary factor for the high-symptom incidence in the adolescent and menopausal groups. That is, the increased production of the sex hormones during adolescence and the decreased production of estrogen during menopause are primarily responsible for producing an increase in sensitivity to and frequency of symptoms. The symptoms themselves are different: adolescents most frequently reported emotional or psychological symptoms, and the menopausal women tended to report somatic symptoms. Neugarten and Kraines feel that the difference reflects the mature woman's ability to cope more effectively at the psychological level.

As early as the 1910s, the origin of the climacteric symptoms was assumed to be some metabolic disruption. Then, as psychodynamic interpretations became increasingly popular, the possible contributions of physiological change receded before the "narcissistic injury" theories (Deutsch, 1945). In the 1960s theories of physiological origin again leaped into prominence as gynecologists attempted to alleviate the symptoms of their menopausal patients with estrogens. "The average urinary estrogen secretion of regularly menstruating women is 2.29 μg per 24 hours; that of postmenopausal women is only one sixth of this amount—0.35 μg per 24 hours" (Wilson and Wilson, 1963).

Greenblatt (1955) has suggested that the autonomic nervous system becomes sensitive to estrogen and dependent upon estrogen for balance. A swift decline in estrogen levels disrupts the balance, and the disruption is reflected in the various body-systems that are under autonomic nervous system control. Judging by the range of menopausal complaints, every body-system seems affected: vasomotor, cardiovascular, metabolic, sensory, digestive, skeletal, muscular, glandular, and the central nervous system in general. Proponents of the estrogen-deficiency theory feel that the hypothalamus is also involved and that hypothalamic–central-nervous-system dysfunctions would account for the psychological symptoms of irritability, depression, anxiety, and confusion.

Most of the enthusiasm for the estrogen-deficiency approach has come from reports of treatment of menopausal symptoms with estrogen compounds. But the reported studies tend to lack good experimental control and tend to overlook the power of suggestion or the influence of a sympathetic physician. We must therefore interpret these results with a certain amount of caution. Wilson (1966) has administered estrogen to about 5000 women and "without exception, every case I treated . . . showed some sign of improvement. In many cases total avoidance of all menopausal symptoms was achieved, and the percentage of marked amelioration was surprisingly high." Wilson maintains that estrogen treatment will significantly reverse menopausal symptoms and if estrogen is administered before the onset of menopause the symptoms will have been prevented.

Goldberg (1959) has found that estrogen alone, or in combination with androgens, will relieve symptoms and create a strong feeling of well-being. In another study by Kantor et al. (1966), fifty women whose ages ranged from 60 to 91 were studied. One group was given estrogens and a control group was given a placebo. Compared with their pretreatment scores, the estrogen group showed significant improvement ($p < 0.01$) in two out of three comparisons. The control group showed no significant improvement. Riley (1959) has also found that many menopausal women gain relief from depression and nervousness through estrogen treatments.

The menstrual cycle data and the menopausal data lead to the tentative conclusion that high levels of estrogen are correlated with high levels of positive moods, and low levels of estrogen and progesterone are correlated with significant negative emotions. These psychodynamic studies are rather crude observational and correlational reports, but at least there are some. Is it because most psychiatrists and psychologists are men that research on the emotional effects of the sex hormones in woman is missing . . . or at least very scarce? Or is it that the long-standing emphasis on the environment has resulted in a psychosomatic blindness toward body contributions? I don't know. I am only certain that psychological papers dealing with the emotional effects of the physical states of menstruation, menopause, pregnancy, lactation, and the elevated sex-hormone levels brought about by the oral contraceptives are conspicuously lacking although the research supports a physical-endocrine hypothesis.

HORMONES AND ADULT SEXUAL AROUSABILITY

Another area that needs study is the possible relationship between endocrine levels and eroticism. The effect of hormones upon the sexual behavior of adults is, however, difficult to establish. There are several reasons for this. The hormones are biochemically related and within the body one hormone is constantly forming breakdown products that may be a different hormone, thereby complicating measurements and correlations; hormones are only one contributing variable toward sexual behavior and their effects are clear only when they are scant or absent; there is not very much research, and what there is gives somewhat contradictory results. Nonetheless, with more courage than wisdom, we will stumble ahead trying to find consistency within apparent inconsistency.

What are the biochemical problems? For one, androgens may be biotransformed into estrogens in men and gestagens (a pregnancy hormone) may break down into androgens in women. Second, inside the body the sex hormones are unstable chemical compounds—androgens, estrogens, and progesterone change into related forms (see Figure 4). Third, and related to the second problem, the assessment of the quantity of the hormones that are functionally active in the body are derived from blood and urine levels. But these levels merely reflect derivative forms and metabolic end-products of the compounds, which are only active inside the body. More accurate measurement techniques have been developed very recently, but most of the research data have been based on the less accurate earlier measurements (Money, 1961). Another confounding factor derives from the central nervous system control of endocrine production. This implies that persons who have different psychological responses to the same stimuli are likely to be producing different hormones, in differing quantities, depending upon their individual reactions to a situation. I have suggested that the woman who reacts to coitus with arousal is likely to be producing different hormones (oxytocins) than the woman who responds with fear or anger (epinephrine and norepinephrine). It is also likely that the hormones interact with each other, and, just to make it more complicated, the individual responds to the increased endocrine level itself (Bardwick, 1967). We might also note that most of the data concerning sexual arousability and endocrine level come from patients seeking help, which is frequently given via the administration of sex hormones. We know that even the placebo rate of success is very high in the clinical relationship and conclusions are necessarily tentative.

Androgens are responsible for the maturation of the genital tract in males. Girls who have virilizing hyperadrenocorticism,[9] with a resulting high an-

---

[9]A disease in which the adrenal cortex is overstimulated and there is an excess production of both estrogen and androgen, especially the latter. High levels of estrogen and androgen depress the production of FSH, the follicle-stimulating hormone. In consequence, the ovarian follicles do not mature and do not produce estrogen. As a result, the uterus does not mature and the secondary sex characteristics do not develop. Simultaneously, the androgens produce masculine effects such as enlargement of the clitoris and marked muscular development.

drogen secretion, have ovaries that fail to mature and a hypertrophied clitoris that resembles a penis in size. A precociously high level of androgens in females is antagonistic to the normal maturation of the reproductive system. Similarly, estrogens are antagonistic to virilized genital maturation in boys, and high estrogen levels in males result in enlarged breasts and the inhibition of androgen production in the testes. The undeveloped penis and clitoris respond to medically administered androgens with an increase in vasculature and size. The erotic effect of androgen seems to be particularly localized to the penis and clitoris. Eunuchs, hypogonadal men (who have markedly small phalluses and testes), and men with total gonadal failure experience a dramatic increase in sexual drive when they are given androgens. The presence of androgens, especially in men, seems to be one of the necessary conditions for sexual arousability.

Among his patients, Money (1961) found that hypogonadal men who stopped taking androgens had fewer erections and less desire to masturbate or engage in coitus. The patients also reported a decrease in erotic dreams and waking fantasy. Erotic episodes were not completely gone but were significantly reduced in frequency (and intensity?). Androgens, especially testosterone, seem clearly linked to sexual maturation in men and to maintaining normal sexual levels.

Most of the literature on estrogens is concerned with their effects on eroticism. Influenced, I suspect, by the psychoanalytic view that the clitoris is a vestigial penis that interferes with mature feminine sexuality, scientists have tended to ignore androgen effects on the clitoris and sexuality and have looked at the hormone responsible for vaginal development—that is, estrogen. Unfortunately, estrogen does not seem to have much if anything to do with female genital sensitivity. Thus Money found that female patients who stopped using estrogen experienced no change in sexual reactions, fantasies, or sensations. We also know that many postmenopausal women whose estrogen production is very low have continued the erotic levels of an earlier time. But some frigid or sexually unresponsive women have responded to androgen therapy with an increase in sexual arousability.

We will return to the topic of the clitoris and its role in sexuality, but at this point I should like to briefly note that the effect of androgen therapy is probably to increase the vascularity and sensitivity of the clitoris—which increases the probability of orgasm. Frequent orgasms will effect an increase in vascularity, which will, in turn, enhance the orgasmic potential. Nothing succeeds like success, and the increased number of orgasms will lead to the psychological anticipation of pleasure in sex. When the hormone levels are normal, increasing them further with additional hormones will not increase the response thresholds nor will it alleviate psychological impotence or frigidity.

Androgen seems to be the hormone most directly involved in human sexuality, but it alone cannot account for sexual behavior. The androgen levels of boys and girls are about equal from the age of 7 or 8 until the middle teens. During adolescence, androgen levels rise in the male while estrogens rise (very significantly) in the female, but the rises do not correlate with the patterns of sexual behavior. At the beginning of adolescence, the boy's sexual responsiveness increases abruptly—but his androgen levels are increasing steadily. The girl's androgen levels also increase steadily until they are at a level two-thirds that of the adolescent boy. But her sexual responsivity and activity develop slowly and gradually and are much lower than comparable activity levels of the boy. The typical adolescent sex patterns of males and females show no clear correlation with the increase in hormone levels.[10]

At this point we might recall an idea I alluded to in Chapter 1. It seems to me that a significant difference between the sexes is the accessible and sensitive genitals of the male, and the inaccessible and less sensitive genitals of the female. Eroticism of the vagina does not normally occur until coitus. In addition, sexual development in the female seems to me to be more radical than in the male, with an extraordinary change in the body and the onset of sex-linked periodic bleeding to cope with. Even when testosterone levels in the sexes are similar, the qualitative effect may be very different. Testosterone acting upon the penis is likely to be more erotically effective than testosterone acting upon the clitoris. In addition, we do not yet know the interactive effects of estrogens, progesterone, and testosterone in women. That is, the androgenicity of testosterone may be altered by the circulating estrogens and progesterone.

No correlation can be found between the frequency of sexual activity and the androgen and estrogen levels of normal men and women. Nor is there a correlation between these endocrine levels and the decline in sexual activity in the older male, nor with the stability of the female response. Kinsey (1953) found no modification in the sexual responsiveness of 123 females who had had their ovaries removed. He also found that castration in mature males caused little or no sexual effect on more than half of the males he studied.

The effect of increasing estrogen levels in women is not clear. Some physicians report an increase in sexual responsiveness and others report no such change. My hunch is that the response to estrogens includes a response to the effect of the hormone upon the bodily sex characteristics. Among other functions, estrogen maintains muscle tone, and I suspect that the crepey skin and the drooping breasts that result from the decrease in estrogen level result in an image of an undesirable or unlovable body. The restoration of the physical tone of the body restores the psychological

[10]August et al. (1969) report finding no significant difference between the plasma testosterone concentrations in prepubertal males and females. Differences between adults are significant. They report a mean of 625 mg/100 ml of plasma testosterone concentrations in adult males compared with 45 in adult females. (As noted before, new assay techniques are changing concepts of endocrine production and there is some uncertainty about these data.)

desirability. Uncertainty about the effects of administering estrogen exists in spite of the data revealing low levels of anxiety and hostility or high levels of self-esteem at ovulation when estrogen production is highest. The lack of certainty about endocrine effects and sexual arousability in women underlines the importance of psychological factors, the complexity of the constantly circulating and transforming sex hormones, and the incompleteness of the data.

For the same reasons, the effect of progesterone is also unclear. Kupperman (1961), for example, sees progesterone as significantly decreasing libido. He has therefore given progesterone to elderly patients who had strong sexual desires and dreams that could not be realistically gratified. Kupperman writes that the reduction in sexual arousability has not always been recognized because the "oral progesterone" (ethisterone) is really ethinyl testosterone, which is androgenic. Therefore the decrease in arousability one would expect from the use of progesterone-like steroid hormones may be nullified by the androgenic quality of such compounds. On the other hand, Sherfey (1966) feels that progesterone itself is androgenic and that high levels of progesterone will increase the sensitivity of the clitoral system. Sherfey believes that estrogens may increase sexual arousability because of their congestive-edemic effect, which is relieved by organism. Androgens stimulate muscular, orgasmic action that increases the sensitivity of the clitoris and enhances the contractile strength of the responding muscles in orgasm. Masters and Grody (1953) have reported therapeutic success with older women using both estrogen and androgen.

I suspect that androgen is more directly related to sexuality per se than either progesterone or estrogen. The responsiveness of the clitoris, which is the primary erotic zone of the female, is probably maintained by testosterone produced by the ovaries plus androgens produced by the adrenal cortex and testosterone derived from progesterone. The response to elevated testosterone levels will probably depend largely on the psychological attitude toward sex. The female who is sexually very anxious may respond to increased clitoral sensitivity with an increase in anxiety and other negative affects. The female who is not psychologically inhibited may respond to increased clitoral sensitivity with increased eroticism—this seems to be a clear pattern for nonanxious women during the menstrual cycle. When androgens are given to adult women there is an increase in activity, aggressiveness, and frequency of sexual behaviors (Kinsey et al., 1953; Kupperman, 1961). Thus androgens seem to be the most effective of the hormones in increasing eroticism in women.

When we turn to the effects of androgens upon male sexuality, the essentially simple and direct sexuality of the male seems well illustrated. Administration of androgenic hormones to males whose androgen levels are below a critical normal level will increase sexual activity and the intensity of fantasy and desire in direct proportion to dosage. Withdrawal of the hormone will result in a decrease in male sexuality. It is not quite that simple, but it is relatively primitive and direct when compared with feminine behavior.

Estrogens, progesterones, and androgens are biochemically very similar, and progesterone and 17-hydroprogesterone are the precursors of both estrogens and testosterone (Ryan, 1963). The progesterone levels increase enormously during pregnancy and during the secretory half of the menstrual cycle. If progesterone breaks down to testosterone (Sherfey, 1966), then we should find an increase in sexual arousability in women peaking several days before menstruation. In her important paper Sherfey has hypothesized that the male embryo must secrete very large quantities of androgens in order to offset its own innate female anatomy and the effects of maternal estrogens. If the androgens are missing, the infant is functionally female in spite of male genitals. The female embryo needs no such endocrine intervention in order to develop normally. Sherfey tells us that as a result of the masculinizing process male embryos develop a high resistance to experimentally injected estrogens. The female has no comparable experience, and as a result female embryos are very sensitive to small quantities of androgen. The androgen responsiveness of the female genitals remains great even in maturity. We should therefore expect an increase in sexual arousability in women whenever the circulating androgen levels increase.

Sherfey refers to Kinsey's finding that approximately 90 percent of American women have greater sexual arousability during the premenstrual phase of the menstrual cycle and prefer coitus at that time. You will recall that progesterone secretion rises markedly after the formation of the corpus luteum, peaks just a few days before menstruation, and then drops abruptly. (Estrogen follows a similar curve after ovulation). The preference for coitus premenstrually has been reported by many researchers, but reports on the other periods of preference vary among the studies. Some have reported a sexual preference postmenstrually—which could not be explained by an endocrine level because progesterone and estrogen are low then—and at ovulation, when estrogen is high. We also lack data about sexual preference and performance during pregnancy when estrogen and progesterone levels are very high. At any rate, there is a fair amount of agreement that most women find themselves more easily aroused premenstrually than at other times during the menstrual cycle. Masters and Johnson (1961) have found that normal women and women with surgically constructed artificial vaginas produce more copious lubricating fluids with arousal premenstrually, which indicates greater vasocongestion and vascular permeability. The increased sexual capacity of women at this time is related, then, to the greater pelvic edema that builds up during this phase of the cycle and to the increased venous congestion. The increase in sexual responsivity is due to the increased progesterone level and to the increased pelvic congestion and edema characteristic of this cycle phase. The edemic response of orgasm provides relief for the pelvic congestion.

It is not that women can be sexually aroused only during this time. Rather, most women report a more spontaneous interest in sex, an increased conscious sexual desire, an increased ease in reaching the plateau level of arousal, and an increased ease in reaching orgasm. Thus women appear to have a biologically based cyclic increase in sexual drive based partly on the erotic effects of endocrines. One reason might be the vascularizing, fluid-absorbing effect of estrogen and the androgenic effects of an increase in testosterone derived from progesterone.

We might point out that this cyclic increase in eroticism and sexual behavior assumes a woman who is neither anxious nor guilty about coitus. It is always possible for psychogenic factors to interfere with, or override, biologically based levels of sexual arousal.

In women, an increase in the androgens that affect tissue capable of erection may or may not increase sexuality. That is true for estrogens too. Why? I would suppose that sex for the female is primarily reflective—a reflection of her relationship with a man, and with herself. The response to increased physical erogeneity can range from delight to disgust. Estrogens do not seem to have anything to do with eroticism directly; their erotic effect may result from their edemic effect, from an increased narcissistic pleasure in a more attractive and therefore sexual body, and, possibly, from low levels of intruding negative emotions. The female response to androgen administration may depend upon whether she is psychologically capable of responding erotically or whether increased body sensitivity will increase previously established sexual anxieties. (It is also possible that endocrine administration for the purpose of increasing sexual arousal, administered by a male physician, is itself anxiety-reducing.)

The emphasis on the effects of androgen in women may seem exaggerated to those who are not embroiled in the disputes about the psychology of women and specifically the sexuality of women. The importance of these data is that they underline the importance of the clitoral system for female eroticism. The sole function of the clitoris is to enhance eroticism, and acknowledgement of the ready sexual arousability of the clitoris ends forever the idea that the human female is not a sexy organism. Conversely, androgen does not seem to affect the sensitivity of the vagina. This is not too surprising, since the vaginal barrel is not very sensitive in the first place. The low level of sensitivity is highly functional—if the vagina were sensitive, one-child families would be the rule.

Infrequent vaginal masturbation in young girls is not the result of inhibitions but the result of the insensitivity of this "silent" organ. Relatively infrequent clitoral masturbation is the result of the small size and inaccessibility of the clitoris. In adolescence, the periodic increase in sexual tension during the secretory phase of the menstrual cycle, the increased erogeneity of the breasts, the sensitivity of the clitoris, and the psychological concept of vaginal fusion will combine to produce a sexual female where a relatively asexual girl had been. But the slow arousability of the human female reminds us that there are differences in the imperativeness of sexual impulses in the two sexes. I think that sex *qua* sex is much less important for women than for men, and I will contend in the pages to follow that love and maternity are more crucial in the self-definition and self-esteem of women.

The genitals, the brain, and the hormones all contribute to human sexuality, and sexual functioning will be impaired if any of the three are not normal (Young, 1961). Within the limits of a normal endocrine range, sexual responsiveness may be increased or decreased by administering or omitting a hormone. The hormones have direct effects on the genitals, keeping them erotically functional, and are in part responsible for the genital and pelvic signals that are relayed to the brain. Hormones are not solely responsible for human sexuality, but the cortex has not emancipated man from hormonal influence.

There is a disjointed quality to the presentation of the data on sex hormones because we have not been able to generalize one phenomenon to another. I would like to be able to say, for example, that high levels of estrogen are associated with feelings of self-esteem and ego integration and are not associated with anxiety, hostility, and depression. We do not know the basic physical mechanism for this correlational observation during the menstrual cycle. Would one find the same effect in studies of pregnancy? Are low estrogens a major cause of menopausal depression? Postpartum depression?

More questions occur: How do the endocrines act upon the central nervous system so as to influence mood states? Does progesterone inhibit or interfere with the effect of estrogen? What does androgen do to the effect of estrogen, or to estrogen and progesterone combined? I cannot answer these questions endocrinologically and I cannot answer them psychologically, but the research cited in this chapter is tantalizing. I urge my peers to explore these general and specific questions.

What can I say with some feeling of confidence? I think that the physiological changes of the menstrual cycle result in significant psychological change. Alternately, phases of the menstrual cycle are associated with characteristic moods that are primarily dependent upon physical state rather than upon attitudes about reproductive function. Our research suggests that changes in endocrine levels result in changes in psychological states and that this might occur during pregnancy, postpartum, in nursing, during menopause, as a result of using oral contraceptives, as well as during the menstrual cycle. This research is only beginning.

chapter 3
PSYCHOLOGY
AND THE SEXUAL
BODY

In the preceding chapter we examined evidence that general shifts in mood or emotions are typical of normal women, that they seem to derive from the physical state, and that they do not seem to be significantly influenced by individual motives, attitudes, or personality qualities. But mood-shift is linked to behavior, and we know that behavior is an expression of motives, attitudes, and personality qualities as well as moods. At the same time that endocrine levels seem to influence general mood states (passivity, content-ment, depression, hostility), specific behavior is being influenced by per-sonal confidence, attitudes about sex and the reproductive system, and qualities of independence and self-esteem. In this chapter we begin to look at the development of the specific content of the female psychological state. We will discuss the female's attitude toward her own sexual body in relation to menstruation, coitus, orgasm, and eroticism.

AMBIVALENCE IN THE YOUNG FEMALE

Perhaps the single most significant threat to a girl's mature sexuality is the extraordinary change in her sexual body at adolescence. She will menstruate and be subject to periodic endocrine fluctuations; she will develop a new body and a new body image; she will be on the threshold of sexual activity and maternity; and she will still have, as her dominant need, the need to be loved. She will eagerly reach out to grow up and enjoy the privileges of maturity—and simultaneously, frightened by the reality and future responsibilities of her new body, she will withdraw and self-consciously play at being grown up.

My 5-year-old daughter just received a gift of an elaborate toy make-up set. My 11-year-old daughter received a bottle of cologne. They are already beginning to learn the future value of their appearance. What is "growing up" to them? The 5-year-old wants breasts and babies and wants to know if she'll be old when she's a grandmother. The 11-year-old wants to grow up so that she can tell her kids what to do, and she would kind of like to be dating because she thinks she'll be in control then too. There is an interesting difference between the two girls. The older one knows all of the details of the reproductive physiology—and so she has, at least for now, stopped talking about babies and motherhood. While maternity in some distant future is still a valued goal, the more immediate threat of menstruation and the threat of the not-too-distant penetration of coitus have aroused anxieties that the younger one cannot imagine. That is one thing we are going to talk about—the real ambivalence toward the reproductive functions so characteristic of preadolescents and adolescents in this culture.

Prepubertal girls, except for verbally expressing a desire for babies to play with and care for, do not find sex and sensuality very important. These girls are very curious but I suspect that their concept of their future roles is ambivalent at best. A child's tolerance of blood and pain tends to be minimal; menstruation means bleeding and perhaps cramps, the "curse"; intercourse is intrusion into the most embarrassingly private part of the physical self; pregnancy is obviously awkward, with the terror of labor at its consummation; lactation is associated with animals, especially cows. Oversimplifying somewhat, we could say that unlike boys, who may associate their genitals solely with pleasure, girls receive a double message: On the one hand sex is pleasurable, menstruation an entry into womanhood, and maternity most fulfilling; on the other hand sex is dirty, menstruation is sick, and ladies can die in childbirth—which occurs in a hospital.

Think for a moment about our attitudes toward menstruation and pregnancy. Ads for sanitary napkins and tampons assure the reader that if these products are used, the user will be able to carry on as if she were "normal." Pregnancy, too. We not only design maternity clothes to minimize the optical shock of that preceding abdomen, we also tell the pregnant woman that she ought to carry on as if she were normal. Not only do we have a widespread symptom of denial—we also, by implication, view the menstruating and the pregnant woman as abnormal. Psychologically speaking, that is not too supportive. The beginning of menstruation, pregnancy, birth, lactation, and prolonged infant care are all periods of *normal crisis.* Generally speaking, as a culture we deny their crisis character and their worth. Except on Mother's Day.

No wonder the girls ask questions. And don't. They reduce anxiety by holding fanciful conversations between themselves and avoiding discussions of intimate reality with their mothers. To the extent that their future reproductive roles are viewed with distaste, I suspect girls will be ambivalent about growing up. In the silence of this culture, they are not likely to receive a great deal of reassurance with which to resolve the fears of normal crisis. In any event, ambivalence toward the sexual body is likely to be a part of the psyche of even our normal women.

THE DEVELOPMENT OF IDEAS ABOUT MENSTRUATION

Only in a few young women have I ever found the feeling that menstruation is a pleasurable reassurance of femininity. My healthier subjects tend to report that menstruation is "just there," "all right," "okay." They mean that it is not too intrusive in their lives. But with very few exceptions, all of the women I have ever interviewed have recalled the circumstances of their first menstrual period and their responses to it. That alone is evidence for its enormous importance in their lives. The onset of menstruation means that a girl is normal, growing up, going to be a woman. Yet, strangely, apparently negative feelings towards menstruation and the menstruating woman are expressed in all cultures. The menstruating woman is dirty, taboo, unclean. This feeling is ancient and widespread,[1] and the menstruating woman is likely to internalize it and also to resent it. I sometimes wonder how much girls resent the fact that men do not menstruate (and do not get pregnant, and so on). Normally, bleeding means damage or injury. It is an extraordinary jump for women to accept the idea that bleeding means health. Therefore, fears of having been ripped (raped?) in the vulnerable body interior are not unusual in young girls who have had no preparation for menstruation. Shainess (1961) found that women who had had no advance preparation

---

[1]Pliny (quoted in Fluhmann, 1966) wrote that "on the approach of a woman in this state, new wine will become sour, seeds which are touched by her will become sterile, grass withers away, garden plants are parched up, and the fruit will fall from the tree beneath which she sits." Menstruating women are described as "unclean" in the Bible; the original Hebrew word also described lepers. In Old Testament law a woman is ritually unclean whenever an "issue of blood" comes from her body; Orthodox Jewish women still go through a purification ceremony.

whatever experienced fantasies of being cut or damaged. But the 75 percent of her study group who had had advance knowledge still anticipated menstruation with anxiety, fear, and dread. (She also found that the majority of their mothers' reactions were not too helpful.) Benedek (1959) tells us that menstruation is the forerunner of the pain of defloration and the injuries that will be felt in childbirth, and that from pain and discomfort will emerge awareness of the uterus and the rest of the internal organs. The girl has the enormous task of accepting the uterus and motherhood as part of her self, and Benedek feels that if this psychological task is accomplished the girl will be able to accept menstruation "without undue protest." To me that is still a very negative attitude, but professional attitudes reflect general cultural values.

Deutsch (1944) points out that puberty is a particularly narcissistic phase. The girl's love for her own body increases, and she shows a particularly anxious concern for its welfare. (It is also the time when she becomes aware of the importance of her body in provoking interest from boys.) At this time ideas about being torn or dismembered internally, ideas of pain, blood, and cruelty, are submerged deeply into the unconscious. What we can observe is a general irritation about having to menstruate, which is a dilute derivative of the original powerful fears.

The extraordinary event of menstruation arouses negative feelings toward blood and pain and a simultaneous narcissistic concern for the welfare of the body. There is now a periodic increase in sexual arousability and masturbation, along with an increase in anxiety about sex and mutilation. There is an increase in emotional lability, with, perhaps, the beginning of a mistrust of the changeable body as the stable core of the world alongside positive feelings of "I'm normal, I'm female, I made it." There is disappointment that the real world and one's role in it has changed so little, and there is also the feeling of having grown up. There is increased pleasure in the sensuality of masturbation and increased anxiety or guilt about that sensuality. There is ambivalence.

THE DEVELOPMENT OF IDEAS ABOUT SEXUALITY

Perhaps most interesting of all is the cultural emphasis on and reward for the cosmetic exterior of the sexual body—as though the developing breasts and hips are attached for seduction alone. Adolescent girls easily verbalize their concern about their (competitive) surface appearance but are given little opportunity to verbalize their concern about internal reproductive functions.

For girls as well as boys, the years before puberty are mainly directed towards the development of skills that are not sex-specific but age-specific. I mean that both boys and girls are preoccupied with mastering techniques in school, with athletics, and with interpersonal relations that are appropriate for their age. Boys and girls tend to play separately, and interaction between them is asexual, or teasing, or a kind of ritualized semiaggressive flirting. In this kind of interaction they are anticipating later adolescent flirting, but in prepuberty the real quality of genital sexuality is essentially missing. Girls in these years rarely masturbate directly and consciously. When boys and girls do engage in some kind of sex play, the primary motive is curiosity. Although girls have been quick to pick up the idea that coitus is a brutal act on the part of the male and therefore very threatening, they also wonder what all the giggling is about, and, to some extent, they experiment too. I find that my children and their friends respond to sex information in the same way my friends and I did twenty-five years ago. They see sex as funny and ridiculous, and too private, and not possibly engaged in for pleasure alone. (Perhaps it is a clear extension of anxiety that many prepubertal children seem certain that *their* parents make love only when they want to make a baby.)

I think that for girls the idea that sex is fused with maternity originates early. This derives in part from the lack of erogeneity of the vagina and the rest of the internal organs, and is also a defensive reaction to penetration and mutilation anxieties. Based on physiology and observations of behavior, we can say it is doubtful that vaginal sensations occur in the prepubertal girl (Sherfey, 1966). I think that for girls the reproductive system presents a psychological threat without the compensation of familiar, significant, genital pleasure. We can see that adolescent girls enjoy flirting, kissing, and petting, but they are not motivated by strong, specifically genital urges.

So we characteristically see in the healthy adolescent who has accepted her femininity an anticipation of her sexual functions, a pleasure in being desired and courted, and an acute awareness of the changes in her appearance. Still responding to others, she will value these physical changes mostly as a means of securing love from new sources. Her sexuality, emerging from the pubertal physical changes, will be confounded by fear and by the anticipation of love. The adolescent crush is a very sexy relationship, but for the girl it is not related to a vaginal sexuality. In addition, the reality of the menstrual cycle and the fear of pregnancy will tend to fuse sexuality with maternity and this will tend to preclude easy vaginal sex play. Fearful of providing a contraceptive, fearful of becoming pregnant, not vaginally aroused, her primary motive for engaging in coitus is not the gratification of her own sexuality but the gratification of her partner's out of her need to be loved.

The boy's sexual development is comparatively simple and linear. The extremely erotic penis, which has been perceptually dominant since earliest childhood, remains the executor of his sexuality. The girl is less invested in the genitals and genital sexuality because of the internal nature of her reproductive organs and the lesser sensitivity of those organs. A general body sensuality and a need for love are more significant for the adolescent girl than physical sexuality.

The sexuality of the adolescent girl fuses with the rewards of dating. Early dating is the testing ground for success in the very new femininity and feminine desirability. As a result the girl is ready to fall in love again and again, and she assures herself of her desirability by her collection of broken hearts—but she is much less aware of the sexual character of her feelings than is the boy. I think she enjoys the power of flirting and is scared to death that the boy will pressure her to intercourse. Her sexuality is more easily sublimated or denied than the boy's. Indeed she is ambivalent toward her genitals—regarding them as something precious and simultaneously as something dirty. They are also a source of danger because gratification of genital sexuality will lower her self-esteem in her own eyes and, she fears, in the eyes of her lover.

The girl's inhibitions have several origins. More obviously, she is afraid of personal and social rejection; less obviously, not being suffused with a high sexual drive she has difficulty in perceiving vaginal sex as pleasurable and confounds sex with blood, mutilation, pain, penetration, and pregnancy. The combination of minimal vaginal arousal and important fears results in minimal genital sexuality.

Attitudes about sex also reveal concepts about the self. An adolescent girl derives pleasure and an increase in esteem from her new womanly body. The responses from parents, girlfriends, and boys add to her narcissistic pleasure. She is likely to spend hours before a mirror experimenting with hair, makeup, and clothes. The whole exciting world of dating, of being courted, is beginning. Her fantasies are likely to be about a dream-prince (in contrast to the specifically sexual fantasies of the boy). Behaviorally we often see crushes, experientially she may know petting. Her sexual feelings are more diffuse than specific although she is increasingly aware that her body is a source of pleasure and a source of (menstrual) pain. Typically, she wants to be loved, but she needs to be esteemed. As her sexual desirability increases, so does parental watchfulness. Her fears of becoming pregnant are reinforced and anxieties about being a "good girl" are increased. Wanting to succeed heterosexually, longing to be chosen, to be reassured that she is lovable and desirable, she is in a bind because she has not yet developed the social skills that will enable her to withstand the pressure for coitus and yet maintain the heterosexual relationship. Simultaneously, she may have found precoital sexual activity pleasurable enough to make her want to experience intercourse, but she is afraid. (Coitus, menstruation, and pregnancy are all intrusions into the self.) She is afraid of the guilt, mutilation, and pain associated with coitus and pregnancy and she is afraid of rejection by her lover, her parents, and the society of which she is a part.

The resolution of this crucial ambivalence toward the sexual body is a task that apparently extends beyond the adolescent years. Sexual attitudes in women reflect their pleasure in femininity, their attitudes toward reproductive physiology, and their general level of confidence or self-esteem. It is therefore not surprising that with few exceptions the woman's sexual life remains more inhibited than the man's. It is also not surprising that the female condition for sexuality is love and trust. Until she has evolved an unambivalent sexuality, it is only in the romantic circumstances of mutual love that the girl can engage in coital activity without feeling that she is being used.

ADULT AMBIVALENCE ABOUT COITUS

We all know that orgasm is at least the vocal goal of women as well as men. Premarital coitus is frequent, pregnancy need no longer be a realistic fear, and women are talking a good game. In other words, there has been an extreme shift in the expectations of both sexes in which the lauded frigidity of the Victorian woman has been replaced by the desired spontaneous sexuality of the Scandinavian. Sex has become an achievement situation for women as well as for men.

So far as premarital sex is concerned, there has been an evolution and not a revolution since the 1920s. Numerically, the overwhelming majority of girls who participate in premarital coitus feel that they have made a deep emotional commitment to a man and that he has made a similar commitment to them. The "justification" for the behavior is love, but all is ambivalence—having given their love they are afraid that they have cheapened themselves and it will become a case of "love 'em and leave 'em." On the other hand, withholding themselves results in the taunt of frigidity, and that may be even worse. Mores *are* changing—but they have not yet changed. The fear is not completely mythological. Ehrmann (1959, p. 269) wrote:

. . . males are more conservative and the females are more liberal in expressed personal codes of sex conduct and in actual behavior with lovers than with nonlovers. In other words, the degree of physical intimacy actually experienced or considered permissible is among males *inversely* related and among females *directly* related to the intensity of familiarity and affection in the male-female relation. . . . Female sexual expression is primarily and profoundly related to being in love and going steady. . . . Male sexuality is more indirectly and less exclusively associated with romanticism and intimacy relationships.

INFLUENCE ON MORES OF THE ORAL CONTRACEPTIVE

One important event in the evolution of sexual mores has been the widespread use of oral contraceptives. The availability of the pill was assumed to be a great liberator. We find that it has increased many young women's difficulties by removing the main realistic reason for virginity. Joan Zweben and I are presently conducting a study on the psychological consequences of using oral contraceptives (Bardwick, 1968). Originally conceived as a study of psychosomatic symptoms, it is turning out to be a study of sexual morality. Since we knew that a very large number of healthy women find the symptoms of pill use intolerable, we attempted to predict which women would react to the pills so severely as to stop using them. Our subjects are for the most part young women—unmarried, engaged, or just married— many of them college students. In our studies we find that attitudes about contraception also reveal feelings about sex, the sexual partner, and the self. Assuming responsibility for contraception is itself an important behavior that our subjects have strong feelings about.

Before they start taking the pills we give the subjects a battery of psychological tests and a long and detailed interview. The initial interview takes from one-and-a-half to two hours, and since there is nothing so pleasurable as talking about oneself to someone who is interested, the subjects all thank us for the opportunity to talk about things they generally cannot talk about. About three months after they start using the pills, we send them a psychological test and a questionnaire. We have completed data on 150 young women.

For the subjects of our admittedly nonrepresentative population, it is very clear that female eroticism is primarily psychological, primarily a function of wanting to love and to secure love. When we ask why they make love, very very few ever answer because it is a pleasure for *them*. This is a sexuality far removed from direct body sensations, and it was true for both the unmarried and the married subjects. The healthier responses included ideas like "It makes us feel close," or "It's an expression of our love"; frequently we hear "It makes him happy," "He wants it," "It's expected." Almost no subjects report reaching orgasm, and yet they say it is all right with them, their sex life is still satisfactory. Is that true? Oddly enough, I think so. There is a kind of conscious disappointment that the delights of orgasm elude them, but it is not terribly important. Most important is the feeling of closeness in the relationship, which they ensure by their sexual participation. But that is a danger too. Without a mutuality of sexual response, where sexual participation is motivated in a one-sided way primarily in order to secure love and from a fear of losing love, there is a giving of self and an increase of vulnerability that overburdens the sexual act itself.

MOTIVES FOR COITUS

The answers to our question "Why do you make love?" suggest that the pleasures of sex *qua* sex are rather rare for this population. Many answers were stereotyped responses, part of the cultural milieu but not really true for the individual—for example, one of the responses was "for the physical release." But these same subjects reported experiencing no orgasm, or something "pleasant" (which is not an orgasm), or "I don't know if I have an orgasm" (which also means no orgasm). Perhaps the most frequent response was the perception of sex as an important technique for communicating love in a relationship which they hoped was mutual—or the observation that if they did not participate sexually the relationship would be ended. For most, the sex act is important because the male makes it important; for these women, it tended not to be important in its own right. Sexual motives revealed general heterosexual motives:

"Because it's a means of getting closer to him."

"I guess because I love him."

"With him it's a giving, sharing, relaxing experience. If I say I don't feel like it, he'll just hold me instead. The ultimate in being together."

"I enjoy it to a certain extent. If I like the person I have a desire to please; desire to please rather than be pleased."

"The emotional commitment resulted in my having an orgasm."

"I enjoy it and make the other person happy."

"Right now to please him."

"Because it's a natural expression of what I feel for him—and it's mutual."

"If I didn't love him I wouldn't enjoy it."

"I like to. It's another way of being intimate with someone, can cement other actions, bring more meaning into other things. Another kind of relationship that depends on other aspects of the relationship."

"A very social thing to do—a way of reaching people."

"I don't know. I think it's really necessary as a symbol of the involvement."

"Some would say that intercourse is not sex for women because all she does is grin and bear it. As far as I'm concerned the pleasure of intercourse has to be learned. Before a woman can accept the fact, that sex is a pleasure, men have a better time of it because they're not so emotionally involved. Once an emotional basis is formed, there's consideration of both."

"It's pleasurable I guess. It's expected."

"I enjoy it. I envy men their freedom and ability to see sex with nothing else attached."

"I don't mind not getting excited or reaching orgasm. It's nice when it happens, but sometimes it requires more work than it's worth.

"Well, a great strain not to. Fairly reluctant for awhile, but then I realized it had become a great big thing in the relationship and it would disintegrate the relationship . . . I wanted to also."

"It seems natural and because at this point it would harm the relationship not to."

"Mostly to see my boyfriend's enjoyment."

"I gave in to Sidney because I was so lonely."

"Besides the fact that it's a natural thing to do and we enjoy each other's company, want to feel united—and it's the first time I made a decision without someone helping me."

"I feel more of a woman because I'm treated as a very special woman. Once we began sexual intercourse I felt more feminine."

"Since we're getting married, it's not wrong."

Overwhelmingly our subjects reported that they made love with one special boyfriend toward whom they felt deeply committed, or had intercourse with their fiancé or husband. Although the absolute contraception of the pill could permit more promiscuous behavior, we saw very few women who had intercourse with more than one partner. Overall, one of the psychological threats of the pill is that it means that contraception is preplanned—the female has made a sexual decision and has difficulty in continuing to perceive her sexual participation as the result of some momentary passion. Taking the pill can arouse anxiety about one's morality and this anxiety is an emotion that is strongly defended against. In spite of any "sex revolution," sexual participation seems to remain emotionally loaded for this population; the young woman feels vulnerable partly because she gets so little real sexual pleasure from the act and partly because she is afraid she has degraded herself and will be abandoned as an immoral person.

"I feel like a hard woman because taking the pill is an admission of what I'm doing. I detest these changes! Every time I have to swallow one of these pills I dislike the relationship we have a little more."

"The pill makes you aware of your sexual actions at all times."

"There's not the risk involved. This is an unselfish thing I'm doing but part of the mystique is gone. Taking responsibility brings anxiety—or sex is great but the purpose of sex is not there—and yet I'm glad."

"I don't expect that I'll become promiscuous. If anything happens I won't credit it to the pills."

"This is a big moral question for me. He was for it. Not sexually inexperienced, but before very sporadic. But now this is more serious and steady. According to my decision—I thought about psychological changes— would it take something away from it because it's so easy—any time of the day. . . . Psychologically I wonder how I'll feel if we broke up—and future husband . . . tell him I took the pill for this other boy. By giving yourself all this freedom and the consequences aren't there. . . . Premarital sex I can justify, but you take the pill when you're alone, not romantic—whether you like him today or not."

Almost all of our subjects have expressed fears in relation to sex, contraception, the loss of love, and abandonment. We also see prostitution anxieties, that is, the fear that allowing oneself to be used, or even consciously seducing in order to secure affection, is deprecating. The anxiety of these women is not simply that they will be abandoned, left alone, but that they have desecrated themselves in a nonfinancial, psychological form of prostitution. This fear we find in the psychological responses of almost all of our subjects, whether or not they are married. They generally fear that they will lose love and be abandoned by their lover; a one-sided, especially a premarital, sexual relationship increases this psychological vulnerability. Without arousal and with fear of abandonment, the female is afraid of simply being used.

On a conscious level our subjects are afraid the male will leave them if they refuse intercourse; on an unconscious level they are afraid he will leave them because they have had intercourse with him. Especially among these young women this conflict cannot be resolved because they do not yet have a sufficient internal sense of self-esteem. It is likely that women with high self-esteem participate in sex as free agents without fears and that they are less vulnerable to feelings of being used because they have not let themselves be used. But the age-group we studied was still dependent upon others' acceptance, with a core of fear of being rejected, and still defined themselves in terms of someone else, especially the man in their lives. We can see, at least in our sample of 150 women, that after having given themselves physically as well as psychologically their anxiety and their vulnerability had not decreased.

It is theoretically logical to assume that some young women enhance feelings of self-esteem as well as feelings of sexuality and femininity when they participate in important sexual relationships. In our research we find that these feelings may be expressed consciously, but the projective data still show preoccupation with the consequences of their vulnerability: prostitution anxiety and fears of abandonment. Startled by these data, we gave TAT tests (the projective measurement) to an additional 150 young women, both married and unmarried. The second group of tests reveals very similar themes. We suspect that this psychological vulnerability is normal, but perhaps not desirable, for middle-class women in this age group.

Unfortunately, we know that unmarried women often justify sexual activity by linking it to a spontaneous and heady passion that dissolves all prior control. I say unfortunately because we see many of these young women in homes for unmarried mothers. Behaviorally this may mean that they do not use contraceptives because having and using a contraceptive is an act of forethought—the negation of this overriding spontaneous passion. Obviously, taking an oral contraceptive every day is a conscious, deliberate, repetitive act. This makes it, among our sample of unmarried and newly married women, an anxiety-provoking act. While on the one hand sex can now be romantic and therefore "justified," taking the pill means the end of sexual passivity and the conscious assumption of responsibility for contraception and therefore for sex. This conscious responsibility tends to increase anxiety and increase unconscious prostitution fears, with the net result that the subjects are even more fearful that men will hold them in contempt and leave them. It is also rather interesting to note their response to the reality of the increased female sexual freedom that the pill allows. Not infrequently our subjects told us that they resent the greater freedom of the male, including his sexual freedom—but they never saw the pill as assuring their own sexual license.

Judging from the subjects we have seen, conflict about the sexual use of the body in young women in the collegiate generation has not diminished in spite of safe contraception and an evolving sexual freedom in the culture. The origin of this conflict is the girl's ambivalence toward her sexual body, her vulnerability in interpersonal relationships, her inability to experience sex as a physical rather than psychological involvement, and the residues of an older morality which are still powerful and which have been internalized as standards of behavior. So we find this odd situation in which many women are consciously disappointed about their inability to experience enormous sexual arousal because the new mythology says that it is their due and because it is regarded as the mark of health. On the other hand, and perhaps with some slight apology, basically they really don't mind—as long as they are loved.

I think we can say that although orgasm is not the important thing in their relationship, the young women are disappointed when they do not achieve it. We do girls an injustice. We inhibit their sexual responsivity through years of reinforcing the inhibitions which define "good girls"; we also, and increasingly, justify premarital coitus so long as it occurs in the context of love—but we do not tell girls that their orgasmic reaction requires considerable deinhibition, experience, and skill. Unfortunately, angels rarely strew rose petals in the bridal chamber. Combinations of fear, ambivalence, and high expectations usually result in disappointment.

THE FEMALE ORGASM

Women experience a range of climactic responses in coitus, all of which are defined as orgasm but many of which are less extreme and definitive than orgasm in men. Even with the inclusion of lesser responses, the percentage of women reporting orgasm is significantly lower. Kinsey et al. (1953) found that whereas almost 100 percent of the males in their study had achieved orgasm by the age of 17, only 30 percent of the females had achieved orgasm before marriage. Maximum orgasmic response in the female was not reached until the age of 35. (Experience and increased vascularity after pregnancy are probably responsible, at least in part.)

Wallin (1960) questioned 540 wives and found that among those who described themselves as rarely or never reaching orgasm, some also reported that they usually experienced complete relief from sexual desires. For these women sex was a psychological and not a physical act so that intercourse was satisfying and enjoyable without orgasm. Similarly, Schaefer (1964) found that the orgasm was not always part of the sexual contentment of her female subjects, that the orgasmic reaction appeared to be learned rather than automatic, and that it was experienced in a subjective and individual way.[2]

It seems to me that these reports clearly infer a lack of strong sexual arousal in the first place—because the female who has reached a high plateau level of arousal is going to need release from the physical tension created by the arousal. Several ideas occur to me. It seems clear that the male model of a strong sexual drive is not applicable to women. In the absence of a powerful physical impulse, the possibility for emotional contributions is stronger. Sexuality for women has a greater experiential component than for men and is more involved with emotional ties; sex as a physical desire may never develop as a strong motive. The absence of high sexual arousal levels has as its consequence a lower probability of orgasm, further contributing to the lack of strong sexual desire. On the other hand, endocrine changes associated with the menstrual cycle and expectations of high sexual responsivity as evidence of successful normalcy create a physical and a psychological need for high levels of sexual performance. The psychoanalytic idea that women are moved by strong sexual drives in the same way that men are has led to the overestimation of sex as a significant variable in the lives of women. There has also been a lack of recognition of the cyclic nature of desire and of the strength of maternity-nurturance as a powerful female need.

PHYSIOLOGY OF THE ORGASM

The publication of Masters and Johnson's data (1966 et al.) has given the world the first objective and detailed portrait of the human female's physiological sex responses. Their work is of incalculable value clinically and theoretically.[3] With the exception of Sherfey, so far as I am aware, psychologists, psychiatrists, and psychoanalysts have not yet begun to respond to this work by modifying existing theories and revising clinical expectations. One of the criticisms leveled at Masters and Johnson's work was that no information was given about the subjects; this was a necessary precaution assuring anonymity for the participating women. A most significant point in their reports is that the physiological responses to sexual arousal and

[2]Here is a slightly irrelevant aside which I would hate to omit. Friedman (1962) wrote a book about virgin wives, or tales of unconsummated marriages. I think that we would all assume this to be a very rare phenomenon. He reports that the ten doctors in one clinic saw *seven hundred* cases during two-and-a-half years of study!

[3]In 1967 I had the pleasure of hearing Dr. Masters address a large convocation at the University of Michigan. Controversy about his work was widespread and the audience was originally pro–con and curious. Within a very few minutes Dr. Masters had charmed us all and had established so much rapport that the main part of his talk was devoted to answering questions from the now enthusiastic and honest audience. Perhaps the most memorable remark he made was that the word "pleasant" never described the orgasm.

orgasm conform to the same pattern in all their subjects regardless of psychological differences. In other words, the physiological arousal and orgasmic reaction will be basically identical in all women—psychological differences will help to determine whether a particular woman becomes sufficiently aroused sexually to be able to achieve an orgasm.

From the anatomic and physiological point of view an orgasm is an orgasm. If sexual stimulation is successful, the response of the pelvic organs is the same. The stimulation may come from clitoral-area manipulation, from natural or artificial coition, or, in some subjects, from breast manipulation. Physiologically, there is no difference in sexual response regardless of the source of the sexual stimulation.

Perhaps the most important conclusions from the Masters and Johnson data are these:

1. Disregarding anatomic differences, male and female orgasms are physiologically the same. In both sexes a reflex stretch mechanism in the responding muscles is set off when the vasocongestive distention reaches a crucial point. The orgasm is initiated by similar muscle components.
2. There is no such thing as a vaginal orgasm without a clitoral orgasm. The clitoral and vaginal orgasm form one anatomic entity. The orgasmic reaction is generalized to all of the pelvic sex organs and is the same reaction regardless of the mode or area of stimulation.
3. Sexual response patterns differ among women and differ for the same woman at different times. Some women, at some times (probably maximally premenstrually), are capable of a response pattern very similar to that of men (see pattern C in Figure 5, page 64).
4. Stimulation of the clitoris in its retracted and tumescent state is achieved by the pressing of the penis against the labia, by the rhythmical pulling of the enlarged clitoral hood, and by direct clitoral-area friction. In any event, and in any position, clitoral stimulation is always achieved during intravaginal coitus, although direct penile contact is not possible when the clitoris is retracted into the clitoral hood.
5. When fully aroused, women are capable of many orgasms. Masters and Johnson report that vaginal coitus can result in as many as six or more orgasms. With clitoral-area stimulation when the woman can control her own sexual tension they have observed 50 or more orgasms in an hour.
6. The woman is particularly susceptible to psychological influences and in order to become maximally aroused must "turn off" the cognitive processes. Indeed, any cessation of stimulation or any psychological intrusion will swiftly reduce her level of excitation.
7. In heterosexual orgasm the female is unable to achieve orgasm herself and is dependent upon the continued stimulation provided by her partner. The orgasmic contractions will cease if stimulation stops.

Sherfey (1966) adds several hypotheses based upon the Masters and Johnson data; I should like to note two:

1. The erotic potential of the clitoral tip (glans) is greater than that of the lower third of the vagina. That is, the major erotic site in woman is the clitoris and not the vagina. Since the function of the clitoris is to enhance sexual excitement and since the clitoris is in any event stimulated during arousal states, the "goal" of giving up clitoral stimulation in the search for "psychosexual maturity" is unrealistic.[4]
2. The orgasm per se, or the maximal orgasm, is best achieved when there is a high degree of pelvic vasocongestion and edema. This congested state is achieved premenstrually probably due to endocrine levels, and is also achieved through prolonged and effective sexual stimulation. Since each orgasm tends to increase pelvic vasocongestion, the more orgasms achieved the more can be achieved—until physical exhaustion occurs.

Conceive of the vaginal barrel as being divided into two parts, a lower third and an upper two-thirds. The upper part does not respond to sexual stimulation with edema or intense vasocongestion. The upward movement of the uterus during the excitement phase of coitus causes this upper portion to balloon out; it remains relaxed and motionless during the rest of the sexual response cycle, and does not participate in the orgasmic reaction. In addition, the diameter of the ballooned-out vagina is approximately three inches, which means that the upper vagina does not touch the penis except at its extreme lower end. At least the upper portion of the vagina is neither anatomically nor physiologically constructed to participate actively in sexual arousal or the release of sexual tension.

The lower third of the vaginal barrel, in contrast to the upper portion, is considered by Masters and Johnson to constitute an erotogenic zone during active penile thrusts, with a sensitivity about equal to that of the clitoral shaft but not equal to that of the clitoral glans. The main portion of the vagina has few sensory nerve endings, but the entire vagina is copiously equipped with a layer of interconnecting veins which are especially thick in the lower third. During the excitement phase the vaginal passageway dilates to about one-and-a-quarter inches, and in the plateau phase the engorged venous sheath presses the vaginal walls inward until the vaginal opening is less than half of its previous diameter. The vasocongestion therefore narrows the passageway, causing the gripping sensations felt by the penis. Just as narrowing induces greater stimulation of the penis through

---

[4]Anyone not in the business of psychology might well wonder why I continually compare the erotogenic potential of the clitoris and the vagina. The answer is that the psychoanalytic insistence upon the vaginal orgasm, orgasm experienced within the vagina, as the criterion for psychosexual maturity has had enormous theoretical and clinical impact, which has also affected the public's ideas of healthy sexual development (see Chapter 1).

friction, penile activity will induce greater stimulation upon the tighter vaginal walls. Thus there is a reciprocal excitation between the penile shaft and the lower third of the vaginal barrel.

The clitoris, the labia, and the lower third of the vagina all respond simultaneously to sexual arousal. Thus the greater the vasocongestion and edema the greater the pressure of the penis, the lower vagina, the upper labia, and the clitoral glans. Anatomically, the surface of the clitoral glans is incredibly packed with specialized nerve endings which make this androgen-sensitive organ the most erogenous of the female erotic zones. Physiologically, when the lower vagina responds to sexual excitement the clitoral complex automatically responds too. The vagina, even the lower third, can never supplant the clitoris as an erotic zone. The labia, the clitoris, and the vagina function as an integrated erotic zone, while the upper portion of the vagina is anatomically suited to receive sperm. My hunch is that the *physical* sensations during orgasm are not separable into vaginal or clitoral origin. Women who report vaginal orgasms in lieu of clitoral orgasms are either consciously aware only of the intravaginal penis or are trying to show their "mature sexuality." There is a *psychological* difference between vaginal coitus and clitoral manipulation without penile insertion, and we will be discussing this difference.

Considering the pelvic physiology of the female sexual-response cycle, it does not seem possible to separate a clitoral from a vaginal orgasm. That rather ridiculous assumption came about only because analysts managed to perceive the clitoris as a masculine-active organ genetically misplaced in a properly feminine-passive body.

In brief, the vagina is not a strong erotogenic zone. Masters and Johnson report that clitoral stimulation that reaches orgasm may be and frequently is as intense as vaginally induced orgasm and is more likely to induce multiple orgasms. They also report a higher frequency of uterine and rectal contractions, indicating a higher level of pelvic congestion. It would seem that women prefer vaginal stimulation for psychological reasons and clitoral stimulation for physical reasons.

LEVELS OF ORGASMIC RESPONSES

We have been describing the physiological responses of women who are arousable and who have achieved high levels of sexual arousal. There are significant differences in the characteristic levels of arousability between the sexes and there are considerable variations among women in ease of arousability. Whalen (1966) discriminates among *sexual identity,* that is, one's male or female gender role, *object choice,* which refers to the persons toward whom one directs his sexual activities, *sexual gratification,* which is the reinforcement or pleasure associated with sexual activity, and *sexual activity,* which refers to the behavior in reality or fantasy by which one achieves sexual gratification. Of immediate interest to us, he also discriminates between *sexual arousal*, which is the level of sexual excitation the individual has achieved at the moment, and *sexual arousability*, which is "an individual's characteristic rate of approach to orgasm as a result of sexual stimulation," that is, the speed with which one can be aroused.

Arousal and arousability are determined by experience or learning and by the physiological state of the organism. Physiologically, the important variables are the hormonal determinants of arousability (which we have described in Chapter 2) and the feedback effect of sexual activity upon subsequent arousability. Physiologically and by psychological preparation, successful sexual activity will in turn lead to more successful sexual activity. This effect is therefore partly endocrinological and partly psychological.

I think that arousability in women is more slowly developed than in men and that momentary levels of arousal generally tend to be lower. We know that the excitement phase for a woman must be significantly longer than for a man in order for her to achieve a high enough plateau phase to reach orgasm. The combination of infrequent masturbation, an unerotic vagina, the absence of significant genital stimulation until middle or late adolescence, and the inhibitions resulting from the "good-girl" syndrome combine to make arousability slower and customary levels of arousal lower. In contrast, the male has had considerable masturbatory experience, an immediate high arousal rate (high levels of testosterone), and an immediately sensitive penis. It is pathological when the male, having achieved an erection, is incapable of achieving an orgasm. It is relatively infrequent that the female achieves an arousal level sufficient to experience a satisfying orgasm.

When I interview women I find many who say that their sexual life is satisfactory although they never achieve an orgasm. I think that they have never reached a sufficiently high level of arousal for the lack of orgasm to result in an uncomfortable or painful resolution phase. Another common response from college-age women is that they do achieve orgasm and that it can best be described as "pleasant." You will remember what Dr. Masters said about that. Very rarely do I find young women who have experienced what I call a major orgasm. I suggest that there is a learned pattern involved, perhaps of deinhibition.

Figure 5 shows three types of orgasmic response.[5] I think it is fairly common for young and relatively inexperienced women to achieve pattern A, which is the achievement of the plateau state of arousal with relatively small and minor surges toward the orgasmic level. This kind of sensation is probably best described as pleasant or tingly and one might call it a minor

---

[5] I developed this model as a summary of my impressions from interview data and discussions in my graduate seminar. I was very pleased to see that Masters and Johnson report finding these patterns (1966, p. 5). My presentation differs from theirs in that I think there is a developmental sequence and I believe that pattern C results in a level of arousal lower than resting levels.

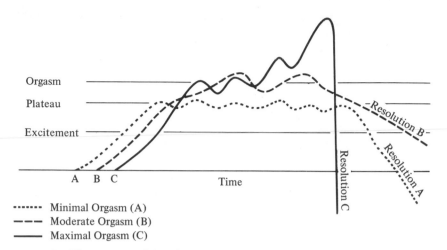

Orgasm

Plateau

Excitement

A   B   C   Time

······ Minimal Orgasm (A)
– – – Moderate Orgasm (B)
——— Maximal Orgasm (C)

Figure 5 Three types of female orgasm.

orgasm. The maximal arousal is not reached, therefore a maximal orgasm is not reached, resolution occurs slowly, and the woman has experienced a "nice" feeling without frustration. I think the primary source of gratification for these women is the feeling of affection or love they achieve. Indeed, this kind of sexual gratification is probably achieved as well through petting as through coitus. Sex as a physical gratification is secondary in this case to sex as an affective, affectionate gratification. In my observations I find that many women never leave this level of arousability.

Through sexual experience and through experimentation that maximizes erotic stimulation, and in the trust of a stable affectionate relationship, some women learn to maximize sensation, feelings, physical pleasure. They learn to forget the self, to deinhibit old inhibitions—they learn to respond more to the physical sensations of sexual arousal.

Since I suspect a learning pattern, I hypothesize that pattern B in the diagram represents an intermediate level of arousability. In pattern B the woman achieves a physiologically defined orgasm but stays at the plateau level and with some stimulation can have recurrent orgasms. I think that there is both a physical and a psychological distinction between patterns B and C.

Pattern C represents an orgasm pattern closest to that of the male. The woman reaches a high plateau state, swiftly achieves a maximal orgasm, and experiences a swift and total resolution phase. Similar to the male, she will take some 15 to 20 minutes at least to recover from this resolution phase. At the end of this type of orgasm the woman, like the man, is at a level of arousal *lower* than when sexual excitement began. Skillful and experienced women report that they are able to control their level of arousal so that they have small orgasms prior to the last large one. They maintain a level of arousal sufficiently high so that body sensations, especially pelvic, are acute, but they postpone reaching the highest level of arousal until they are ready for an explosive orgasm which will mean the end of their immediate sexual excitement.

The decisive, imperative, pattern C orgasm is the least commonly reported among the women I interview. This kind of excitement is not "pleasant"—it has a desperate, imperative quality to it. At this level of arousal the physical sensations of the body are all-important and sex as a physical drive is demanding. Physically it can be described as waves of pure sensation centering especially in the lower pelvic area. At this time sex as a means of giving love or getting love does not exist; this is a body-state and not a psychological condition. Of course, for most women, feelings of affection are important as the psychological precondition for arousal. For those women who have achieved a level of arousability represented by pattern C, not achieving that kind of definitive orgasm is very frustrating. This is true both because they have an expectation of that level of gratification and because the pelvic congestion and edema resulting from their unrelieved high level of arousal leaves them physically (as well as psychologically) uncomfortable.

In summary, I think that the female orgasm, although physiologically always similar in pattern to the male orgasm, occurs in a far greater range of variability. That women can achieve levels of arousability and arousal and orgasm similar in intensity and gratification to men should not lead us to forget that the majority of women never do. I suggest that the multiple-orgasm pattern reported by Masters and Johnson and commented upon by Sherfey represents an intermediate stage in levels of arousability for women. There is the corollary hypothesis that the explosive orgasm, which results in a lower level of arousal than before sexual excitement, represents the most mature and the most elusive sexual-response pattern in women.

Sherfey would, I think, disagree with me. Because an orgasm is promptly followed by the re-engorging of the venous chambers and with edema, each orgasm creates more tissue tension. As a result, Sherfey sees the human female as sexually insatiable because each orgasm actually increases the orgasmic potential of the body. Therefore, according to Sherfey, the idea that the woman should strive for one intense orgasm that will reduce all sexual tension is fallacious. I cannot argue with the physiology and it is perhaps true that the intense orgasm is preceded by a series of smaller orgasms, the total resulting in physical exhaustion and psychological satiation in spite of bodily insatiation. My impression is that women who do achieve an extraordinary, intense orgasm achieve the same kind of orgasmic release as men do—and that their subsequent level of sexual arousal is significantly lower than their original or resting level. Everyone agrees that the male orgasm is satiating and requires a recovery period. I therefore contend that the more closely the female orgasm approximates the intense orgasm of the male, the more satisfying, satiating, and "final" that orgasm is.[6]

As reported by Moore (1961, p. 578), Benedek has said:

. . . female sexuality cannot fit into the male model of sexual maturity upon which psychoanalytic concepts are based. Pregnancy and lactation constitute the completion of psychosexual and reproductive maturity in women, and the drive organization of these phenomena is not "genital" in the same sense as is mating behavior.

And Sherfey has written (1966, p. 90):

In all women, so long as obstetrical damage does not intervene, pregnancies will increase the volume capacity of the pelvic venous bed, increase the volume of the sexual edema, enhance the capacity for sexual tension, and improve orgasmic intensity, frequency, and pleasure. I suggest that natural selection has taken advantage of every random opportunity to make enhanced sexual pleasure the insurance that motherhood will continue unabated.

PSYCHOLOGICAL DETERMINATION OF EROTICISM

Sherfey (1966, p. 34) agrees with both Deutsch and Benedek that vaginal frigidity has not decreased along with the increasing sexual freedom of girls; rather, clitoral eroticism and fixation have increased. I think this is likely to be true because I interpret it as meaning that sexual erogeneity, or sex as a physical sensation, increases with the increasing sexual freedom of girls. As a result, awareness of the physical sensations that derive from clitoral stimulation would naturally increase and not decrease. I regard this as indicating a healthy increase in sexuality. Sherfey also comments on the difficulty women have in describing their sexual sensations and she wonders if this is due to women knowing that they do not experience what they are "supposed" to. That is, women are afraid that what they are feeling is not what the healthy woman should feel and they wonder whether they are normal. It is very likely that they expect "normal" to mean that the vagina is the site of important erogenous sensations.

There *is* an important difference between vaginal and clitoral sensations, and the difference is psychological. For all women, and I am including young girls who masturbate and pet, the primary source of sexual excitation is the clitoris. But for the psychologically mature woman, sex is conceived of within a relationship, with love, to a specific man. This is an active female attitude—but receptive. *Coitus is perceived as the physical and psychological*

---

[6]I do not wish to give the impression that I generally disagree with Dr. Sherfey. Hers is an insightful and valuable paper which I strongly recommend to those interested in the Masters and Johnson data and its effect upon psychoanalytic theory.

fusion with the loved man. This is a psychological change from an essentially egocentric, masturbatory activity to receptive activity linked to another. The logical, the dominant organ of fusion is the vagina. The primary source of physical sensation remains the clitoris; the site of physical-psychological fusion is the vagina. In this *psychological* sense there is a change from a clitoral to a vaginal orgasm.

In women, thinking gets in the way of sex. Sherfey puts it more scientifically when she observes that the participation of the higher cortical and intellectual centers is nil during sexual arousal. From our discussions in Chapter 2, you will recall Benedek's finding that when estrogen levels are high the direction of a woman's emotional life is turned outward to the interpersonal and to achieving. You will also recall that sexual arousability seems highest in the second half of the cycle when attention is drawn inward, into the self (this is also reminiscent of Eriksen's observations). A task orientation, an activity directed outward, seems antithetical to sexual arousal. Masters and Johnson have also noted that female eroticism is very vulnerable to psychological disturbance—like thinking. How difficult! The female will be most arousable when she stops thinking about her sexual participation, her elusive vaginal orgasm, her desired (and observable) responses, what she is supposed to do and say and think and feel. She has to unlearn learning; she is sexiest when she thinks least and feels most.

The female who is sexually arousable has to be tactilely sensitive, psychologically able to give of herself, and able to enjoy the psychological awareness of body penetration. I hope it is clear that women can be, and some are, spontaneously and honestly sexy; it just seems more difficult for the female of the species than the male. The sexuality of the human female seems to be a developed ability. It is more vulnerable to a lack of development, more fragile and easily disturbed, than is usually true for the sexuality of the male.

The interpretation of body signals and environmental stimuli as erotogenic (and therefore as pleasurable or threatening), and the range of stimuli perceived as erotic, will differ widely between individuals and between the sexes. That is, the range of possible erotogenic stimuli will have a developmental history that has emerged from the ease and dominance of body sexuality, which itself also interacts with the individual's history in the particular culture. The range of stimuli that are erotogenic for women seems likely to be far narrower than the range for men.

The absence of a powerful sex motive in women is not only the result of massive repressions and denial; it is a logical extension of the anatomy of the female body and of the girl's relationship to the sexual body. Surely a large part of feminine sexuality has its origin in the need to feel loved, to be reassured about that love, and to feel that one is actively creating an intimate and mutual love.

A man may fail in sex and that failure is public. Impotence, premature ejaculation, or an inability to satisfy his partner are critical failures that cast doubt on his masculinity. The woman can never fail—at least that is what some people think. If she lies passively and at least is not rejecting and perhaps adds some particularly cooing noises near the end, she can fake sexual excitement and resolution. Her anxiety has been seen not in terms of successful performance but in terms of fears of being left or of not being attractive enough to stimulate erotic interest in a man. But this seems to be no longer true. Increasingly, we have an assumption on the part of both partners that the female requires an orgasm and that her orgasm is the sign of the successful performance of both. Now the woman can fear her inability to become aroused—and at the same time, because she can participate without being aroused, she can regard herself as a sexual vessel for the man, or a prostitute. The new sexual freedoms are also bringing new potential areas for anxiety. Now, for everyone, orgasm is an "achievement." This preoccupation with successful orgasm as the sign of successful masculinity or femininity is perhaps related to our pervasive uncertainty about our masculinity and femininity.

Actually, all of this preoccupation with sex is a little revealing. I think that sex, like health and money, is a commodity that the successful purchaser and user can ignore. If your sex life is satisfactory, you can forget it. You're certainly not going to worry about it. In that case, sexual activity is but one activity in a life of diverse activities, and it is no more important than most. The cultural preoccupation with sex reveals a generalized lack of sexual success or security. I daresay for women a much more important preoccupation will be with the quality of the emotional relationship, or the feeling of being loved, or role conflict, or the daily activities of their children. Sex is a behavior to which we bring all of our core attitudes, hopes, and anxieties, in relation to ourselves and in the way we relate to others. It is therefore a particularly revealing behavior. But sexual behavior is not, by itself, character-determining—rather, our attitudes and attributes direct the quality of our sexual behaviors.

For healthy men and women, sex and love, and love and paternity, will fuse. Those who are most able to enjoy themselves, their work, their beloved, and their children, will, on the whole, be most able to enjoy the sensuous pleasures of physical eroticism. They will also not be preoccupied with the subject. Maslow (1954) finds that self-actualized people don't need sex but enjoy it when they have it; although they enjoy sex more than most people, it is also less central in their total frame of reference. "These people do not *need* sensuality; they simply enjoy it when it occurs."

In summary, I think that, far more than for men, the mature woman *is* her body—it is the way in which she attracts men, manipulates them, loves them, secures love, and gratifies both of their sexual and reproductive needs. Her sexual development is more complicated and fragile than that of the man, more vulnerable and easily disturbed. The vagina, which is not erotically prominent, will have to become a part of the sexual self through psychological change. Rather than a body image centered on the genitals, women have a more diffuse eroticity, in the clitoris, the breasts, and the skin. The entire body image is more diffuse, and the entire body is perceived as a sexual object. The reproductive functions of the body are psychologically dominant, but the internal, unobservable, vaguely perceived, not consciously controlled female organs are regarded as mysterious and potentially threatening as well as creative and life-giving. The development of the self as a sexual rather than reproductive organism, with genital primacy, is helped by a cyclic increase in masturbation and arousability, but it is difficult. There is in the female an ambivalent relationship to her own sexual body as she anticipates blood, pain, and mutilation as well as love, pleasure, and creativity. She has come to expect maximal sexual arousal and orgasmic success and is likely to be disappointed should they not occur. If her arousal levels have not climbed high enough she will regard sex primarily as a means of pleasing her partner. She will need to be reassured that she is precious and loved and that by loving she is being good. Her lack of self-esteem will make affiliation very important and sex an emotionally loaded useful tool for garnering love. But this will also be a source of danger because if she uses sex in order to create love she may feel she is prostituting and degrading herself. When sex is psychologically overdetermined, reflecting one's attitude toward oneself and the need for approval from others, when sexual attitudes are an expression of needs that are not directly sexual, a romanticism will result. But if a woman accepts herself as loved, and if the derivatives of early fears are resolved, she can become very erotic.

chapter 4

PSYCHOSOMATIC
DYSFUNCTIONS
OF THE FEMALE
REPRODUCTIVE SYSTEM

Emotionally related dysfunctions of the reproductive system in men seem limited to the two symptoms of impotence and premature ejaculation. Women experience a range of dysfunctions astonishing in their variability and frequency—every one of the reproductive-system functions in women can develop symptoms. The frequency and diversity reinforce our assumption that this system is central in the self-concept of women.

In this chapter we are going to see what the studies of psychosomatic responses contribute to our understanding of the psychology of women. But first, what are the psychosomatic responses? A partial list of symptoms cited in the literature suggests the range: dysmenorrhea (painful menstruation), oligomenorrhea (scanty menstruation at long intervals), amenorrhea (the suppression of menstruation for months or years), vaginismus (painful vaginal spasms), pseudocyesis (false pregnancy), unexplained infertility, premature labor, incoordinate uterine contractions, menstrual and menopausal tension, premature dilation of the cervix, premature rupture of the membranes, habitual spontaneous abortion, and inhibition of milk production. Such symptoms may have either psychological origins or direct physical causes. The presence of the symptom does not tell us its origin.

We have described earlier how under normal conditions the cyclic functioning of the reproductive system creates mental changes in women. How can mental attitudes be responsible for changes in the reproductive system? The answer is to be found in the same mechanism: the endocrine glands and their messenger hormones. Let us briefly review this chemical feedback system.

The way in which people experience the world, what they perceive or ignore, what they are emotionally affected by and how, are all transmitted through the senses to the brain. The brain transmits the information by way of the hypothalamus to the pituitary gland. The pituitary sends its messenger hormones into the bloodstream, from which they affect the other glands of the endocrine system—the thyroid, the pancreas, the adrenals, the sex gonads, and probably the parathyroid. These glands will in turn send messages back to the pituitary, the hypothalamus, and the brain. The endocrine balance affects the individual's psyche and behavior; emotional reactions produce changes in the endocrine levels. Everyone experiences this continuing and changing pattern of interaction between the outer world and the internal physiological system. Literally, mind and body are one, and there is no barrier between the mind, the body, and the outside world.

PERSONALITY AND PSYCHOSOMATIC SYMPTOMS

Research in psychophysiology has shown connections between personality type, conflicts, styles of coping or failing, and the general development of psychosomatic symptoms. Some researchers believe that specific symptoms have meaning to the sufferer on a symbolic level. While investigations have shown reasonable connections between personality qualities and particular symptoms, the relationships are still not clear; there are many important unresolved questions. For example, given similar personalities and the same kind of stress, why does one person develop stomach disorders and another migraine headaches? Are some personality types more likely than others to express emotions through physical change? Are other types more verbal, or more behavioral? When similar symptoms occur in different personality types, are they expressing basically similar problems and resolutions? Does a symptom always have a "meaning" or can it be a general response to stress? When do physical symptoms express emotions, conflicts, defenses?

Most of us are aware that emotional stress may be expressed through physical reactions—headaches, belly aches, diarrhea, constipation, and sweating are somatic responses to tension that are within the experience of normal people. Psychologists feel that much can be learned from persons whose experiences are more severe. They assume that the severe responses are exaggerations of basically the same phenomena that we see in less extreme cases. But there is an important technical problem involved because the overwhelming majority of psychosomatic studies are done on patients who have come to physicians seeking help. The analysis of their personality dynamics is correlated with their symptom, and correlational studies can tell us that patients who have certain symptoms also generally have particular needs and conflicts. This does *not* tell us about persons with similar needs and conflicts who do not have these symptoms. Correlation can only infer causation. On the basis of the studies we have, especially when the function of the symptom is very clear in the life of an individual, we can make hypotheses that seem valid. But we cannot demonstrate direct causal links between the symptom and the motive and we cannot assume a psychological origin when we see the symptom.[1]

Psychosomatic symptoms include exaggerated concerns and fears over minor or normal body changes, or even concerns where there are no changes. We are especially interested in those disorders that reveal a symbolically understandable relationship between the emotion and the symptom through an actual change in the normally autonomous functions of the reproductive system, which is normally independent of voluntary control. When we look at pathology and dysfunction in the reproductive system, we find that changes can be used as a psychological defense, as a means of keeping the personality intact, as a way of coping with threats to one's specifically feminine identity. Because the reproductive system is so salient it can become for some women the most logical and obvious vehicle for the expression of aggression, anxiety, and desire—especially relating to their sexual feelings, their maternal longings, and their relationship with themselves and with the important people in their lives. Symptoms often express a strong conflict that cannot be revealed more directly, resolved more efficiently, or sublimated healthily.

We know that specific body organs play different roles in different situations, and that dissimilar personalities can have the same symptom—but the same symptom may have a different meaning for each person experiencing it (Ibor, 1960). The symptom itself does not tell us the meaning. Women with differing specific motives will use the reproductive system to express their individual conflicts. We even find that the symptom expresses ambivalent motives simultaneously within the same woman. For example, pseudocyesis, a hysterical false pregnancy, can simultaneously express the conscious wish for a child and the unconscious fear of begetting a child. But

---

[1]For example, Seward and Myerhoff (1965) compared 41 patients in an infertility clinic with 41 postpartum women. They hypothesized that the infertility patients would differ significantly from the multiparous, postpartum mothers. Using many of the same psychological measures used in other studies which did find expected differences, Seward and Myerhoff found no significant differences between the two groups. In these samples there were no real differences on the dimensions of dependency, aggression, or relation to authority, and no differences in feelings about menstruation, childbirth, sex, orgasm, marital happiness, and men.

while we cannot expect to find a universality of the specific motive, we can make a good case for a general similarity of personality and motive in women with the same psychosomatic disorders of the reproductive system. This is really the problem of organ choice, and we assume certain similarities among women who have selected the same organs. In a sense we are saying that the symptom expresses an attitude that could be expressed in language, but isn't, and that this attitude has been associated with a particular body system (Grace and Graham, 1952; Graham and Graham, 1961; Williams and Krasnoff, 1964).

PERSONALITY CHARACTERISTICS OF PSYCHOSOMATIC PATIENTS

The self-concept and self-esteem of women are closely linked to the appearance and function of their bodies because the life goals of women are closely tied to their bodies. Women experience their body boundaries more definitely than men do and have clearer criteria for conceptualizing their bodies as psychological objects (Fisher, 1964). Their self-evaluation as women depends largely upon their physical attractiveness and their sexual and maternal behavior. Their awareness of internal sexual functions is reinforced by the menstrual cycle. Normal femininity includes the acceptance of menstruation, pregnancy, and maternity as the normal and desired consequences of being a woman.

When compared with healthy persons, persons who use psychosomatic symptoms as an important defense—as a primary technique for solving a conflict which is essentially self-created—seem more dependent, inadequate, immature, and anxious, and seem afraid of the aggression that they could direct upon the world or themselves (Ibor, 1960). Oversimplifying, I nonetheless think it fair to say that the majority of these patients are typically unable to directly express their aggression, resentment, and dependency, and use the indirect technique of somatic change instead.

We find that menstrual and pregnancy symptoms are associated with certain personality characteristics. Gynecological and obstetric difficulties are more likely to occur in women who are both dependent and passive. These are two surprising personality variables considering the assumptions of the psychological literature that dependence and passivity are normal generalized personality characteristics of women. Although these traits are more characteristic of women than men, I believe that their generalization to most relationships and situations is abnormal. Normal women are dependent and have a strong need for affection, but the need is limited to relatively few significant persons such as husbands, children, and parents. Normal women have an ability to cope with episodes of hostility and rejection, although in less close relationships they will be more vulnerable than men to interpersonal rejection. The healthy woman has a self-concept that is influenced by, but is not wholly dependent upon, continuous unalloyed affection from others; she has a strong ego and has developed an independent self. In her important relationships there is a need to be loved, frequently expressed as a need to be taken care of, and normal but limited passivity. There may be a limit to the amount of aggression she will express in her very important relationships, but there is not a pathological withdrawal from all hostile expression.

The woman whose self-esteem is so fragile that she is afraid of expressing hostility in any externalized form because she fears the loss of affection has little recourse but to behave nonaggressively in all situations with all people. We find that such women tend to act out their hostilities and fears psychosomatically. They avoid an obvious, overt aggression by developing a symptom that effects a subtle aggression (such as a wife denying her husband a child because she has ceased menstruating). It seems to me that in this way women are able to effect an external, observable, good-life adjustment by nonverbally expressing hostilities and anxieties through symptoms. As a result they are able to interact with others in a way that tends to reduce the threatening qualities of their anxieties and aggressions.

It is not by accident that certain women wordlessly act out anxieties, fears and hopes specifically and repetitively in the reproductive system. There is no more economical or relevant way for a woman to express her core attitudes towards her femininity, towards sex, her husband, or her children (born and unborn) than through the functioning of this critically important system. In addition, the system is internal, nonobservable, it is not only mysterious and liable to be integrated into fantasies but its unseen working seems to be automatic, independent of one's own volition—and therefore its nonworking has the same automatic, involuntary quality. We are not responsible for what is not voluntary, therefore dysfunctions of this system are not guilt-producing.

FEMININE IDENTITY AND SYMPTOMS

When asked what being a women means to them, women with psychosomatic symptoms talk about self-sacrifice, responsibility, suffering, the ability to master a situation, and the need to cater to their husbands—all of which they resent and fear. Because their need to be dependent enforces nonaggressive, passive behavior, the resentment and fear is never expressed directly. Such women tend to control their husbands, but obliquely, never openly.

They are characteristically ambivalent about being female and equally ambivalent about assuming the traditional feminine role. Their ambivalence is closely related to strong passivity and dependency needs. These patients tend to be unwilling or unable to give up infantile dependency satisfactions and so they defer to their husbands in order to secure affection. Simultaneously they resent the husband's affectional and role demands as a threat to their dependency needs. These women want to receive rather than give in a relationship.

We often find that these patients do not identify with their mothers and, with some awareness, seek to assume the characteristics of their fathers. They describe their mothers as able and responsible women, which strongly implies that their fathers are dependent and passive. Consciously, they report that they prefer their fathers; unconsciously, they may have identified with them. The question of identification is not clear and I think it is probably not necessary to assume an identification with a passive and dependent father as a part of this syndrome.

What is clear is that these patients do not have a secure and normal feminine identification. On the one hand they fear and are unable to cope with the usual female responsibilities. On the other hand they have few other resources for a strong and independent self-concept. They are not able to set and achieve other goals. It therefore becomes necessary for them to perceive themselves as successful women succeeding in traditional role responsibilities, because if they do not succeed in this one available area their immature and fragile self-concept will become even more vulnerable.

Women who are highly passive, dependent, and conformist assess themselves by the reactions of others. When asked, they are likely to tell an interviewer that they are independent and that they pride themselves on their independence, but this is patently untrue and reflects the use of denial, a primitive defense mechanism used by immature people. Because they behave in a manner designed to fulfill their percept of others' expectations, we find a conscious wish for pregnancy and sex, but we also see an unconscious rejection of these feminine functions.

Women who resort to psychosomatic dysfunctions are caught in and maintain an infantilizing vicious cycle in which they accept responsibilities (especially those that are normal in the traditional female role), are frustrated by failure (and, based on a lifetime of experience, probably anticipate failure), feel anger, fear rejection if they act upon their anger, feel guilt about their hostility, and behave compliantly so as not to threaten the interpersonal relationship. Their hostility cannot be expressed directly. The psychosomatic symptom both obliquely expresses hostility and removes the sufferer from the reality of an unsolvable conflict. Characteristically, women with psychosomatic disorders have restricted social outlets. They are not adaptable, they are unable to take on real responsibility and act independently, and they are therefore unlikely to be able to achieve independence and a strong sense of self in new interpersonal relationships or in work. They expect to fail, their personality characteristics tend to assure that they will fail, they do fail, and their frail sense of self-esteem is, with each new failure, even more vulnerable than before.

Fearful of rejection, psychosomatic patients tend to use indirect forms of aggression instead of direct ones. We find them suffering pain and nausea during menstruation and pregnancy and punishing their husbands with their not-too-silent suffering. We often see a crippling kind of dependent behavior in which the other person, especially the husband, is punished and bound, in which there is great anxiety over separation and the possibility of rejection. These women cannot express themselves by having bouts of depression because depressed women are as unlovable as aggressive women. So strong negative effects which might threaten the relationship are not expressed and lead to psychosomatic symptoms.

Women who are excessively dependent, passive, immature, with low self-esteem, who use the defense of denial, who behave in order to conform, and who have a history of psychosomatic symptoms may effect an external, observable, good-life adjustment by nonverbally expressing their anxieties and hostilities through conversion symptoms in that most salient physical system, the reproductive system. They are then able to interact with others in a way that reduces the threat of acting out their anxieties and aggressions, and they are simultaneously able to secure compassion for their fragility. They alter their physical selves in order not to jeopardize the important relationship. But since their defense is neither mature nor adaptive, they are unable to break out of the self-injurious pattern that they have defensively erected.

When asked what their motivations are to have children, psychosomatic patients typically list external rather than internal motives. Ambivalent toward the pregnancy and the child, they will say they want a child because their husband wants one, or that this is known to be a woman's main accomplishment, or that when you don't have a child you reveal your inadequacy. This way of expressing desire for a child really reveals a repetition of the pattern of conformity. Some patients reveal more clearly the fear of a loss of love if they do not gratify their husband's desire for a child. These women fear the loss of dependency gratifications either because they do not satisfy their husband's desire for paternity or because they do—they additionally fear that the presence of a baby will necessitate nurturant behavior from them or decrease the attention their husband pays to them.

A core-intense anxiety about sex is characteristic of these psychosomatic patients. Sexual arousal increases in normal women when they can give of themselves as well as receive. But for these women the former is impossible; they may fear pregnancy as a consequence of sexual activity or they may fear coitus as an intrusion into their vulnerable body interior. But, characteristically, they deny difficulty and often say that their sex life is "the best part of this marriage." It is possible that under certain specific circumstances their sexual activity is gratifying. Because they are preoccupied with helping themes and guilt themes, especially sexual, they may be able to "justify" sex by perceiving it as helping their husbands. One has difficulty in imagining them actively enjoying sex, but it is possible that they take pleasure in sex because it indicates that they are loved and needed. More commonly, the basic response to sexual demands from their husbands is resentment.

Denial is a primitive and generalized defense mechanism that can be easily somaticized. In amenorrhea, for example, there is in effect a denial of the menstrual flow, which is a regression to prepuberty. This sometimes seems to clearly symbolize a desire to return to a time in life when dependency was normal and responsibility was minimal. The regression is also a return to an asexual time and can therefore ameliorate sex anxiety. Amenorrhea symbolizes a denial of being an adult female; at the level of reality, it prohibits conception.

When we turn to patients who were not so ill as to preclude the possibility of conception, and who successfully delivered babies but suffered severe postpartum reactions, we sometimes find that the crisis was not in the pregnancy but in the real existence of the child.[2] These patients often seem to have intense, mutually dependent relationships with their husbands which had been transferred from their relationships with their mothers. The baby could become a source of danger in the balance of the relationship if the wife became so attached to it that the husband suffered or if the husband's affection for the baby was seen as a withdrawal of affection from the new mother. We would expect these women not to be as pathological as those who preclude the possibility of conception through amenorrhea or who reject the child through habitual self-generated abortions. But these patients also seem to be excessively dependent and vulnerable in their affiliative relations.

When we examine the literature on pseudocyesis we again find that the same personality characteristics are cited as important. This mock pregnancy seems to be unconsciously motivated by the woman's wanting to secure her husband's wavering affection, prove her ability to conceive and therefore be a successful female, achieve parity with other women, and effect masochistic self-punishment through symptoms of illness associated with pregnancy. Pseudocyesis is the most elaborate of the reproductive-system dysfunctions. It can symbolically represent the needs, the anxieties, and the defenses of pathologically passive, dependent, insecure women.

Since the origin of these personality variables lies in childhood and adolescence, we would expect to find that somatic defenses began early and that patients showing psychosomatic symptoms have a history of psychosomatic illness. We hypothesize that from puberty on most of the symptoms were related to menstruation. Studies have found that patients who had severe

[2]Vanden Bergh et al. (1966) tested the hypothesis that habitual aborters are unwilling to accept the role of motherhood. Nine patients were followed during successful pregnancy after corrective surgery. Five developed postpartum psychoses. These data must be interpreted cautiously since we are not certain of the origin of postpartum depressions.

pregnancy symptoms also had many premenstrual symptoms. They also show a high acceptance of the sick role. It is likely that these women have consistently acted out their anxieties and anger somatically and that psychosomatic conversions are as much a part of their life style as passivity and dependence.

I suspect that women with psychosomatic dysfunctions start having menstrual problems early in adolescence and that the problems increase as the sexual aspects of dating grow more important. The symptom severity is probably strongest during their twenties and thirties, when the marital pressure for pregnancy is strongest and most threatening. So long as this type of woman can perceive herself as young enough to bear children she will be increasingly anxious, but consciously she will be running from one obstetrician to another looking for the miracle of pregnancy. Menopause is likely to come as a relief and be relatively symptom-free.

The woman who is psychosomatically ill unconsciously assumes that because she is ill she will not be abandoned. But control of other people through passive methods rests on chivalry in the controlled, and she remains psychologically vulnerable. Illness is a fragile technique for resolving conflicts.

STUDIES OF PREGNANCY, CHILDBIRTH, AND BREAST-FEEDING

The psychosomatic symptom can also be a simple sign of anxiety or a cry for marriage; we can see this in the temporary amenorrhea of the unmarried girl. When I interview young women I am impressed and upset by the ambivalence they feel toward pregnancy as such. Aside from the deeper anxieties we have just been describing, one sometimes sees a panicky fear of the body changes in pregnancy and hears a description of the fetus as a (gnawing) parasite. For the most part, the subjects I have seen describe pregnancy as a period to be tolerated, something to be curious about—the terms they use are sometimes very negative, usually ambivalent, rarely positive. These subjects are not patients, they are not seeking help. We can also see a relationship between the needs and fears of a woman and her sexual body in situations in which there is no obvious pathological syndrome. It is important to remember that biological femininity has annoying, bloody, or painful components, but in addition to realistic fears the underground folklore transmits terrifying ideas.

In the past few years, stimulated largely by the natural childbirth movement, there has been an increase in the number of published studies in which the experimenter hypothesized a psychosomatic correlation between the anxiety and complications of pregnancy and delivery in the mother and deviancy in the newborn child. I do not think that any of the studies have been really conclusive and there are also published negative findings, where the hypothesis was not supported. Nonetheless, as one surveys the recent literature one does get the impression that anxious women have more pregnancy and delivery complications. Basically the hypothesis is that high levels of fear or anxiety will result in incoordinate uterine contractions.

Many studies have found that the number of unsatisfactory labors increases as fear and anxiety increase. In two samples of clinic patients, Davids et al. (1961) found that women who scored significantly high on the Manifest Anxiety Scale had a greater number of complications during labor and more frequently gave birth to children with abnormalities. Similarly, Zuckerman et al. (1963) found significant positive relationships between somatic complaints during pregnancy and a history of menstrual symptoms, manifest anxiety, and marital conflict. Anxiety during pregnancy was directly related to the amount of analgesic required during delivery. They wrote, "The significant correlation between the Manifest Anxiety Scale and somatic complaints during pregnancy supports the idea that many of these complaints reflect somatic expressions of their anxiety, and their relationship with the Marital Conflict Scale suggests the origin of this anxiety." Some studies have found a relationship between vomiting during pregnancy and a negative attitude of the mother toward the child. Fetal asphyxia and uterine inertia occurred much more frequently in Swedish women who had been negative about their past life, their marriage, sex, pregnancy, and the fetus at midterm (Engstrom et al., 1964). A significantly higher incidence of interpersonal, economic, and job problems was found in Australian women who had prolonged vomiting and toxemia during pregnancy (Hetzel et al., 1961). McDonald (1965) found that patients who suffered premature rupture of the membranes, excessive weight gain, and preeclampsia made significantly higher scores on the Minnesota Multiphasic Personality Inventory (MMPI) anxiety, social introversion, and hypochondriasis scores, than did pregnant women who had no somatic symptoms. Similarly, women with inefficient uterine action during labor were significantly different from women with a normal labor in respect to the now familiar variables: their attitude toward motherhood, sex, marriage, their relation to their mother, their adjustment to pregnancy, their attitude toward their first menses, their attitude toward the father of the child, their habitual anxieties and habitual body complaints (Kapp et al., 1963).

The physiological mechanism by which the fetus is affected by the affect levels of the mother were surveyed by Ferreira (1965). In addition to the studies I have just briefly described we can note that Ferreira, Grimm (1961), and Davids and DeVault (1962) all report that women who were significantly anxious during pregnancy and suffered from high degrees of tension had a significantly higher incidence of infants who were hyperactive, deformed, or dead.

We have just been describing women who were not suffering from the obvious and severe and classic psychosomatic conversion syndromes. The implication is clear that there is always a range of attitudes toward the functions of the sexual body, that the reproductive system is always crucially important in the psyche, and that this system is likely to be the site of emotional expression.

Increasing efforts have been made in the past decade to encourage mothers to breast-feed their infants, but there are few published reports comparing the mother's success or failure in nursing with her psychological attitudes. Niles Newton (1968) has published a paper on this topic and it is of interest to us in this context because basically the same psychological variables seem to be important. Newton has not measured all of the variables that we have found significant, but those that she does report on are all in the anticipated direction.

The mother's ability to produce milk depends upon her attitude towards nursing and towards sex. Women who are afraid of sex and dislike nudity are aversive to breast-feeding. In contrast to women who prefer bottle-feeding, women who breast-feed their babies have a greater tolerance for masturbation and social sex-play in their children (Salber, 1959; Adams, 1959; Sears, 1957; all reported in Newton, 1968). Newton found that success in breast-feeding was closely related to the mother's attitude. Successful nursing mothers expressed more delight when they saw their infants for the first time, more frequently expressed a desire to nurse them, frequently felt that women have a more satisfying time in life than men, and actually had shorter labors during the delivery of this first child.

A STUDY OF UTERINE ACTIVITY

I should like to describe an experiment that S. Jan Behrman and I (1967) conducted with normal women in which the relationships were clear between psychological passivity, dependence, sex anxiety, the use of denial, and psychosomatic changes in the reproductive system. We gave our subjects sexual and nonsexual stimuli and measured changes in the contractions of the nonpregnant uterus as the women read and reacted to the experimental materials. Each woman was seen at four different times of the menstrual cycle. We used 10 highly paid subjects, each of whom was given a battery of psychological tests before the experiment began. The psychological measures were scored after the experiment was completed, and we found that by accident we had selected two groups of women. Five of the women were clearly passive and sexually anxious, four were neither passive nor sexually anxious, and one woman scored at the mean on the psychological measures (and was later to show both kinds of uterine activity).

We found no relationship between the menstrual cycle phase and the stress effect. This means that the ovarian hormone balance of the cycle phase did not alter the stress-response of the contractions. (There were differences in the nonstress or resting-period contractions during different cycle phases). Certain uterine responses were generally characteristic of all subjects: When our subjects were emotionally aroused there was an increase in the amplitude and the variability of the contractions. This occurred whether the emotion experienced by the subject was fear, anger, or sexual arousal.

We also found that when they were confronted with sexually relevant stimuli, subjects who were anxious about sex showed a greater increase in galvanic skin responses, basal resistance levels, and uterine contractions. That is, the sexually anxious groups were made more anxious by the sexual content of the stimuli than were the nonanxious subjects. Thus the sexually anxious women consistently responded with a greater number of significantly deviant galvanic skin responses and uterine responses to the sexual stimuli than they did to the nonsexual stimuli.

We also found that the two groups of subjects consistently had two distinctly different uterine patterns under the arousal condition. We measured the uterine contractions by means of a small water-filled balloon which was inserted into the uterus. Anxious subjects extruded the intrauterine balloon and nonanxious subjects had uterine spasms. Women who were passive and sexually anxious extruded the balloon into the vaginal tract without being aware of it; extrusion usually occurred when they were confronted with the sexual stimuli or shortly afterwards. Extrusion was a consistent response, which means that it occurred during at least three of the four menstrual cycle phases.

We felt the extrusion of the balloon could be interpreted as both a response to the experimental materials and an aggressive ending of the experiment. Unconsciously, but aggressively, the subject ended the experiment, ended the exposure to the threatening material, frustrated the experimenter by the lack of data, but still managed to get paid. For our subjects who were unconsciously anxious about sex, our experimental stimuli were hardly arousing—at least not of sexual impulses. In this case the stimuli aroused anxiety ("I don't like this"), depression ("I'm no good at this"), and unconscious hostility ("I didn't like this *last* time"). As it happened, our subjects who were sexually anxious were also passive and were unable to express their aggression directly, overtly, consciously. These women ended the experiment, unconsciously but decisively, by expelling the intrauterine balloon.

Under the same experimental conditions, the women who were neither passive nor sexually anxious never extruded the balloon. When these women were most aroused, their uterine contractions consistently revealed brief uterine spasms superimposed upon the basic large contractions. Other experiments have suggested that these muscle spasms might be the normal response of the uterus during coitus and that this response may have the effect of increasing the probability of conception. The expulsive pattern of the anxious women would seem to have the opposite effect.

In addition to whatever fundamental differences may accrue from central nervous system differences in the sexes, the psychology of women is closely related to the physiological functioning of their reproductive system and their attitudes toward it. The reproductive system generates direct effects upon the personality of women, and psychological states will induce effects in the physiology of the system. Psychologically salient, the reproductive system will be perceived as a source of threat, as a source of satisfaction, as the crux of femininity.

In this section of the book we have examined the relationship of the female personality to the female body.[3] I think it should be obvious that we don't have to resort to phantom organs, to phallic disappointment, to castration trauma; the real and existing body of the female creates needs and conflicts and satisfactions in its own right. Women who have low self-esteem, who think their bodies are ugly or dirty, who are anxious about themselves and biological femininity, are likely to have disruptions of their reproductive system. These may take the form of menstrual problems, problems in conceiving or carrying a baby to term, in mothering a child, in achieving orgasm, or any other of the large number of obstetric and gynecologic disorders.

[3]I should like to reinsert a note of caution. We have oversimplified in this discussion and generalized from incomplete data; the dynamics of each patient can be more complex and contradictory than we have suggested. Although the basic ideas we have discussed are probably valid, there are many unanswered questions in the entire field of psychosomatics.

chapter 5
DIFFERENCES
BETWEEN MALE
AND FEMALE BRAINS

Recent evidence suggests the development in the embryo of a male brain and a female brain. It is a reasonable guess, although still only speculative, that the influence of the sex hormones before birth involves the shaping of neural circuits in the hypothalamus, which is the part of the brain that directly influences the endocrine system. The research is recent and still limited, but evidence of sex-linked differences in the hypothalamus makes it plausible to hypothesize that there are also other sex-linked differences between males and females in the central nervous system.

In this chapter we will review experiments in which the brain functions of animals have undergone sex reversal after injection of hormones at a crucial stage of development; we will examine differences in infant responses to stimuli, differences that seem to be constitutional in origin; and, finally, we will describe a problem in sexual identity that may be related to a critical stage in the development of the central nervous system—the phenomenon of the transsexual.

ENDOCRINES, BRAIN FUNCTION, AND SEX REVERSAL

Experiments in animals indicate that gonadal hormones in the embryo organize the developing tissue that is responsible for mediating sexual behavior. In fishes and amphibians, the administration of the hormone appropriate to the opposite sex during embryonic and larval stages resulted in a complete and functional sex reversal. In the guinea pig a prenatal injection of testosterone in female fetuses resulted in the formation of hermaphroditic females characterized by a low capacity for feminine behavior. The guinea pigs were born with masculinized genitals, and at maturity they displayed distinctly masculine characteristics in their sexual behavior (Young, Goy, and Phoenix, 1965). Normally, the female hormones of the mother and of the developing female embryo support the development of female behavioral potentials. A male embryo offsets the influence of its mother's hormones with its own production of testosterone. If androgen is administered to female rats when they are 5 days old, the postpubertal sexual cycle is permanently impaired. At maturity the rats are sterile, are in a constant anovulatory state of estrus, and are always sexually unreceptive to male rats (Money, 1965).

During the various stages in the development and life history of an organism there are certain critical periods, and the exact time of these critical periods appears to be different for each species. But in mammals the critical stage for sex-linked development appears to be plus or minus one week from birth.[1] The presence or absence of the sex hormones at this specific time will induce permanent changes in the psychophysiological processes of the animal. The sex hormones in newborn animals alter the reproductive-system patterns (the cyclicity of the female or the acyclicity of the male) and probably also the amount of hormone secretion in the adult. Evidence also indicates that the sex hormones present in the infant determine which hormones the brain centers of the adult will respond to.

If the male rat is castrated following birth and as a result cannot produce testosterone, he will display the female receptive behavior at maturity in response to doses of estrogen or progesterone. If, on the other hand, a large dose of testosterone is given to female rats during the first 120 hours after birth, they will be incapable of responding with the normal female pattern when adult. Most studies conclude that at birth all rats are physiologically female but are capable of masculinization if testes are present. Adult male

---

[1] New techniques are enabling endocrinologists to measure plasma concentration of testosterone. A recent paper reported finding no significant sex differences in the umbilical venous testosterone levels of 12 infants at birth (August et al., 1969). But Robert Jaffe of the University of Michigan Medical School informs me that he has found significantly different testosterone levels in male and female fetuses. Jaffe has observed that the fetal male testis can synthesize testosterone; no testosterone synthesis could be demonstrated in the female fetal ovary. If sex differences can be observed in fetuses but not in infants after birth, it is plausible that the critical stage of development in humans may occur significantly earlier than just before birth.

rats who had been castrated at birth and who therefore were unable to produce testosterone developed corpora lutea in the normal female cyclic pattern when they had ovarian transplants. Either the administration of testosterone or the normal secretion of testosterone by the gonads during the first week after birth in the rat will markedly and irreversibly affect adult reproductive and behavioral functions. There is a critical stage; if the testosterone is administered after the first week, there are no effects (Levine and Mullins, 1966).

In 1967, Goy (cited in Valenstein, 1968) experimented on a more sophisticated species, the rhesus monkey. He found that when androgens were injected into pregnant mothers the female offspring were hermaphroditic or masculinized. They displayed much more "rough and tumble" play than normal females and exhibited as much chasing behavior as the males. They demonstrated as much "social threat" behavior as normal males when they played with peers. There was also more "mounting" behavior. These masculinized female offspring demonstrated either a significantly increased number of male sex patterns or an increase in behaviors, such as aggression, that are precursors of normal male sexual behavior. Similarly Young, Goy, and Phoenix (1964) compared the behavior of two normal female rhesus monkeys and two pseudohermaphroditic female monkeys and found that the behavior of the pseudohermaphroditic females was much closer to that of the normal male in terms of play initiation, rough play patterns, and aggression. These results suggest that in addition to the specific sex behaviors, other behaviors are being influenced by the steroid hormones.

The first experiments in this area were done by Carroll A. Pfeifer, an endocrinologist, thirty years ago (cited in Levine, 1966). He removed the ovaries of a young female rat, implanted testes, and found that the rat was in effect now male, showing no estrus at maturity. In some of these young female rats he left the ovaries intact; the production of testosterone from the implanted testes prevented the normal functioning of the ovaries. Similarly, when the testes of a young male rat were removed and an ovary was implanted, the ovary functioned and the animal was functionally female. If, however, the ovary was implanted in a young rat whose testes were not removed, the output of testosterone prevented the ovary from functioning. The crucial factor, then, was the presence or absence of testosterone during the critical stage.

Under the direction of Geoffrey W. Harris, Levine (1966) conducted a series of related experiments, but instead of transplanting organs he exposed rats to sex hormones within four days after birth. When female rats were given a single injection of testosterone propionate (a long-acting testosterone compound), they never developed the normal female pattern of reproductive physiology. If a normal female rat received an injection of testosterone when mature, it exhibited some signs of male sexual behavior. If the rat was injected with the male hormone within four days after birth and received another injection when adult, it exhibited full male sexual behavior. If it received the male sex hormone within the critical period after birth, it failed to exhibit female sexual behavior when mature in spite of an injection of estrogen and progesterone.

The feminization of male rats could be accomplished only if the young rats were castrated and deprived of all testosterone during the critical period. Thus a normal male rat was unaffected by an injection of estrogen and progesterone when mature. But if the male rats were castrated within the first four days, they assumed the female sexual posture at maturity if they received an injection of estrogen and progesterone or if they had an ovary implanted.

Permanent control over the hormonal action of the pituitary was established by the presence or absence of testosterone in the first few critical days after birth. When there was no testosterone, the pituitary regulated the female cyclic pattern with its release of the hormones FSH and LH. If testosterone was present, this normal female cyclicity was abolished. (Levine notes that essentially the same effect has been demonstrated in guinea pigs and monkeys, but for these species the critical stage is before birth and the testosterone effect is accomplished by injections into the mother during the fetal stage.) Normal female rats can occasionally be observed making male sexual responses, especially "mounting." If the normal female rat receives an injection of testosterone when adult, it will go through some of the male activities of copulation. But the masculinized female rats go beyond these partial behaviors; when, as adults, they are given a dose of testosterone they go through the entire male sexual ritual, including the motion of ejaculation. In a similar fashion the male rats who had been deprived of testosterone soon after birth reacted to an adult injection of even very small doses of estrogen and progesterone with normal female sexual responses. The central nervous system response to the female hormones had been changed.

Levine thus concluded that in some way testosterone determines the sexual differentiation of the brain within a few days after birth. In female rats, early presence of testosterone results in an adult sensitivity to testosterone and insensitivity to the female hormones. In the male, the absence of testosterone within the critical period makes the animal sensitive to female hormones. "To put it another way, the absence of testosterone at the differentiation stage would leave both males and females sensitive to the female hormones and capable of displaying female behavior; the presence of testosterone, on the other hand, would desensitize females as well as males, so that both sexes failed to display feminine behavior when they were challenged with female hormones."

It would seem that the gonadal hormones have two influences on the central nervous system—an organizational influence during development and an excitatory influence in the adult. The presence or absence of testosterone in young organisms alters the sensitivity of the controlling brain structures so that at maturity they will respond to certain types and sequences of hormones. Even small amounts of male hormones given to 5-day-old female rats will alter the gonadotropin-releasing mechanism in the adult rat from the female cyclic pattern to the male acyclic pattern. The reverse is also true: The absence of testosterone in the young male rat will result in the establishment of the gonadotropin-release mechanism in its female cyclic form.

Levine and Mullins (1966) therefore concluded that testosterone would seem to be the active hormone that organizes the sexual system. It also seems clear that "nature's primary impulse is to make a female—morphologically speaking at least" (Money, 1965). The idea that development of the male is somewhat more complex leads to the idea that it is also more hazardous. In other words, sexual pathology among men would then be more common than among women. We will return to this idea when we discuss sexual pathology in the transsexual.

The change from the cyclic to the acyclic pattern of pituitary gonadotropins is the result of hormonal action not on the pituitary but on the neural centers of the hypothalamus. The hypothalamus, you will recall, controls the release of hormones by the pituitary. Endocrinologists believe that the steroid hormones act on the central nervous system via the hypothalamus rather than directly on the pituitary. The cycle would be from the hypothalamus to the anterior pituitary to the gonads and back to the hypothalamus. In this model the endocrine cycle interacts with psychological and environmental changes via the hypothalamus—behavior, thoughts, and perceptions of the environment can, through the central nervous system, affect the production of the steroids. It is equally likely that different levels of the sex hormones circulating in the blood can affect the central nervous system so as to make certain behaviors, moods, or perceptions more or less probable.

Harris (1964) has stated:

The sex hormones seem to exert a double action on the central nervous system. First, during fetal or neonatal life these hormones seem to act in an inductive way on an undifferentiated brain (as they do the undifferentiated genital tract) to organize it into a male type or female type of brain. And second, during adult existence the gonadal hormones act on the central nervous system in an excitatory or inhibitory way, and are thus concerned with the expression of overt patterns of sexual behavior.

Gagnon (1965) enlarges on this idea. He states that during the early critical period the organism may be especially sensitive to certain interactions with the environment, and that following this critical period the organism will be resistant or immune to such interactions.

The character of the sexual reaction depends upon the neural substrate that the hormone is acting upon. It would thus seem likely that as a result of the sex-typing of the central nervous system, endocrines and stimuli would be responded to differently by the sexes. We assume, especially in humans, that we are dealing with some normal range of sensitivity to stimuli, or a range of predispositions to respond to stimuli. We also assume that this sensitization to stimuli, since we are dealing with the central nervous system, is enormously influenced by experience. *On the other hand, and to the extent that there is central nervous system sex-typing, the predispositions to perceive and respond to stimuli will be influenced by the sex-type of the brain.*

Before we leave this particular idea, I should like to point out that there is the possibility of sexual pathology if the sex hormone appropriate to the genitals is not present during the critical stage. We are suggesting the possibility of two independent critical periods in development: the first would be the fetal development of the internal and external genitals; the second would be the development of the appropriately typed brain. In other words, the development of femininity or masculinity in the central nervous system could be independent of the development of reproductive organs. This idea has occurred to several researchers who work with transsexuals in whom it is common to find a gender-role inversion before the age of 3. In fact, it is the absence of clear genetic or endocrine or environmental pathology that has led Pauly (1965) to hypothesize that this syndrome has resulted from a nondetected prenatal or postnatal sex-hormone imbalance. Stoller (1964) has suggested that there is an early and irreversible establishment of sexual identity that is largely the result of a biological force that can sometimes be powerful enough to counteract one's upbringing and even one's anatomy. Benjamin (1966) feels, in an idea similar to Gagnon's, that an error in conditioning depends ultimately on an abnormal physical constitution.

I think that this whole idea would be of limited interest if it affected only sexual behavior. Ford and Beach (1951) tell us that as we go up the phylogenetic scale, mating behavior becomes increasingly less dependent upon the sex hormones. We are interested in the origins of masculine and feminine behavior, and this interest is clearly not limited to sexual behavior. Therefore it is very relevant that Young et al. (1965) found that the hormonal effect on the central nervous system in young organisms results in the establishment of behaviors which are part of the masculine or feminine repertoire of behaviors but which are not directly related to the reproductive process itself. Gagnon (1965) also states that this central nervous system substrate is likely to make the organism differentially ready to receive the inputs of masculinity and femininity from the parents. We find, for example, that some human female hermaphrodites who had been virilized in utero from an excess of adrenal androgens report erotic arousal from visual and verbal stimuli, which is more characteristic of normal males. If testosterone is administered to normal adult females we find that their levels of physical activity and their general level of aggressiveness may increase to levels normally found in males.

Levine (1966) has reported on the few experiments that have looked at the question of this early hormonal effect upon non-sex-related behavior: Richter had observed that when female rats run on an activity wheel measuring the amount of voluntary running an animal will do on any day, they show a cyclic pattern peaking at ovulation. Males perform more uniformly every day. When Harris applied this activity measure to male rats who had been castrated during the critical period and who had had an ovary implanted as adults, he found that these male rats ran with a cyclic pattern of activity corresponding to the ovulation cycle. In the open-field test, female rats tend to be more exploratory and to defecate less than the males. When female rats who had been given testosterone at birth were put through this test, they displayed the male pattern of defecation. Levine reports Young's finding that female monkeys who had been given testosterone before birth displayed male types of play patterns. These females were rough and active, aggressive, and made more use of threatening facial expressions. The experiments have been few and the evidence limited, but there is a suggestion that sex differences in the brain of a mammal influence not only sexual activity but other forms of behavior as well.

We have been discussing the effect androgens have on organizing neural tissue in young organisms and on activating sexual responses in adults, but normal adult behavior can occur only if the neural, hormonal, and experiential developments all have been within a normal range. The behavioral dispositions that may result from the sex-typing of the brain are the infant's personality qualities that will be socialized by being punished, rewarded, or ignored. It is unreasonable to ascribe human motivation solely to experiential factors and animal motivation solely to endocrine-constitutional factors. Both sets of factors contribute to the development of the personality in the human and in other animals.

When we think of the sex hormones we immediately think of adult sex behavior, but if we want to see their possible effect on young organisms we have to look for different behaviors. Infants are not terribly sexy. The literature on animal behavior suggests sex-linked differences in curiosity, aggression, play initiation, roughness of play, passivity, and levels of physical activity. High levels of aggression, play initiation, rough play, and general physical activity are characteristics of young males. Lower levels of these characteristics but a high level of curiosity are characteristic of females. This list is reminiscent of the sex-appropriate behaviors in human children and adults, which seem generally universal.

Most cultures may be reinforcing behavior tendencies or predispositions that are basically characteristic of the sexes due to sex-typed neural–endocrine development. If this is true, then it would be so pervasive that we would notice the contribution of the body only in fairly rare cases of pathology, as in the transsexual. That is, we would not notice the constitutional contributions to sex-identity because the appropriate relationship of the genital system to the central nervous system occurs naturally, and, therefore, so does the appropriate behavioral predisposition.

INFANT DIFFERENCES

In the preceding section we found that endocrine research led to the hypothesis of differences in the central nervous system of males and females. If such differences really exist, we should expect to find them clearly demonstrated in differences in the behaviors of male and female animals and children. Even before socialization, there ought to be measurable differences in the general behavioral dispositions of the two sexes.

I have been personally impressed with the basic and consistent personality differences between male and female infants and would like to be able to present a long list of infant researches that support this idea. This I cannot do for several reasons: Infant research is just beginning, and little of it has been directed towards sex differences. Most of the studies have used fewer than 40 infants and those infants were divided into male versus female, breast-fed versus bottle-fed, first-born versus infants with siblings—with the number of infants in each category extremely small. The length of gestation of each infant has been omitted, so we have no estimate of differences in maturity at birth. (Normal gestation time is from eight-and-a-half to nine-and-a-half months, which could well mean a significant difference.) An even more important reason, which should be obvious to anyone who handles infants, is that because infants lack control of their bodies they display a great deal of irrelevant and meaningless activity. This makes it difficult to validly interpret the infant's behavior, especially if the researcher is unfamiliar with that infant except for the testing hour. There is another equally important difficulty—the behavioral repertoire of the infant is very limited. This also makes interpretation difficult and reminds us that the behaviors we are especially interested in do not appear in recognizable and specific form until the infant is about six months old. Many of the studies have used infants just a few days old.

I therefore find especially interesting the longitudinal studies of children that have found consistent sex differences over a period of time in the dimensions of activity, passivity, introversion, and extroversion (Kagan and Moss, 1962; Schaefer and Bayley, 1963; Macfarlane, Allen, and Honzik, 1954; Murphy et al., 1962). Generally speaking, these studies find that the basic response to the environment is consistent from early childhood to adulthood, if the personality parameters are conceived in abstract terms and not in terms of age-specific behaviors. Females tend to be more passive, less active, more introverted. It seems most likely that only some of the personality variables will prove to be sex-linked, but in an ultimate sense, we may find that the sex-linked dimensions are broadly related to the reproductive functions of the two sexes.

If we look at other mammals, particularly other primates, we find that the sex differences are consistent with the findings for humans. Within a month after birth, male rhesus monkeys are wrestling, pushing, biting, and tugging while the female monkeys are beginning to act shy, turning their heads away when challenged to a fight by young males (Goy, 1968). Harlow (1962) has found that male macaque monkeys show a greater likelihood of making a threatening gesture in the face of attack and are less likely to withdraw from an attack. Jensen and Bobbitt (1968) also found that in the first few weeks of life the male monkeys develop behavior patterns quite different from the female monkeys. The males quickly surpass the females in the rate of achieving independence from their mothers (which was helped by the mothers punishing them more, paying less attention to them, and holding and carrying them less). The males had higher general activity levels, did more biting, hitting, pushing, shoving, yanking, grabbing, and jerking. They also did more thumbsucking and more manipulation of their genitals.

In 1962 Harlow observed that male monkeys threaten other males and females but that females do not threaten immature males. Females display a much higher incidence of passivity responses. "In all probability the withdrawal and passivity behavior of the female and the forceful behavior of the male gradually lead to the development of normal sex behaviors." Grooming patterns sharply differentiate the sexes: "Caressing is both a property and prerogative of the females." Play behavior in the playroom is seldom initiated by the females. Play involving body contact is far more frequent among the males and is almost invariably initiated by the males. "Real rough-and-tumble play is strictly for the boys."

Harlow went to a second-grade school picnic where he observed sex differences in human play that were very similar to the patterns he had seen in monkeys. "These secondary sex-behavior differences probably exist throughout the primate order, and moreover, they are innately determined biological differences regardless of any cultural overlap." Harlow concluded, "We believe that our data offer convincing evidence that sex behaviors differ in large part because of genetic factors."

We know that when girls enter school they are developmentally ahead of boys of the same age. Kagan and Lewis's observations (1965) seem pertinent:

The data are persuasive in suggesting that girls display more sustained attention to visual stimulation, and prefer more novel auditory patterns than boys at both 6 and 13 months of age. The 6-month data suggested greater cardiac deceleration to the matrix of lights among girls, and longer fixation times to the film-presented pictures. Moreover, girls displayed greater attention to the novel music pattern at 6 months, whereas the boys preferred to listen to the simple repetitive tone.

At 13 months of age, the girls sustained attention to the blinking lights across all 12 trials, whereas the boys showed rapid habituation. Finally, the girls' preference for more novel auditory patterns noted at 6 months was still present at one year of age. For girls showed greater cardiac deceleration than boys to the low-meaning–high-inflection paragraph, and it was argued that girls may have a preference for auditory inputs with greater stimulus uncertainty.

If one assumes that sustained attention and a preference for deviation from the familiar are *mature* attentional habits, it appears that girls are developmentally advanced over boys as early as 6 months of age. These data support the general belief that there are basic biological differences between boys and girls in rate of psychological development during the opening years of life.

The differences we see in human infants that seem to be constitutional in origin are shown in Table 1. What I think generally happens is outlined in Table 2.

The girl is constitutionally less likely to gratify impulses in activity that the parents find offensive, such as aggression or masturbation. In addition, she is better able to make accurate assessments of the demands of people in the environment and to behave so as to minimize stress. She will, earlier than the boy, cope with discord verbally. As a result of her own behavior potentials there is less parental-cultural stress on girls to give up infantile behaviors. Dependency upon adults, which later forms part of the feminine role but which is part of the normal disposition of infants and young children, will be permitted. Because of the lack of external stress and the lack of internal impulses, she will develop fewer internal controls over impulses. She will have a more diffuse body image and a self-concept still linked, through dependency, to the evaluations of others. She will have a higher need for approval and acceptance, and a greater motoric passivity. The lack of internal ego controls and an independent concept of self leads to a dependent sense of self-esteem. This makes her more amenable to cultural patterning, to more conformist behavior, to better school achievement.

For boys, there is a greater and earlier cultural pressure not to act out impulses. There are few mothers who can tolerate impulsive physical activity that leads to continuous injury, to physical aggression that might injure siblings and playmates, or to public masturbation. In addition, at about the age of 2 to 2½, when children are clearly no longer infants, the dependency behaviors that were normal for both sexes are now seen as babyish or feminine in boys. Girls can be tomboys without undue notice; boys can never be sissies.

Because the culture interprets infantile behavior as feminine, and because it rejects many of his early impulses, the boy is soon pressured to conform

Table 1 Sex Differences in Infancy and Early Childhood

Boys	Girls
At Birth	
Larger size and weight (Terman and Tyler, 1954); more muscle mass (Garn, 1957, 1958) More activity Correlation of low sensitivity with higher prone head reaction (Bell and Darling, 1965)	Greater motoric passivity (Bell, 1960; Kop, 1946) More sensitivity to stimuli; sensitivity to a greater number of stimuli Greater tactile and pain sensitivity; higher skin conductance, greater irritability during an anthropometric examination (Bell and Costello, (1964; Lipsitt and Levy, 1959)
6 Months	
Better fixation response to a helix pattern of lights	Longer fixation time to visual stimuli, less motoric activity, and greater cardiac deceleration (Lewis et al., 1963) Better fixation to a human face (Lewis, Kagan, and Kalafat, 1965) Greater responsiveness to a social stimuli; more social orientation (Bayley, 1964)
Greatest cardiac deceleration (a measure of attention) to an intermittant tone	Greater cardiac deceleration to complex jazz music (Kagan and Lewis, 1965)
13 Months	
Maximum response to a verbal stimulus high in meaning and low in inflection	Maximum response to a verbal stimulus high in meaning and inflection; implies a response to a person (Kagan and Lewis, 1965)
Preference for low complexity stimuli	Preference for high complexity stimuli (Kagan and Lewis, 1965) Earlier language development, especially inflection
Possible better figure-ground differentiation	Greater field dependency; less likely to eliminate irrelevant stimuli, awareness of contextual relationships

to parental expectations in direct opposition to his predispositions. This necessitates an early development of internal ego controls. The boy who is considered excessively passive and withdrawing will be pushed to conform to an active masculine image, while the very active and aggressive boy will be pushed to conform to a less egocentric active style. The percentage of boys who are pushed to change their life-style is high, and the cost shows up in a higher evidence of male psychological pathology.

To the young boy, the prohibiting parents can no longer be seen as a stable and undemanding source of self-esteem. As a result, slowly and with difficulties, with frequent outbursts of aggression, he gives up the parents as his primary source of self-esteem and develops a self-regard system relatively

Table 2 Socialization of Early Sex Differences

Boys	Girls
Testosterone	
More physical activity	Less physical activity
Greater aggressiveness	Less aggressiveness
Less pain sensitivity	More pain sensitivity
More insistent sexual impulses	Lower sexual impulses
More masturbation	Less masturbation
Figure Ground	
More inclined to focus on figure as distinct from ground	More influenced by entire context
More likely to ignore what is irrelevant to problem being solved or to goal	More attention to complexity, to visual, aural, social stimuli
Personality	
More intent on own purposes, more likely to be unaware of or resistant to parental demands	More aware of social demands, better able to assess parental wishes and anticipate them
Receives more parental pressure to inhibit or channel aggressiveness; more likely to be rewarded for achievement, to have to struggle for sense of autonomy against parental pressure	More likely to conform, to be rewarded for goodness, to remain dependent on others for self-esteem
Higher self-esteem based on achievement	Higher self-esteem based on being loved
Independence, achievement, objectivity	Interdependence, conformity, subjectivity

independent of the evaluations of others. His self-esteem is more likely to be based on his achievements, which are more likely to be objective and tangible. The girl's self-esteem is more likely to depend on her acceptance, which is personal and intangible. This is an extremely important difference between the sexes. The girl rarely achieves a sense of independent self-esteem until she is a young woman—if then. The difficulty of this process in the boy is attested to by the frequency of behavioral outbursts, the higher incidence of psychological pathology, and, perhaps most important, by the intrusion of emotion into his perceptual-cognitive spheres so that he does worse than the girl in school until about the fifth grade. It is as though he is too preoccupied with the development of his identity and with the control of his important and prohibited impulses.

The cultural pressure on boys, the reaction to their constitutional behavioral predispositions, is great. The cultural pressure on girls is much less, because their general predispositions and the cultural interpretation of what is acceptable are more nearly matched. The differences in impulses plus the greater perceptual-cognitive sophistication of the girl will enable her to experience a less stormy childhood. As a result she is cognitively mature, in an interpersonal and scholastic way, earlier than the boy. But emotionally, she leaves the relationships of childhood slowly, if at all.

I am suggesting, then, that children are born with personality characteristics that lead to behaviors, and that these behaviors are reacted to evaluatively by parents. The child with these behavior potentials is a member of a specific sex, and the behaviors are evaluated by what is acceptable for members of that sex. I would also suggest that most parents respond to the infantile quality of the child for the first 2 to 2½ years, and then significant sex-role discrimination increases as he or she comes to be seen as less of an infant and more of a child. The very early sex differences do not originate as a response to parental actions.

It is not, then, that children are born with a built-in set of responses that will determine their behaviors irrespective of environmental reactions. Nor is it true that children are "tabula rasa," or blank clay, destined to be molded solely by the imprint of a parental (and heavy) hand. Predispositions to respond and to perceive similar stimuli may be significantly different between the sexes because of genetically determined differences that have their roots in physiology. The endocrine data and the infant animal and human studies lead to the assumption of general behavioral tendencies that are sex linked and that may be related to the presence or absence of testosterone at a critical stage in development. The behaviors of the organism, whether animal or human, will be responded to, rewarded, punished, or ignored in the process of socialization. I suggest that most cultures may be reinforcing behavior tendencies or predispositions *characteristic* of the sexes. In that case these behavior tendencies would be so pervasive that we notice body contributions only in exceptional circumstances such as that of the transsexual.

THE TRANSSEXUAL

Transsexuals know that they are trapped inside a body of the wrong sex. They have identified completely with the role of the opposite sex. Despising the genitals of their body, their single aim is to rid themselves of these disgusting parts and achieve through surgery and endocrine therapy the body of the opposite sex, which is their "true" sex. The transsexual is not a homosexual; the homosexual has the normal psychological investment in his own genitals. Moreover, the transsexual is, by and large, not mentally ill. He is able, excepting this syndrome, to function normally. It is important, however, to understand the intensity of emotion involved—autocastration by male transsexuals is not uncommon.

What is the origin for this extraordinary motive and conflict? Pauly (1965) reviewed the clinical material on 100 cases of male transsexuals and found that gonadal development was generally normal, that the steroid levels were within normal limits for those patients for whom information was available, and their secondary sex characteristic development was also within normal range. The absence of a clear physical pathology in the majority of transsexuals has been noted by many researchers.

Transsexuals appear in Greek mythology and in histories of ancient Greece and Rome; they have been described in many cultures around the world and throughout history (see Green, 1966). They are not found in any particular family constellation with consistency—although many patients are described as having an excessively loving and permissive (seductive?) mother and often a weak or absent father (Stoller, 1967; Hampson, 1961; Benjamin, 1966; Pauly, 1965), the frequency of this family constellation is too low to account for the frequency of the pathology. Of Benjamin's 152 male patients, only 20 percent could be definitely classified as having this form of childhood background, whereas 52 percent showed no such possibilities. In addition, siblings of the transsexual, both older and younger, are normal and have not been affected by this familial background.

While the familial contribution to this syndrome does not seem to be supported by strong evidence—Pauly writes, for example, that the "intrafamily dynamics are varied and there is no common pattern which allows for generalization"—the distortion in sex identity commonly has occurred by the age of 3. Rejection in boys of the male role, ranging from simple rejection of masculine activities to the assumption of a female role and dress, does result in their being rejected by their peers. Transsexual patients are often socially withdrawn and friendless. Puberty increases their anxiety because the development of the secondary sex characteristics of the despised sex makes denial and fantasy even more difficult. Although male transsexuals have been known to marry and father children, they tend to have low levels of sexual activity unless they take up overt homosexual behaviors or can secure a change of sex through medical-surgical sex-conversion procedures.

Psychological therapy with these patients seems to enlighten the psychotherapist but not the patient. No form of psychotherapy has proved to be helpful (Benjamin, 1966). Pauly has written (1965) that "intensive psychotherapy, hypnosis, aversive deconditioning, chemotherapy, and behavior therapy have been generally unsuccessful." On the other hand, the sex-conversion operation generally leaves the patient happy. Hastings reported a good social and emotional adjustment; Pauly reported that only 12 percent of his cases were unsatisfactory; Benjamin found only 2 percent unsatisfactory. This is a remarkable record of success for the most drastic kind of surgery and identity revision, on patients with histories of social withdrawal, alienation from peers and family, and a general culture-wide revulsion towards their abnormality.

It is interesting to speculate about the origin of this pathology. The literature seems clear in asserting that the normal causes for pathology, especially those from the family constellation, or from deviations in the mature body, seem absent. In 1961 Hampson and Hampson listed seven variables of sex: chromosomal, gonadal, hormonal, internal accessory reproductive structures, external genital morphology, sex of assignment and rearing, and gender identity (psychological sex). When they studied 110 pseudo and true hermaphrodites they found that the most critical factor seemed to be the assigned sex of rearing. But when they discuss the transsexual they state that "neither the purely genetic explanation nor the purely environmental explanation supplies all the answers to the questions posed by the disorders of psychologic sex (the transsexual)." They postulate that imprinting and critical periods could account for this phenomenon since these patients can recall having fantasies of being of the opposite sex as early as the age of 3 (Hampson and Hampson, 1961; Money, Hampson, and Hampson, 1957).

Stoller (1964) feels that gender identity is determined by the external genitalia, which includes the ascription of sex at birth and the consequent rearing, parental preference for a child of one sex or the other, and, finally, a "biological force." The term "biological force" is a name for the unknown factor inside of the mother, the fetus, or the infant which causes a child to later perceive himself as a member of the opposite sex despite his anatomical sex, his upbringing, and his parents' desires. It must be underscored that the patient's conviction that he is in the wrong body and can achieve happiness only by a change to the body of the opposite sex is in opposition to every force that the culture can pressure him with. This pathology, in the legal, psychological, and interpersonal sense, can bring him only rejection and grief.

What might Stoller's "biological force" be? What could be the origin of the "critical stage" described by the Hampsons? You will remember that the studies of the effect of testosterone upon animals revealed changes in the central nervous system, in the establishment of the masculinity and femininity of the organism independent of the reproductive organs. At birth the infant's genitals are large and well developed, but the central nervous system is not yet complete; that is, the developmental rates are different for the genital system and for the neural system. In that case it seems likely that the critical stages in development are also different. Organisms could reach normal *genital* development of one sex at the critical stage before the sex is established in the *neural* system's critical stage. If testosterone were present from outside sources during the critical neural-system stage of a female infant, the infant could have normal female genitals and a "masculine" brain. On the other hand, the male infant whose gonads produced insufficient testosterone at this second critical stage would be likely to have normal masculine genitals and a "female" brain. This could be the source of the feeling as he developed that he was trapped in the wrong body. If this situation were true we would find evidence, as Stoller suggests, of an early and irreversible core-gender identity "which is the result of a biological force sometimes powerful enough to contradict one's anatomy and upbringing."

It is interesting that most researchers report a ratio of between 3 and 4 to 1 (Hamburger, 1953; Pauly, 1965) and even 7 to 1 (Benjamin, 1966) in the proportion of male to female transsexual patients. I suspect that this may be a true finding and not simply the result of shyness on the part of female transsexuals. If our hypothesis is correct, the pathology will be more frequent in males. The female fetus is feminized by the sex hormones of the mother, and the animal data indicate that she would be female simply in the absence of testosterone—which, at least in the early stages of fetal development, her ovaries do not produce. The male fetus must produce and secrete testosterone from its own gonads in sufficient quantity and at the critical stage in order to produce masculinity or to offset the possible effect of circulating maternal hormones. This hypothesis suggests that masculinization of the central nervous system at the critical stage is more liable to error than feminization.

The sexual identity of the human child and adult is not determined by his sex hormones or his reproductive system alone. The predispositions to sexual identity originating in biological forces are a part of a self-aware human being who more or less conforms to accepted cultural norms and who has internalized the cultural values into his individual psyche. No one of these factors will by itself determine identity; in a very real way they interact. But it is important to realize that sexual identity does have origins in early constitutional factors, and that experiential factors are not solely responsible for its development.

chapter 6

SEX DIFFERENCES
IN PERSONALITY
AND LEARNING ABILITY

During the 1950s my husband and I spent some time on Okinawa while he was in the Air Force, and I had a temporary job teaching kindergarten. I was unskilled, inexperienced, and optimistic. After a while I noticed that most of my time was spent disciplining bored bright children and wiping tears from the eyes of dull children who were devastated by the simplest directions. The mass of the intellectually average children were fortunately quiet—and therefore ignored. We had 100 children and four teachers. I made an offer to the school director: On my own time, for free, I would individually test each of the children and then we could take the brightest 25 and put them in one class, do the same for the dullest 25, and have two classes for the average middle. The director heard my proposal in icy silence and then informed me that my suggestion was completely intolerable because it was "undemocratic."

Traditionally, or, if you will, democratically, we have denied the importance of genetic differences between children, preferring to ascribe observed differences to variations in experience. This is probably a case of the baby and the bath water. It is obvious that environmental factors significantly influence development, but constitutional factors also contribute to the variance. In this chapter we will examine the literature on sex differences in learning behavior and personality in children.[1] Some of these differences will appear to have a genetic origin. Of course there is interaction—any constitutional differences will mean that the infant or child has a tendency to interpret or respond to the world in a specific way; simultaneously, the child's response proclivities will be responded to in specific and unique ways. We will find that there are not only differences between children of the same sex but there are modal differences between the sexes. These early modal differences are consistent with those later found in adults.

The male mind discriminates, analyzes, separates, and refines. What is masculine? "Masculine" is "objective, analytic, active, tough-minded, rational, unyielding, intrusive, counteracting, independent, self-sufficient, emotionally controlled, and confident." The feminine mind knows relatedness, has an intuitive perception of feeling, has a tendency to unite rather than separate. What is feminine? "Feminine" is "subjective, intuitive, passive, tender-minded, sensitive, impressionistic, yielding, receptive, empathic, dependent, emotional, and conservative" (Silverman, in press). Even in infants we find precursors of these cognitive styles; early differences in motor, sensory, and autonomic responsiveness are consistent and correlate with later personality dispositions. Infant dispositions will tend to make some stimuli perceptually dominant and more meaningful than others. While it is true that temperament, which includes the relative ease of arousal of an innate pattern of response, is itself subject to modification by experience (Diamond, 1957, p. 50), behavioral differences in infants imply that constitutional primitive adaptation mechanisms exist which are precursors of later adaptive mechanisms (Escalona, 1963; Bridger and Birns, 1963; Schachtel, 1959). For example, there seems to be an infant response style of "approach" or "withdrawal" behavior to stimulation and differences in readiness to perceive and respond to stimuli (Bridger and Birns, 1963; Dayton et al., 1964; Lewis et al., 1965a, 1965b; Stechler, 1965; Steinschneider et al., 1965; Kessen and Hershenson, 1963). Thus Escalona and Heider (1959) found that children with high sensory thresholds in infancy had concrete, nonimaginative, literal play patterns in kindergarten. On the other hand, two-thirds of the children with low sensory thresholds in infancy had imaginary playthings, imaginary companions, and an involvement in fantasy situations when they were older. Escalona and Heider concluded that a low sensory threshold (originating in infancy) is a necessary although not a sufficient precursor for the later development of a rich

---

[1]Much of the information in the first part of this chapter comes from a paper by Julian Silverman of the National Institute of Mental Health, entitled *Temperament, Sex, and Cognitive Style*. A revised version will be published in a book called *Attention: Contemporary Studies and Analysis*, edited by D. Mostofsky (Appleton-Century-Crofts). Dr. Silverman's chapter will be titled "Attentional Styles and the Study of Sex Differences."

fantasy life. Murphy (1958) and Schachtel (1959) also feel that an active imagination, a pleasure in subjective personal experience, and a readiness to assimilate new experiences also depend upon some innate capacity to perceive and register an unusually broad range of stimuli.

ACTIVITY AND ATTENTION

Muscular activity and attention to stimuli are inversely correlated. When attention is arrested, the heartbeat perceptibly slows. Using this cardiac deceleration as a measure of attention to stimuli, the data clearly demonstrate that the hyperactive infant or child does not have the same high level of attention to stimuli as the less active child (Kagan and Moss, 1962; Kagan, 1965; Escalona and Heider, 1959; Rosenblith, 1964; Schaefer and Bayley, 1963). Less active infants respond to stimuli with cardiac deceleration; more active infants respond to the same stimuli with cardiac acceleration. It is as if the hyperactive infant becomes motorically agitated as he responds to stimuli and this precludes his perception of the stimuli; the less active child responds with a decrease in motor activity which allows him to register the stimuli. (Of course the interesting question for us is whether there is a difference in activity levels between the sexes; I think there is). Schaefer and Bayley (1963) found that children who were hyperactive at the age of 1 showed little attention to intellectual problems when they were 5 and 6 years old. Kagan and Moss (1962) and Kagan (1965) found that children who displayed excessive motion between the ages of 3 and 6 were not involved in intellectual activity when they were adolescents and adults. The more impulsive children were unable to inhibit impulsive answers to problems, were restless and distractible, and were not able to sustain their attention for long periods of time. The children who were not motorically reactive were less active out of doors, less distractible in class, less impulsive in solving problems, were motorically quiet in the laboratory and in class, and had the cardiac deceleration pattern to stimulus input.

I suspect that the motoric hyperactivity peaks at certain ages. It can be a response to conflict, and it requires sublimation instead of suppression. The experience of being with a group of 8- to 9-year-old boys is illuminating. They fight, run, jump, hit, twitch, climb, and in all manner of ways ignore the demands of authority to "cool it." When forced to sit still long enough to produce artwork and stories, boys in this age-group will use themes of war and aggression or more subtly express the bursting-out of activity. The originality of the products reflects the impulsive, exuberant quality of the motoric child. Cub-scout leaders for this age-group of boys are probably doing penance for past sins.

In Chapter 5 we examined sex differences in infants (see page 93) and noted that six month old girls have a longer fixation time to visual stimuli, less motoric response to stimuli, a larger magnitude of cardiac deceleration, and a preference for complex stimuli (Kagan and Lewis, 1965). These response proclivities all correlate with the "analytic attitude"—an ability to perceive similarities or relatedness (Silverman, in press).

The preference of six-month-old girls for faces (Lewis et al., 1965a) is more marked than in boys of the same age and is consistent with findings for older children; this suggests that infant girls have a greater sensitivity to social stimuli (Anastasie and Foley, 1949; Witkin et al., 1962). They also have a greater reactivity to physical stimuli, as evidenced by their lower tactile and pain thresholds, their greater irritability during physical examinations, and their higher skin conductance. The idea that this early sensitivity is a necessary precondition for empathy and imagination is supported by studies of older girls and women. Obviously a lot of learning occurs in the years after infancy, but older females are more prone to fantasy than older males (L'Abate, 1960), are more emotional (Castaneda and McCandless, 1956; Goldstein, 1959), have a swifter perception of details and subtle cues (Anastasie, 1958; Bakan and Manley, 1963; Pishkin and Shurley, 1965), have a better memory for names and faces, and have a greater sensitivity to other persons' preferences (Exline, 1957, 1962; Witryol and Kaess, 1957), as well as a greater freedom of emotional and intuitive experiences. Female infants seem to be perceptually precocious when compared with males (McCall and Kagan, 1967) and, at a minimum, this may allow them to establish more detailed and accurate perceptions of the stimulus-world earlier than boys, especially that stimulus-world composed of people.

We know of four longitudinal studies in which children were observed in their earliest years and were followed until adolescence or early adulthood: Kagan and Moss (1962), Schaefer and Bayley (1963), Honzik and Macfarlane (1963), and Murphy (1962).

Since behaviors tend to be age-specific, it is necessary to use broad patterns of reaction tendencies in longitudinal studies in order to perceive behavioral consistency in one child over a time span. These four studies, using different terms, are in general agreement about the consistency of behavior in a dimension of active, expressive, and extroverted versus passive and introverted. Bayley (1964) reports the greatest consistency in those behaviors characterized as active versus passive or as extraverted, outgoing, and impulsive versus introverted and controlled. Girls are more consistent than boys in this dimension. Thus activity and rapidity during infancy were correlated with outgoing, extraverted behaviors in adolescence, especially in girls. Macfarlane found the most consistent dimensions were reactive-expressive or retroactive-inhibitive styles of behavior. Murphy found most consistent in her sample dimensions of energy or activity level, the intensity of the affective response, and an impulse or drive level. Kagan and Moss found a continuity from the preschool years to adulthood in the passivity and dependence of females and in the aggressiveness of males.

That the culture pressures the sexes to adopt one form of behavior or another, forcing greater conformity along behavioral dimensions, is both true and not true. For example, consistency over the years in a boy's relative aggression level means that he has not changed his relative position on this dimension. Since the culture permits aggression in males, there is not a general inhibition of this behavior in boys and men. On the other hand, the original relative aggression proclivity is not significantly altered by cultural permissiveness. If the boy is not aggressive as a young child no amount of permissiveness will lead to generalized aggressivity, especially motoric. The low correlations for aggression as a behavioral response in girls is probably due to the cultural rejection of direct and overt forms of aggression in females (as well as their lower level of motoric aggression in the first place), which leads to subtle sublimations of aggression in girls. The relative level of passivity and dependence in girls, which correlates over a large part of the life span, does not mean that girls become more passive and dependent because the culture encourages this form of behavior. It means that the culture allows greater freedom in this dimension for girls, and therefore girls show a greater tendency than boys to retain their general level of passivity and dependence. If the culture successfully pressured boys to become aggressive and girls to become passive, the correlations would approach zero instead of being statistically significant and there would be no consistency in these dimensions over the age span. Honzik (1964) has written: "Perhaps the extraordinary finding here is that boys maintain their position on the aggressive continuum and the girls on the passive-dependency continuums, in spite of cultural pressure. It would seem to me, with my admittedly biological bias, more reasonable to consider constitutional factors within each sex as contributing to the observed constancy." We may also note that Bayley found that girls are more socially oriented than boys, even in infancy, and that this is also a consistent behavior.

Perceived in the most general way, the broad, general reactive tendencies of children, their original response proclivities to the world, seem to form a consistent life style, although specific behaviors will clearly reflect the sophistication and abilities of a particular stage of development. The extraverted, impulsive, motoric child will tend to continue to respond to the world that way—and such a child is not likely to engage in intellectual pursuits when he or she is older. And, generally speaking, the more passive, inhibited child will be the more passive, inhibited adult, and such a child (especially a boy) may well be successful in intellectual pursuits. The motoric, hyperkinetic child is less likely to respond to a wide range of stimuli than the passive child, and he is likely to be less fanciful, more concrete, in his perceptions. The less active child is more likely to be able to attend to details and to accurately appraise interpersonal perceptions. There will be a consistency in the aggression levels of boys and in the passivity-dependency levels of girls because, for each sex, these behaviors are permitted; aggression in girls and passivity-dependence in boys will show low correlations because these are behaviors considered inappropriate.

The culture may inhibit the direct expression of disapproved behaviors, it may force the repression or sublimation of disapproved behaviors, but it will not be able to reverse the original behavioral disposition. It can act on the qualities that a child already has; it cannot generate basic qualities that the child does not have. The girl who is motorically active, impulsive, and extroverted will learn sublimations of these tendencies which will stand her in good stead or she will be deviant. Nonetheless, we should not be surprised to find that the active-extroverted girl is more objective, less empathic, less imbued with fantasy than the average girl—and the passive, introverted male is more likely to be empathic, interpersonally oriented, and subjective than the average boy.

Sublimations are more or less available at different ages. For example, the motorically active, preadolescent girl will achieve status through competitive sports. Later, in adolescence, especially when teenagers are cruel in their demands for stereotyped conformity of behaviors, she will undergo a deep crisis unless she can divert her activities and aggression into competitive academics. That will be a solution and simultaneously a problem. The motorically passive and inept boy will face derision until his peers accept academic success as a successful route to status. For both sexes, academics offers a prominent route for sublimations.

Differences between the sexes do not originate solely in genetic differences. We know that there are genetic differences between boys and girls that result in differences in abilities and temperaments. But children and their parents and their peers and their teachers all have expectations of characteristics that are normal or desirable for a boy or a girl. The child is aware of those expectations and he or she knows whether his behaviors or dispositions are normal for that sex or whether they are deviant. In addition, expectations are age-specific, and each child is more or less able to cope according to the demands placed on his behavior at a particular age.

Let us, for example, compare boys and girls when they enter the first grade. At this level, the school requires at least a minimum of controlled behavior and an ability to memorize; first-grade children are expected to learn to read and write. For whatever it means (I'm not quite certain, but I read the phrase often enough), at this age girls are more mature than boys, perhaps by as much as a year. They are less overtly aggressive, they are less threatening to parents and teachers, they are well motivated to being "good" and loved, they are more socially oriented, and they are more verbal.

And the boys? The poor boys! Boys are less mature, and their impulsive and agressive qualities threaten authority. Their higher impulse level requires greater inhibition in order for them to quietly concentrate and learn. There is more early stress on boys to conform to a sex model: thus the active boy has to restrain himself in order to do problem solving (under the threat of banishment to the principal's office) while the passive boy is rejected by his peers. The boy must meet early demands for inhibition in temperament, for the acquisition of verbal skills in which he does not excel, and for conformity to interpersonal norms. In addition, some of the areas in which he could excel, such as space manipulation and exploration, are not part of the problem-sets the school engages in. Thus the stress from the culture is greater on boys and the capacity for resolution is less. It is not surprising that the incidence of personality pathology in boys is much higher than in girls. Ego integration in boys probably takes many years, perhaps until the age of 11 or 12, at which time we see the boys taking giant strides in cognitive skills, at least in school.[2]

It seems to me that parents and teachers have to understand what is happening to the boys and cease insisting upon feminine standards of performance. I have before me a composition which my 9-year-old son wrote:

Hi I'm a hawk I live on top of a giant saquara. Im a hundered years old, wich is pretty old. Im so old I had to hire a snake to do my hunting.

So one day he did not come back, and I got a scorpio-gram saying he was ded. So I called the non-employment desk and hired a tarantula to get me food, but I had to fire him because he was to slow and he poisined the food and it did not taste good.

So I hired another snake but he poisened the food and the seckend I took a bite I died?!?!

The sublimation is clear and the creativity derives from the sublimation. We will discuss differences in creativity in a later chapter, but for now I should like to note that the greater creativity of boys is easily observed even in the lower school grades. The artwork and writings of girls are much more predictable in style and content. Creativity has an element of deviancy, and girls are more conformist. I sometimes think this leads to different goals. Thus, my 11-year-old daughter is very pleased that she has missed only one spelling word in two years. This goal is not only beyond my son, I am sure it has never occurred to him. I also know that their IQs are almost identical in the total score. My son took enormous intellectual leaps when his teacher ceased being an inhibiting enemy, and he began to take pleasure in his evolving skills.[3] Simultaneously, the pecking order of the boys in the class

[2]The European "elevens" exam which determines whether or not children can go to college is likely to be very unfair to boys. The predictive power of the exam would be increased if testing took place when the children were 12 to 13 years old.

[3]An additional difficulty for boys is the preponderance of female teachers in grammar schools. An increase in the number of male teachers and male-oriented learning tasks might help the boys greatly.

was established, and once the order of dominance was settled the boys could attend to intellectual problems. It should be obvious by now that girls do not usually face similar problems in the early school years.

THE INFLUENCE OF BODY TYPE

Male children seem to be more muscularly reactive than females. Newborn infants and nursery school children show similar differences: boys exceed girls in motility, they have greater motor tension, they jump and squeal excessively, and they are tense during rest periods and stay awake at nap times (Terman and Tyler, 1954).

Walker (1962), attempting to repeat and extend Sheldon and Stevens's findings correlating body type and behavior (1942), studied children aged 2 to 4. The sex differences were already evident at the age of 2 and were the same as those at 4. Just 25 percent of the boys reached or exceeded endomorphy (fat) by the time they were 4, but over half of the girls did. On the other hand, over half of the boys reached or exceeded mesomorphy (muscular, heavy bone structure) by 4, while only 16 percent of the girls did. This is only a verification of what we can see: a greater number of boys than girls have a muscular, large-boned body, which is correlated with an assertive personality, a high level of energy, and a quality of directness. Interestingly, the endomorph in this typology is characterized by passivity, orality, and a need for social approval—which sounds a great deal like the female personality qualities that we have derived from other psychological models.

In Walker's study the mesomorphic body-build was more predictive of personality traits than either the endomorphic or the ectomorphic (lean). Boys and girls who were mesomorphic were assertive in play, were competitive, self-assertive, easily angered, energetic, and fearless. The boys were hostile and impulsive, the girls combined these traits with cheerfulness and warmth.

I do not know whether there is any genetic linkage between these body types and personality dispositions. In any event, from our point of view, the most important observation is that more than half of the boys have mesomorphic bodies as against only about 15 percent of the girls. It should also be clear that children of either sex can have body types and personality dispositions that are more typical of children of the opposite sex. Although this is likely to result in a personality type more typical of the opposite sex, the sex-identity, or the percept of one's self as a member of a sex, is not at all abnormal.

I suspect that there is an outgoing, assertive kind of self-confidence which comes easier and earlier to children of the mesomorphic body-type because so much early learning and interaction is primarily physical. Cortes and Gatti (1966) found a strong and significant relationship between body build and temperament. Rating themselves, endomorphs characterized themselves as kind, relaxed, and warm-hearted; mesomorphs saw themselves as adventurous, confident, energetic and enterprising; and the ectomorphs rated themselves as detached, tense, shy, and reserved. In the 1966 study they compared 100 delinquent and 100 nondelinquent 17-year-old boys. They found that the boys who were high in the need to achieve were high in mesomorphy. Thus physique seems to be one intervening variable that predisposes towards certain types of behavior.

We know that boys tend to have higher activity levels than girls. Now the question is, is this an intellectual advantage or disadvantage? Maccoby et al. (1965) predicted that general-activity-level scores would not correlate with IQ but that ability to inhibit motor movement would. The literature (cited by Maccoby, 1966) is contradictory: Murphy (1962) found a positive correlation between activity and the ability to cope with the environment. Witkin et al. (1962) found that assertiveness, striving, and an interest in being active correlated with field independence—which itself correlates with the WISC (Wechsler Intelligence Scale for Children) performance scale. Sontag et al. (1958) found that passivity correlated with a declining IQ score, whereas aggressiveness, competitiveness, independence, and self-initiation correlated with a rising IQ score. But other studies provided opposite conclusions. Grinsted (1939) found a large negative correlation between movement and IQ. Kagan, Moss, and Sigel (1963) found that children who had an analytic style in approaching problems, which correlated with performance-scale IQ scores, were quiet, contemplative, cautious, and not very active.

Maccoby felt that the problem is really one of specificity rather than a more general activity trend. Thus a child needs to be able to inhibit expressive movements during problem-solving tasks when the movements would constitute an interference, but at other times the child can be very active. Using nursery school children, she did find that the ability to inhibit movement was positively correlated at the 0.01 level with a Stanford-Binet IQ. The more intelligent children were not characterized by any general low level of activity, but they were able to inhibit their movements in a situation which required them to do so in order for them to complete a task successfully.

Within the normal experiential range there is probably no correlation between body build and intelligence. But there may well be a correlation between physical type and the characteristic way of approaching or attacking a problem: a difference between a more reflective, calm, and rational approach and a more aggressive, impulsive, swift approach. The major point is that the more active children have to learn motoric control in order to problem-solve successfully—and more boys than girls are motorically active.

The physical reactivity of boys is also shown in the ways in which they cope with frustration—by aggression. Studies of children as young as 2 show boys to be more aggressive and angry than girls. With other children they tend to grab toys and attack; with adults they refuse to obey or they ignore requests in that common syndrome of "perceptual deafness." Boys quarrel with more children, they do more striking, they tend to precipitate fights, and with the exception of verbal bossing they exceed girls in all forms of aggressive behavior (Terman and Tyler, 1954). They are also under more strain, and it shows.

Although the live-birth ratio of males and females is approximately equal, the incidence of still-births, deaths, and diseases during the first year of life indicates that the male has a greater vulnerability to stress and trauma than the female. We permit children to enter school according to their calender age, but at the age of 6 the girls are approximately twelve months ahead of the boys in developmental age, and by the time the children are 9 this developmental difference has increased to eighteen months (Bentzen, 1963, 1966). In children of the same chronological age, boys have three to ten times more learning and behavior disorders. More than two-thirds of those kept back to repeat grades in school are boys. Approximately four times as many boys as girls stutter, and this difference increases in each grade up until the eighth. In addition, boys stutter more severely than girls and fewer of them "outgrow" it (Kelly and Berry, 1931; Schuell, 1947). In the first three grades, Mills (1947) found that 46 percent of the boys had errors in articulation whereas only 28 percent of the girls did. Kopel and Geerded (1933) found that 78 percent of the children referred to reading clinics were boys. Sarason (1959) concluded that until puberty the incidence of problems or pathology is clearly greater among boys than girls.

It would seem that everything—their biophysical immaturity, their temperament dispositions, expectations for their behavior, the stress of conformity—all conspire to produce in boys a much higher incidence of learning and behavior disorders than occur in girls. The early stress on the boys will either tend to result in independence, self-confidence, and a strong sense of self-identity, or it will tend to produce pathology. The route to maturity for girls has far fewer dangers, but the attainment of an independent sense of self-esteem is less likely. This can only occur when early dependent relationships are given up, and that is not as likely to happen when the relationship has little stress, does not threaten, and tends to sustain.

VERBAL AND SPATIAL SKILLS

The middle-class route to social success is through talking, and here again girls have an early advantage. I do not think anyone knows why, but all of the measures of verbal skills tend to indicate that girls master verbal speech before boys (McCarthy, 1930). I use the phrase "verbal speech," which looks like a redundancy but isn't. It is my impression that boys learn to understand verbal messages as early as girls do but they do not respond in kind. While they understand speech, they do not talk. Perhaps the most fashionable explanation for the difference in linguistic maturation is the identification hypothesis. Thus McCarthy (1953) suggests that girls talk earlier because they identify with their (verbal) mothers, while the speech and voice of the father are frightening to the son. Another hypothesis is that girls may be preferred, held warmly, and spoken to more frequently and affectionately. Still another hypothesis is that girls practice speaking more than boys do and girls' games are more linguistic.

Maccoby (1966) addresses herself to the identification hypothesis and finds it lacking—as I do. A child begins to talk at a very early age, before he can perceive which parent is the same sex as he is, and long before he is aware that he is supposed to model his behavior after that of the like-sexed parent. We will return to problems with the identification hypothesis in Chapter 8, but for now I should like to note that this sex difference tends to be common and clear. I do not know the origin, but I do suspect it is enormously important. (I have various hunches: a slower neural maturation in boys, or possibly a preoccupation with things rather than people, or a tendency to communicate by doing rather than talking). In a culture that demands and rewards verbal skills, the boy is at an early disadvantage— although ultimately he will catch up.

The mean age of learning to talk appears slightly lower in girls, and girls have a tendency to begin talking in short sentences earlier (Terman and Tyler, 1954). Girls articulate speech more clearly and earlier than boys, use longer sentences at an earlier age, and are generally more verbally fluent throughout the preschool years. Girls learn to read earlier (though by the age of 10 the boys have caught up), and throughout the school years girls do better in grammar, spelling, and word fluency. By the beginning of school, there are no significant differences in the vocabularies of boys and girls (Maccoby 1966). Before the age of 5 girls learn concepts faster and seem to do better in solving problems that require flexibility or listing. Boys do better on tasks that require spatial or mechanical reasoning or analogies. Between the ages of 9 and 16, girls excel verbally, especially in grammar, spelling, and logical memory.

Boys do much better on spatial tasks, but unfortunately there is not much demand for that in school. There is not much sex difference between pre-school children on tasks like form boards or puzzles, but beginning with the school years and on through college, this superiority continues for boys. Sometimes one hears that the reason for the difference is that the toys girls play with do not make spatial demands. But building a house out of blocks is a spatial task, as is filling a baby buggy. What we observe is that girls elect not to play with the specifically spatial-mechanical toys although they are available. Perhaps this difference is best explained by

Erikson's observations (1951, 1964) of the difference in the play modalities of even very young children—a difference he hypothesizes is related to their experiences of their physical selves.

Girls learn to count at an earlier age (which may relate to their verbal skills), but there are no significant differences in the arithmetic abilities of the sexes during grade school. Beginning in high school, however, and continuing through college, boys do better in tasks of arithmetic reasoning. Aside from the possible effect of the cultural expectation that boys will do better in the mathematical skills—resulting in a decrement in the girls' performance—I suspect that there is a general and consistent selectivity in cognitive skills where boys have some tendencies toward the objective and "thing-related" and girls toward the intuitive, verbal, and "people-related." The cognitive skills that are developed become congruent not only with the current role expectations but with the personality characteristics of the sexes. It is not surprising, therefore, that most professional women who have doctorates are in education, certain aspects of medicine, and psychology— professions in which interpersonal sensitivity is an advantage.

There is another set of sex differences which at first glance might seem to be an isolated phenomenon but which is actually consistently related to general personality characteristics of the two sexes. Witkin et al. (1962) have found sex differences in three tests of spatial discrimination, the rod-and-frame test, the tilting-room test, and the embedded-figure test. Males do better, at least after the age of 8, on all of these tests. In the rod and frame test the subject sits in a darkened room facing a luminous rod and frame. The subject's task is to tell the experimenter to move the rod until it is in a true vertical position. The subject's chair and the frame may both be tilted. People differ in their ability to ignore the perceptually misleading cues of the tilted chair or frame and discern when the rod is truly upright. On this test, women perceive the rod as upright in relation to the frame, irrespective of body cues that indicate the rod is tilted. In the tilting-room test, where the room, including the subject's chair, is off the vertical, women perceive the room as straight, ignoring body cues even when the room is as much as 63 degrees off. In the embedded-figure test, the subject is asked to find simple figures camouflaged by more complex figures. Women are less able to break the perceptual set and isolate the figures from the misleading background. Men are more able to use an analytic approach to the test, and they can isolate one aspect of the stimuli from misleading cues.

Witkin has found sex differences on the embedded-figures test and the rod-and-frame test in school-aged children. Sigel et al. (1963) did not find this difference in 5-year olds on the embedded figures test, nor did Maccoby et al. (1965) among a group of 4-year-olds. People who group objects together on the basis of some selected element are also less influenced by the background, and here again boys are more likely to use analytic groupings than are girls. Sigel did not find a sex difference in analytic grouping among 4- and-5-year-olds, but Kagan et al. (1963) did find clear differences between the sexes in second grade and fourth grade children.

People whose personality tests indicate that they are more analytic and cope with the environment more actively are more independent of the context of the field in these perceptual tasks. People whose personality tests indicate that they are more passive and dependent on their environment for support and direction are also more suggestible to environmental cues in the perceptual tests. There seems to be a relationship between personality characteristics and characteristic ways of responding to the perceptual tasks. Witkin et al. have written:

Passivity signifies inability to function independently of environmental support, an absence of initiating activity, and a readiness to submit to forces of authority. Activity, on the other hand, involves ability to function with relatively little support from the environment, a capacity for initiating and organizing, and the power to struggle for mastery over social and other environmental forces. [1954, p. 457]

In the mode of approach, in both perceptual and intellectual situations, men are relatively more independent and more analytical than women. These differences are observable at least as early as the age of 8, but it should be noted that there is a considerable range of response within one sex.

In the rod-and-frame test and the tilting-room test, it is as though women "choose" not to attend to the body cues although they are available. If they are told to close their eyes, they then give accurate responses and the sex differences are eliminated. The sex differences exist where the task requires analysis, and the female response reveals a passive acceptance of the field rather than an objective analysis of the perceptual problem. Men consistently deal with the field in an active, analytic way—that is, they selectively isolate tasks of different structures and demands. Women accept the given situation in spite of internal body cues, while men always use the internal cues even when the situation doesn't specifically call for it. Perhaps the integrative style characteristic of women means that all cues, contextual and body, are perceived equally or that the contextual cues have enough priority for body cues to be ignored. Although men are equally susceptible to the originally induced set, they break the set more easily and they also restructure the set more easily.

In 1962 Witkin speculated about the possible origin of differences in perceptual behavior. Perhaps, he wrote, the internal, nonobservable nature of the female reproductive system results in a less clear body concept that may affect articulation of experience. Actually we know that women have a clearer body image than men do, but it is a whole, diffuse, complete body image. The body concept of the male, perhaps related to the demanding insistence of penile erections, is likely to be more differentiated than the global body concept characteristic of women. How well one discriminates between separate elements or how global one's perceptions are seems to be related to the articulation and differentiation of the self from the environment.

Maccoby (1966) enlarges on Witkin's idea, pointing out that we know from diverse studies that girls are more dependent, more conforming, and more suggestible than boys, and that these are the characteristics associated with global perceiving, or field dependency, and with the lack of the analytic ability that allows one to break a set and restructure a problem. Persons who are dependent (and therefore conforming) are more likely to be perceptually attuned to the cues that emanate from others and may find it difficult to ignore those stimuli in favor of internal cues. A task that requires breaking the percept of misleading physical cues is not helped by a reliance on interpersonal cues. In addition, the dependent person tends to be passive and these tasks require activity for successful solution. So it would seem that the personality characteristic of dependency, along with the other derivative personality characteristics of passivity and conformity, tend to preclude success in tasks that basically require an independent, analytic, specific approach. But there are other tasks, especially verbal ones, at which girls ought to do extremely well—like vocabulary, spelling, the recalling of names—verbal tasks that require the rather passive acceptance of information and its later recall.

I think it likely that this kind of difference in skills has important repercussions. For all of the reasons we have discussed before, girls do best in the cognitive tasks that are least demanding of independence, assertiveness, initiative, analysis, and activity. These learning behaviors, and therefore the passive-dependent-conformist personality dimensions underlying them, are being disproportionately rewarded in school at a time when the influence of the teacher is maximal. Because of the combination of the original personality disposition and the consistent academic reward, girls have little incentive to effect much change in their personality tendencies or cognitive skills. I think that girls are likely to end up with a perception of themselves as academically able (and academics constitutes a very large part of the life space of children and adolescents), skillful in scholastic techniques, able to achieve, but not innovative or creative.

The way a child uses his cognitive skills has an important effect on the development of his personality characteristics. It seems likely that the boy's active, analytic, focused, goal-oriented activity leads him to many more situations than the girl and he learns from first-hand experience. He is likely to learn the real consequences of various actions, cause and effect, how things work, and the results of what he himself initiates as an articulated, separate individual. Girls are more likely to learn from reading or talking about actions rather than by participating, and they learn to value or devalue less from their own experience than from the opinions of authority. These dispositions are reinforced by the behavior of teachers.

In a study by Sears and Feldman (1966), more than half of their sample of teachers said that they differentiated in their behavior toward boys and girls but that their educational aims for the sexes were identical. It is illuminating to see the differences in interaction between teachers and children of opposite sexes. While the boys receive more disapproval and blame than girls, there is a more active interaction in other dimensions as well: approval, instructions, and listening to the child. The boys are receiving more of the teacher's attention than the girls are (Meyer and Thompson, 1963; Spaulding, 1963). Teachers make more supportive remarks to girls and more critical remarks to boys (Lippitt and Gold, 1959), but they also reward the creative behavior of boys three times as much as the creative behavior of girls (Torrance, 1962). It is of course very possible that girls are making far fewer responses that the teachers can react to in the first place, but in any event, the message to girls is that one does best by being good and by being conformist; creativity is reserved for boys. (I also think that the personality characteristics of dependency, passivity, and conformity preclude much original and creative behavior because creativity seems to require the capacity to be original, to be deviant.)

Boys and girls are disapproved of in school for somewhat different reasons. Spaulding found that lack of attention accounted for about 40 percent of the negative responses by the teacher to both boys and girls. But another 40 percent of the negative remarks that teachers made to girls were because the girls gave the wrong answer or did not know the answer. This accounted for only 26 percent of the negative remarks to boys. Only 9 percent of the negative responses to girls were made because of infractions of rules, as against 17 percent to boys. According to the study, sixth grade boys got into at least eight times as much trouble as girls, and while this may reflect the difficulty boys have in controlling their impulses, it is equally likely that the boys have learned that they can generate a lot of teacher interest by misbehaving. It is also one route to peer status. Although the boys receive a disproportionate amount of the teacher's attention, a lot of that attention is unpleasant. When teachers criticize a boy they are likely to use a harsh and angry tone, while criticism of girls is likely to be made in a normal voice. I think that in spite of the goodly amount of negative affect, the boy learns that he can command attention and a kind of respect by nonconforming activity, either in behavior or cognitive skills. In addition to the greater independence that is generated by parental prohibitions of his impulse gratification, teacher responses are likely to lead him, for similar reasons, toward increasing independence, autonomy, and activity.

The sex differences that are present when children enter the school system are most likely to increase until girls and boys are very different. Dependency, affiliation, passivity, and conformity versus independence, achievement, activity, and aggression are the important variables. The origin of the differences lies in early constitutional proclivities which the culture enhances by reward and punishment along sex-specific lines.

chapter 7
DEPENDENCE, PASSIVITY, AND AGGRESSION

In previous chapters the idea emerged from various sources that levels of dependence, passivity, and aggression are particularly important in discussions of sex differences. Here we will elaborate upon these three qualities. An examination of the data may not lead us to any surprising conclusions —on the other hand, the consistency of the data is startling.

DEPENDENCE

What is dependence? In the beginning it is the normal infant's way of relating to people. Later, in children and in adults, it seems to be a way of coping with stress, a reaction to frustration, or a protection against future frustration. It can be affectional—the grasping and forcing of affectionate or protective behavior from someone else, especially from an adult. Dependent behavior can also be a coping behavior—one gets help in order to solve a problem that he cannot solve himself. It can also be aggressive—by grabbing attention or affection for oneself someone else is prevented from re-

114

ceiving it. In all cases, dependence means a lack of independence. Dependence is leaning on someone else to supply support.

By itself, "dependence" is a neutral word. Like many terms in psychology its meaning is clearest when the behavior it describes is extreme. Both dependence and independence can refer to normal and healthy personality qualities or to deviant and unhealthy qualities. Extreme independence can be maladaptive, meaning an inability to relate to people, a "tuning out" of others. Extreme dependence can mean a hypersensitivity to other people's reactions from an egocentric rather than a shared point of view.

In women, healthy dependence means a sensitivity to the needs of persons who are important to them, which allows appropriate nurturant or supportive behaviors. Unfortunately, we often see women who depend almost entirely upon other people's reactions for their feelings of self-esteem, and this is both a symptom of their feelings of inadequacy and vulnerability and a cause of that vulnerability. The woman who is markedly dependent feels less able to cope independently and is aware of it, feels a greater need for support, and is further dependent. We can see unhealthy dependence when people lean on others for activities they can or ought to be able to do for themselves, when they try to maintain a relationship through weakness rather than through a more egalitarian interdependence, or where they are tuned into the evaluative responses of people and are so afraid of being rejected by others that they cannot assert themselves or act aggressively.

Independence develops from prior dependence and is probably related to self-confidence. Independence in achievement behaviors results from learning that one can accomplish by oneself, can rely upon one's own abilities, can trust one's own judgment, and can become invested in a task for its own sake. Similarly, healthy interdependent interpersonal relationships seem to call upon the ability to trust the other person and upon the confidence that allows one to permit the other person to come close, to be dependent, to love, and even to reject.

Failure to achieve independence can result from numerous experiences of frustration. Continuing dependence results from frustration of attempts to be independent or the continuous reinforcement of dependent behaviors. I have children in mind especially. I have been tremendously impressed with the push toward independence in young, normal children. My impression is that in the first two years of life independence is begun simply by the child being allowed to do those things that he wants to do by himself. I suspect that the imperative, "Me, do!" in words or actions generally accompanies early motoric, cognitive, and feeding attempts. In this case, the frustration is of the early attempts at independence.

Children with very different characteristics are likely to use similar dependent behavior for ameliorative defense. Motives that result in dependent behavior can include the need for power, the expression of aggression, the enhancement of self-esteem, and the grasping of affection. Dependent behaviors can therefore have different origins and meanings in different people. Part of the evaluation of dependent behaviors depends on the sex of the person being evaluated. Since we know that girls are socialized to be dependent in comparison with boys, we expect to find that many dependent behaviors in girls are not only common but normal and adaptive, and our evaluation of the level of dependency in girls depends upon the appropriateness of the behavior, or, conversely, upon a generalized inability to be independent. In contrast, in this culture we socialize boys to be independent, and the boy who has not attained independence is quite likely to be evaluated as maladjusted, insecure in his masculinity, and immature.[1]

It seems to me that independence is achieved when the child (or adult) is able to see himself as generally successful in achieving goals. The goal may be cognitive, or motoric, or interpersonal—what matters is not so much the content of the goal as the nature of the resolution. The content variables that have occupied much of psychology for so long, like toilet training, weaning, and masturbation are important, but in this context they form only a small part of the relevant content. As children grow older, the nature of the crises and goals changes, but the important question seems to be whether the parent has the patience to allow the child to solve the problem for himself. It seems to me that we underrate the independence motive in children. When they try to dress themselves, comb their hair, color a picture, clean their room, finish a puzzle, they are not only mimicking adult behavior, identifying with suitable people, improving specific skills—they are also, in numerous and diverse ways, teaching themselves that they have skills and that they can cope (more or less) all by themselves. The child who is confident in his abilities and who explores the world and his skills from the basis of a secure parental affection is less likely to use dependent behavior as a means of punishing, exploiting, and manipulating. That child will be slower to use dependent behavior in order to master tasks because he will try to perform the tasks himself before asking for help. And that child will enjoy affection but he will not need it in continuous doses in order to reassure himself that he exists and is estimable. Does a child do things in order to be rewarded, praised, or even punished (at least that's some sort of attention), or does he do it for himself and then share the pleasure of accomplishment with someone else?

Children, like adults, are never entirely independent. There are always critically important persons whose love and esteem are essential. There are narrow margins for success and failure here because a parent rewarding dependence is seen as loving whereas his consistent training for independence can be perceived as rejection. For example, when a child comes home and says, "Somebody hit me!" the mother who responds with "Oh, my poor

---

[1]This is a somewhat exaggerated version of the socialization model. There are significant differences between the sexes but they are also relative. Girls, for example, are encouraged to achieve but less independently than boys. And boys are expected to be affectionate to their families but less overtly than girls.

dear" fosters dependence, the mother who says "Who hit first?" may be fostering guilt, and the mother who says "What happened?" and hasn't taken sides may be fostering independence. In different proportions, an emphasis of the "What happened?" response with only a bit of the other two is likely to result in a child who leans on himself first and who looks for objective criteria to assess life's happenings.

An additional variable may contribute to the sex difference. The toys and tasks of boys may foster objective, independent criteria of success; if an erector-set model works it is largely irrelevant what people say although it is nice to hear praise. Whether or not the decoration of a doll house is pretty really does depend upon the judgment of others.

Since we know that girls are both more mature and cognitively able than boys when they enter school and are more dependent too, it would seem that there are other factors also operating. A quick survey of the experimental literature shows that the greater dependency behavior of girls is not as significant and consistent when they are very young as it is at the age of 8 or older. Kagan and Moss (1962) found that the correlations in the dependency behavior of girls in childhood, at adolescence, and in early adulthood were higher than for any other behavior dimension that they measured. This means that girls are consistent in their patterns of dependency over this span of time. High-dependent girls become high-dependent women, and low-dependent girls become low-dependent women. This correlation does not indicate that girls are being forced to become more dependent as they become older; rather, it indicates that the culture permits a range of dependent behavior in girls that is not tolerated in boys. But we also know that most studies show girls to be more dependent than boys, and this difference persists as the children grow older. Several possibilities suggest themselves. Girls may tend to be more dependent-passive in the first place, or boys may, relatively speaking, be forced to become independent. I suspect that both are true.

Dependent children feel less adequate and are less able to try to cope by themselves. A lack of independent achieving results in less adequate coping techniques, less self-confidence, and a continued need for support from others. The child who is pushed or encouraged to cope by himself is more likely to experience the satisfaction of achieving by himself. If the child is frequently successful he will develop confidence in himself and have a self-concept that includes, or depends upon, independent coping. This is not necessarily sex-linked. Girls who have frequent successes in coping by themselves are also likely to achieve high levels of self-confidence and low levels of emotional dependency. But the response tendencies and the socialization patterns of girls make this a less frequent development for them.[2]

[2]We are going to discuss this at length in Chapter 10 on the motivation to achieve, but I should like to tantalize your curiosity now: The data suggest that the most independent, aggressive, and competitively achievement-motivated girls are those who receive the least affection from their mothers. A little alienation in this case seems to have big repercussions.

Perhaps the critical issue is, to what extent and in what ways is the child encouraged or forced to perceive himself as a separate person responsible for his own behavior, and to what extent have adult help and affection discouraged this development? The girl who is verbally adept and relatively mature is likely to have better controls and greater resources in coping with frustration than the boy. The boy who copes with frustration and reacts with aggression is likely to be punished, to feel alienated, and to be rejected for both aggressive *and* dependent behaviors as he grows older. When children are very young, in spite of blue booties and pink booties I think that parents respond to their children in terms of their ages and not significantly in terms of their sex. I do not mean that parents are unaware of the sex of their child, or that they do not find particular delights in the dimples of the female infant or the burly chest of the 6-pound son. I mean that most of the interactions of parents and young children are in terms of the helplessness and slowly developing abilities of the young child. Feeding, rocking, bathing, and so on, are not sex-specific. In addition, even if the parent gives the youngster many sex-related cues, the perceptual and cognitive apparatuses of the infant do not allow for much awareness or sensitivity. I always suspect that people who talk about the omniscience of the infant never had one.

But with increasing age, certainly by the time the child is 2 and is seen as a child and not a baby, significant changes occur. For the boy, the affectionate and dependent forms of relating are seen as sissified. Gradually (if not decisively), dependent behaviors will be rejected, especially by the father, and the son will be pushed toward and rewarded for independent behavior, and his aggression will be socialized into acceptable or even commendable forms, such as athletic competition. As girls grow older and acquire more coping skills, they too ought to grow more independent. But the majority of girls, not significantly alienated from adult authority, continue to perceive their worth in terms of interpersonal acceptance and evaluation and still depend upon the good will of others. This may or may not result in dependent behaviors as a preferred mode of relating to others. Probably the psychologically healthy girl is really dependent only on some few trusted people in addition to the family nucleus. Anyone who is critically dependent upon the good will and symbolic help of the majority of her acquaintances has no self-esteem to call her own.

I think that girls will be more emotionally dependent upon males than upon females. It is not only that dependency is permissible or even desirable in that kind of relationship, it is also that females have a considerable amount of experience with aggression from other females. The girl's relationship with her mother is more ambivalent than with her father, and her girlfriends are often obliquely, interpersonally, verbally hostile. The triadic friendships of preadolescent girls remind me of *La Ronde*—the number stays the same but the partners are ever changing. Thus I suspect that girls are more emotionally dependent upon their fathers, that this emotional intimacy is rewarding for both, and that if the girl is successful she will transfer this dependency, trust, and intimacy to her husband. Dependent behavior is vulnerable, and while girls may become more sure of themselves and more independent, new relationships, especially with males, are likely to resurrect old needs, vulnerabilities, and reassurances. In other words, the healthy girl will be selectively dependent, especially in the important emotional relationships and especially when she is not quite sure of her status within that relationship. I suspect that there are very few women who are really independent of the affectional resources of husband and children.

It might be helpful at this point to divide dependence into three categories: *instrumental* dependence, in which objective help is sought; *emotional* dependence, in which affection, support, and comfort are the goals; and *aggressive* dependence, in which the objectives are negative and manipulative. While emotional dependence is fairly acceptable for girls, it is definitely not acceptable for boys. Although the boy may receive affection from his mother he is pushed to identify with his father, who is a relatively nonnurturant model (although he may receive a goodly amount of help from his father in instrumental skill development). The boy is also pushed into competitive relationships with his male peers, who are also products of identification with the male role. In their relationships with adult males one should expect boys to become increasingly less emotionally dependent, although specific instrumental dependencies should continue longer. The boy who is unfortunate enough to have a father who is completely nonnurturant is likely to continue emotionally dependent upon that father in an attempt to gain affection. This is certain to fail and may leave the boy overdependent upon his mother. Boys, as well as girls, can give up emotional dependence when they are fairly certain of the basic love in the relationship. For girls, emotional dependence is likely to remain important, especially in their relationships with men. If the girl is neither mature nor independent, aggressive dependency, the behavior that I call the "tyranny of the weak," is likely to become a preferred mode of ego enhancement.

The father's tolerance or enjoyment of his daughter's emotional dependency is likely to be connected with his general paternal indulgence of her behavior. The boy's similar relationship with his mother has parallel implications. Cross-sexual emotional dependence, associated with the parent's general indulgence and nonevaluative pleasure in the existence of the child, creates a sexual overtone. If this is not excessive and the children can generally regard themselves positively (so that they are not too dependent upon this kind of reinforcement for self-esteem), it is likely to be a functional set of expectations in their adult love relationships. Emotional dependency in boys is likely to take oblique or derivative adult forms because the stereotype of the male is to be strong and independent. The girl's emotional dependency, if it is not aggressive, is seen as a positive future attribute and is less likely to take sublimated forms. For both boys and girls, instrumental dependency ought to decrease as they increase their cognitive skills and enjoy independent achievement. Aggressive dependency, in which the child manipulatively intrudes into the lives of adults, forces adult attentions, or uses adult power, is an indication of pathology in the child and weakness in the adults. Dependent behaviors reflect general sex-role expectations and the personal qualities of the individual.

The girl's reliance upon others stems from the relative lack of alienation from adults, perhaps from a genetic perceptual sensitivity to others, and from cultural role expectations. McCandless et al. (1961) found that boys and girls did not differ in their total and instrumental dependence behaviors but that girls scored much higher in emotional dependency behavior. And emotional dependency, especially if it took some negative attention-seeking form, tended to interfere with a girl's popularity but not with a boy's. Sears et al. (1957) and McCandless found that girls show more emotionally dependent behavior towards adults, that when such behavior takes a negative form it is perceived as aggressive in girls but not in boys, and that this results in a rejection of the girl. Here we have the implication that the emotional dependency of the girl is permitted only if its form is in accord with the rest of the sex role.

Emotional dependence upon adults offers subtle advantages. It can serve as a way of enforcing impulse control, because the nearness of the prohibiting adult precludes acting upon impulses. (Although the boy has more impulses to control there is a certain indulgence of his less extreme aggressions and there is also an earlier development of internalized impulse controls.) And it can serve to vicariously gratify an impulse through the protective response of the adult; for example, when an adult intervenes and settles a child's argument by acting aggressively, the child does not have to acknowledge his own aggressive feelings and can enjoy the aggression as an innocent bystander. But whatever the advantages of emotional dependency, and there are many, the underlying need for support and reassurance that dependency reflects will leave the dependent person vulnerable even as an adult.

When we review a sample of the experiments on dependency, we find that dependency behaviors in boys and girls tend to stem from different motives. Girls may be motivated by their high needs for affiliation and not by needs for achievement. The boys' responses may derive from their struggle in the early school years to gain impulse control and independence, to move from an affiliation motive to an achievement motive. Although the frequency of dependency behaviors in young children of both sexes can seem fairly similar, the early sensitivity of the girl to interpersonal sentiments and of the boy to achievements means that, very basically, these can be different behaviors.

Sears et al. (1965) studied 40 nursery school children and hypothesized that the more reinforcement of dependency behavior a child had experienced as an infant, the more dependency behavior could be observed when the child was 4 to 5 years old. This hypothesis was not supported. In truth, the less frustration the child had experienced and the more caretaking or nurturance, the less dependency at 4 to 5. That is quite understandable if one thinks of dependency behaviors as inversely related to feelings of security about the self. Most of the data suggest that the general levels of self-esteem of very young boys and girls are fairly identical, and that differences in dependency behaviors reflect the characteristic and particular anxieties of the sexes. The increased dependency of older girls implies a relative reduction in self-esteem as well as a favored and approved coping mechanism.

To be honest, I do not regard frequent dependency responses as healthy in children or adults of either sex. I think emotional dependency, especially in females, toward a few important persons is common and probably functional in the relationship. I think that generalized dependency is really a response to feelings of some kind of inadequacy.

Girls are characteristically more dependent, in either direct or indirect forms, than boys. Girls are also interpersonally oriented. We cannot tell from the data whether girls become more dependent as they grow older or whether the increased differences between the sexes comes about because of increased independence in boys. I suspect that the interpersonal vulnerability of girls, which itself is the result of the lack of independence, means the maintenance of early kinds of dependent interactions. Certainly, the boy who is psychologically healthy has increased his independence. Dependence is usually accompanied by conformity and passivity since they all originate from the lack of an independent esteem—but that is my own value judgment.

Kagan and Moss (1962) studied 89 children, 44 males and 45 females, over the years from 1929 to 1954. Dependency was one of the personality variables that they measured and followed over this 25-year period. They found that dependence was remarkably stable for girls over the 11-year span from the ages of 3 to 14. While the correlation on this variable was a positive .64 for girls, the comparable correlation for boys was a negative .33. The high positive correlation for the girls means that the girls remain consistent with their own early behavior as they grow older. The correlations, in conjunction with other information, also tell us that the boys are not consistent and become more independent as they grow older. Boys who are dependent when they enter school are likely to suffer rejection from peers and adults, so that these boys should shift towards greater independence. The boy who is initially independent may become even more independent, but he will not become dependent. In other words, dependency as a normal childhood way of interacting is likely to be as common for boys as for girls, but girls, given greater leeway, are less likely to change their original disposition. The cultural pressure on boys is greater, and most of the change is probably due to the dependent young boy becoming an independent older boy. Kagan and Moss found that dependence conflict was an important integrating principle for men but not for women.

I find an interesting variety of conflict about dependence in the college girls whom I interview. They are highly motivated to perceive themselves as independent and in the beginning of the interview characterize themselves as independent. They talk about earning their own living, living alone, and so on. At that point in the interview they usually say that their relationship with their boyfriend or husband is "50–50" and neither dominates. After a while, when they describe the masculinity and successful characteristics of their partners, it usually becomes clear that either the male does dominate in having a final say in decision-making or the female wishes that he did—so she either perceives him as dominating or puts him in a position of making final decisions. They also perceive masculinity as independent and femininity as dependent. Their dependency, then, is channeled into this single relationship.

Kagan and Moss found that both passivity and a dependent orientation towards adults were stable dimensions in girls into adulthood. The girl who was passive in the first three years of life remained passive in early adolescence, and the girl who was passive in adolescence was withdrawn and dependent on her parents when she reached adulthood. For women, dependence on a love object and dependence on parents was highly correlated —but this did not apply to friends. The girl who is dependent upon her parents transfers these needs to her husband or boyfriend, but not to her friends. The girl who is dependent on particular persons may be generally self-assured in other relationships. The adult male who is dependent on his love object has similar dependency relations with his friends. This implies that the dependent male is insecure in his own esteem and seeks reassurance in all relationships. Alternately, the inference may be that the girl's dependency relationships may be with superiors (parents, teachers, husband), while boys transfer their dependency needs to peers. Peer dependency may be closer to mutual interdependency and may be allied to the adolescent's need to detach himself from the family and develop his independence. Douvan and Adelson (1966) found that the urge to be independent is almost exclusively a masculine goal. They found that up until the age of 18 girls showed no drive towards independence, felt no need to confront authority in rebellion, and made no insistence on their right to form and hold independent beliefs and controls. Instead, the girls had a more compliant relationship with their parents, identified with the parental standards, and differentiated rather little between their own and their parents' standards and controls. In comparison with boys this is likely to be true but I also find, again in college students, that the girls are actively seeking an independent self, insisting on the end of parental and college controls, and are just as alienated from their parents as are the male students. Of course this could be a later development than in the boys, and the girls may be suffering from all kinds of guilt and anxiety. For girls the greatest threat is a loss of love and therefore they will be less independent than boys. But the portrait of a high *generalized* dependence sounds like very few women and girls whom I know.

PASSIVITY

It is strange how the portrait of the passive woman fails to resemble anyone we know, but we all know that women are passive. Are they? Imagine my surprise when in my first experiment in feminine psychology I found that all of the subjects who scored high on passivity were neurotic, anxious, dependent, and inadequate. That shook my stereotype.

Deutsch (1944) tells us that the feminine woman is passive-narcissistic. Passivity, in her definition, does not mean inactivity, emptiness, or immobility, but rather activity that is directed inward and has a vital content. But when we look at Deutsch's explanation for passivity, we see she doesn't really mean it. According to Deutsch, in all of the cultures and races with very few exceptions, feminine-passive and masculine-active are the norm. She attributes this to the internal hormonal-constitutional qualities of the sexes and to anatomy. The sexuality of the young child, in the psychoanalytic theory, has active and aggressive components which the boy is better able to gratify. The clitoris is an inadequate sexually active organ, the passive vagina awaits stimulation, and so the frustrated girl gives up the sexual, active, aggressive components of her personality. On close reading, passivity to Deutsch really does mean the end of activity and aggression.

Are women passive? That depends on the meaning we give to the term:

1. Passivity can be conceived as receptivity, as the vaginal tract is receptive. But the contractility of the tract is active. This is an internal, nonobservable, active taking within oneself and is not a withdrawal from activity. Receptivity can be similar to Erikson's concept of activity directed inward, elaborated inward within oneself, and is normal and observable in girls and women. This intraceptive tendency can mean a rich inner life.
2. Passivity can mean being dominated, allowing and preferring domination because it is perceived as love.
3. Passivity can also be a means of manipulating someone else to do what one ought to be doing oneself. Similarly, passivity can mean a lack of outward aggressive behavior, with the use of passive-aggressive techniques in order to manipulate and dominate.

4. Passivity as a normal component of the ego may relate only to the loved object, especially during coitus. In this sense passivity may mean pleasure in being fondled, made love to, and dominated.

5. Passivity, or a withdrawal from activity in the outside world, may be cyclical, dependent upon progesterone production. In this case, passivity would be increased during pregnancy and during the second half of the menstrual cycle.

6. Passivity can also mean using an oblique form of aggression such as a reaction-formation (where you "love to death"), or a turning of aggression against the self because of a fear of loss of love. Similarly, aggression may be turned against other women instead of men because relationships with men are more valuable and vulnerable.

7. Passivity can be, rather than an expression of helpless choicelessness, a behavior in which the ego makes a conscious and adaptive choice (Hart, 1961). When it is a specific behavior and not a generalized personality quality, it may be an adaptive coping mechanism in response to cultural expectations. Since people are surprised and dismayed by the active, aggressive woman, her deliberate use of passivity and femininity is both manipulative and adaptive.

8. Passivity is neurotic if it is generalized to most situations and objects. Hart (1961) describes this very well: "Anxiety over passivity (choicelessness) is as marked in the female as in the male, and extreme passivity or submissiveness is an ego-abnormality in either sex. . . . Passivity, defined as the wish to have things done to and for one, is the manifestation of an ego that is weak in techniques of mastery, weak in integrative capacity, impoverished in choice of defenses, having few alternatives available to meet traumatic or frustrating situations, and prone, therefore, to regression to infantile levels of functioning."

9. Since direct expressions of aggression in women are regarded negatively, passivity can also be a response to frustration by an elaboration of compromise solutions in fantasy and thought. In a successful sublimation there will be a fantasy projection of aggression; if the expression of aggression is followed by guilt, then there was little sublimation.

10. Passivity can mean quietness.

Traditional definitions of passivity refer to activity and aggression. The female is less active than the male, and the female is less aggressive than the male. This is true for most if not all mammals. It is also true that maternal activity, which is the essence of femininity, is not passive but very active. The world of most girls today requires cognitive activity as well as the assumption of responsibility. The very passive female, like the very passive male, seems infantile, completely dependent upon others for esteem, fearful of rejection, and obliquely aggressive. I think there has been an exaggeration of the *global* character of feminine passivity. The normal female is less aggressive and less active in a general way toward the outside world but can be aggressive toward particular persons (especially when she can tolerate potential rejection from them) and usually in distinctly feminine ways. The contribution to feminine passivity from cultural molding is obvious; there have also been suggestions that there is a constitutional contribution. The fact that only one-third of females are likely to be mesomorphs, the lower activity rate in infancy, the early low levels of testosterone, the female's preoccupation with internal and closed space, her early sensitivity to people, will all tend to make the girl less active and less aggressive.

Kagan and Moss (1962) found that passivity was a more stable dimension for females than for males, and they, too, found that passive and dependent behaviors are more frequent in females. Reviewing the literature they also conclude that there seems to be a passive-active behavioral continuum which has a constitutional origin (other longitudinal studies also found this to be true) and which is reinforced by the culture. The presence of high levels of passivity in response to an environmental threat in young girls resulted in women who were dependent and who withdrew from stress.

The portrait of the passive girl is exaggerated and reflects the acceptance of the male model of physical and overt aggression. Girls do not withdraw from aggression or from activity—only from direct physical aggression because it is prohibited and probably because they are physically weaker. I think that the early maturity of the girl, especially her verbal maturity, coupled with her sensitivity to interpersonal relations, results in more sophisticated methods of coping with or diverting aggression. The withdrawal of friendship, verbal slams, and the use of adult intercession do not simply hide aggressive tendencies—they quite realistically handle problems aggressively. In addition, the more oblique kinds of coping are reinforcing because they achieve the desired result without the threat of alienating people.

Passivity in the sense of indrawing, of elaborating and evolving a rich, empathic, intuitive inner life—in contrast with activity directed outward— may be a necessary part of the personality equipment of healthy women. It is also probable that this tendency is a preferred coping technique at particular times such as during pregnancy or in those years when one is nurturing very young children.

People are complex and everyone evolves personality characteristics that may seem contradictory. The pregnant woman may need to withdraw into herself in order to best cope with the demands of that crisis, but when this same woman cares for her children or returns to the labor force she will direct her activities outward. While there is a range of characteristics, healthy women probably evolve techniques for relating and coping directed both inward and outward. At different times in their lives women will use one technique more than the other. Compared with men, women are more passive or inner-directed as well as less motorically active and less obviously aggressive, but normal women have outer-directed activities and appropriate aggressions as part of their personalities.

It makes sense that the little girl, the bearer of ova and of maternal powers, tends to survive her birth more surely and is a tougher creature, to be plagued, to be sure, by many small ailments, but more resistant to some man-killing diseases (for example, of the heart) and with a longer life expectancy. It also makes sense that she is able earlier than boys to concentrate on details immediate in time and space, and has throughout a finer discrimination for things seen, touched, and heard. To these she reacts more vividly, more personally, and with greater compassion. More easily touched and touchable, however, she is said also to recover faster, ready to react again and elsewhere. That all of this is essential to the "biological" task of reacting to the differential needs of others, especially infants, will not appear to be a farfetched interpretation; nor will it, in this context, seem a deplorable inequality that in the employment of larger muscles she shows less vigor, speed and coordination. [Erikson, 1964, p. 598]

AGGRESSION

Although the experimental literature in psychology avers that the female is very passive and nonaggressive, I know in my soul that it isn't true. The apparent discrepancy seems to come from an expectation that girls are not aggressive and boys are, with the resulting assumption that aggression has to conform to the male pattern. Here is an enlightening excerpt from the Detroit *Free Press* for March 3, 1966:

Test Shows Little Girls are Not as Nice as Boys

If you think that little girls are made of "sugar and spice and everything nice," you're mistaken.

So says Los Angeles research psychologist Norma Feshback who has just finished a behavior study of little girls and boys.

Dr. Feshback, a 39-year-old mother of three, including an 8-year-old girl, organized 84 first-graders into two-member "clubs" with special names and badges. One club's members were all boys and the other girls.

Then she introduced a child from another classroom to each of the clubs.

Boys, it turned out, were much nicer to the newcomer.

"The initial response of girls to a new member, whether it was another girl or boy, was more likely to be one of exclusion and rejection," reported Dr. Feshback.

She said that while previous studies have shown boys to be more aggressive than girls, such findings seem to relate to the greater physical activity of boys.

Girls are not likely to hit, kick, bite, and wrestle, which are typical forms of aggression in boys. But girls are likely to use passive aggression (getting a powerful adult to intervene for them), verbal slings and arrows, and subtle interpersonal rejection frequently masked as solicitous caring. The assumption that the male model of aggression is the only form leads to the perception of low levels of aggression in girls. Differences in form need not mask similarities of motive. I think that girls are, in general, less disposed toward aggression, especially the direct and overt forms characteristic of boys. I also think that most cultures reinforce that tendency, so we should expect to find a decrease in overt forms of aggression in girls as they grow older. But in the spheres that are especially important to girls, notably the interpersonal, we find sublimated forms or oblique forms that are neither guilt-producing nor retaliation-inducing. As usual, three variables are interactively operating: temperament or disposition, cultural values and specific reinforcements and punishments, and a standard of expectations derived from the dominant male behavior.

The data in this section come from observational studies, ratings of behavior, experiments, projectives, self-report studies, fantasy-aggression measures, and studies of anxiety and guilt about aggression. They encompass work done from the 1930s to the present. The large number of studies, using different methods over a wide range of ages, report with near unanimity (a rarity in psychology) that the male is more aggressive, that his aggression takes physical forms, is directed toward his peers as well as toward adults, is accompanied by flings into danger, by high activity levels, and by trouble with everyone. But these are relative comparisons. To say that boys are more aggressive does not mean that girls are not. Girls are verbally aggressive especially toward other girls, but they are also guiltier about expressing aggression. We therefore find a minimum of overt aggression, especially physical, and the use of passive negativism, stubbornness or withdrawal, or social or verbal aggression. This difference in forms of aggression shows up very early—indeed, most of the studies seem to have been done in nursery school. Because the difference shows up so early, because of the conclusions of endocrine studies and body-type and temperament studies, and because there is probably less parental insistence on sex-typing in very young children than we usually assume, I suspect that some of this difference in levels of aggression has some constitutional origin which is then reinforced. The higher levels of aggression in the boy will lead to an expectation of peer aggression, to ego and superego development, to competitiveness which will be functional when he is an adult, to independence in the long run. If he doesn't crack up. The use of more indirect and subtle forms of aggression by the girl, at least with adults and males, is, we know, functional in the extreme.

In the 1930s hypotheses and techniques were simpler and we only dealt with one variable at a time. Terman and Tyler (1954) reviewed the 1930s literature and found the reports agreeing that from early childhood boys showed more aggression and anger than girls. For example, Hattwick (1937) observed 579 nursery-school children and found that boys more frequently grabbed toys, attacked other children, refused to comply with adults, or simply ignored adult requests. The girls more frequently withdrew from play, gave in too easily, sought praise from adults, stayed near the adults, and criticized others. The boys exceeded the girls in all forms of aggressive behavior except verbal bossing. Terman and Tyler felt that these sex differences, frequently found in other studies as well, could not be due to social pressures since they were found with similar frequency in children of 2 through 4½ years. They also felt that sex differences in aggressive and dominant behavior are likely to derive, at least in part, from gonadal or endocrine factors. Giving somewhat more weight to the idea of a constitutional contribution to sex differences in aggression was Whiting and Whiting's field observation (1962) of children aged 3 to 6 in six cultures. In all of the cultures the boys showed significantly more physical aggression.

Green (1933) observed children in nursery school and reported that boys quarreled with more children and their quarrels were physical, while the girls were usually verbal. Boy–boy interaction led to the most quarrels, boy–girl next, and girl–girl interaction least. (They also observed that girls reject other girls who quarrel. Children condemn aggressive girls and they are not popular, whereas aggression does not have an inverse correlation with the popularity of boys.) Dawe (1934) reported results almost identical with Green's. She also found that boys were more likely to quarrel over possessions while girls quarreled because of interference from someone. Boys often precipitated quarrels, whereas girls retaliated to an aggression someone else started. In their free-play activities boys were more pugnacious than girls, and that takes us back to the wrestling grounds of my children's schools. One might say that many forms of aggression, competition, and leadership are considered desirable in boys, and that aggression in boys will therefore not be controlled or sublimated to the extent that it is in girls.

More recent studies use more complex methods and give us greater detail, but in the main the data of the 1930s have been replicated over the years. Bach (1945) watched children play with dolls and found that the fantasies of the boys were often socially unacceptable, hostile, and aggressive whereas the themes of the girls were socially approved and dealt with affection, although the girls did use more verbal commands. Pintler et al. (1946), in another doll-play study, found that the themes of girls were stereotyped and conforming while the themes of the boys were aggressive. Muste and Sharpe (1947) found the most aggression in boy–boy interactions; in response to aggression boys used counteraggression and girls used verbal resistance. In studies that measured verbal aggression, sex differences in the amount of aggression tend to disappear (Sears, 1951; McKee and Leader, 1955). Walters, Pearce, and Dahms (1957) found that boys in nursery school and kindergarten choose boys more frequently for aggressive acts. This seems to be a fairly replicated finding and I suspect that it reflects an early preoccupation of boys to ascertain the pecking order of the group and establish a place in it by the most direct means—physical aggression.

We find that boys tend to be organized in gangs that are rather stable and probably protective against the incursions of adult requests. Prepubertal girls continue to socialize in groups of two or three, the triad changing with some frequency. The girls are never able to overtly establish an order of dominance within the group because the forms of aggression are subtle and because they continue to depend upon the good will of others and cannot afford the possible rejection they might incur by overt aggression. But they are aggressive and they are establishing their relative abilities, popularity, and likability in the friendship relationships. On the one hand, the girls do not need a group bastion against the onslaughts of adult restrictions to the extent that boys do, nor can the triadic relationship serve that purpose; on the other hand, personal support is not provided in these changing relationships. The girls tend to work out the quality of their interpersonal relationships one by one, and since the relationships are both emotional and changing, I suspect that this is one more reason why girls are relatively slow to achieve self-identity.

Sears et al. (1965) found that boys were higher in almost all measures of aggression and more consistent in their levels of aggression. I think it fair to say that boys perceive their world as more aggressive and competitive, both in regard to peers and fathers, than girls do. Tending to support our idea that this difference in aggression level is at least partly influenced by temperament, Gordon and Smith (1965) reported that boys were more aggressive in a doll-play situation than girls, but that the mothers of the boys and girls did not differ in their permissiveness for aggression, in their general strictness, or in their use of physical punishment. Certainly parental responses significantly alter children's behavior, but I suspect that parental reactions alter the form of a behavior more than its intensity. The Gordon and Smith study (1965) found that if the mother was strict and did not use physical punishment, the girl was aggressive and the son was not. It is as though the daughter can cope with the mother's verbal aggression with a verbal aggression of her own, and we suspect that the father (who was not interviewed) served as the affective and supportive base for the daughter. The son may well be devastated by aggression from the mother, especially in a verbal form, when he is probably receiving a goodly amount of punishment from the father too. In that case the son may be less likely to be aggressive because he is fearful of the loss of affection from everyone—mother, father, teacher, and playmates.

As boys and girls grow older, less physical punishment is directed at girls. Mothers are more prone to use verbal and psychological forms of aggression, and they serve as models for this form of sex-appropriate aggressive behavior in their daughters. I also suspect that fathers (who were once aggressive boys) are more prone to use physical force than mothers and are more likely to use it with their sons than with their daughters. All of this is still rather consistent: girls are probably less prone to use physical aggression than boys by virtue of temperament; their early maturity and verbal skills probably allow them to cope with frustration verbally and interpersonally rather than physically; their physically aggressive fathers are likely to be supportive and warm with them; their mothers, who do serve as frustrating agents and as models for the expression of aggression, are more likely to use nonphysical forms of aggression, preferring the verbal; female models for sex-appropriate behaviors who are outside of the home are also likely to use verbal and oblique sex-appropriate forms of aggression. Girls seem to have every reason not to use direct, physical, overt forms of aggression.

We are talking about one behavior at a time, but the girl who has a wicked tongue is also the girl who is motivated by high affiliation needs, who fears rejection, and who conforms to general norms and the expectations of others. The girl who is overtly aggressive is likely to be the girl who is anxious and testing limits, or the girl who has evolved a concept of herself and a feeling of independent worth that permits her to alienate some people and still retain a sense of worth.

Sears (1961) found that sixth-grade girls scored higher than boys on prosocial aggression and on anxiety about aggression. The anxiety was the result of a conflict between the desire to be aggressive and the girls' knowledge of appropriate sex-typed behavior. The boys scored higher on antisocial aggression, as one would expect. What is particularly interesting about the study was the correlation between high scores on a femininity test and high prosocial aggression and aggression anxiety. Conversely, low scores on the femininity test correlated negatively with antisocial aggression. This means two things: more girls than boys will score high on the measure of femininity and will use the more appropriate form of (prosocial) aggression —but boys who score high on the femininity measure will also use the more feminine form of aggression.

Children whose personalities are like those of the opposite sex in some important ways are likely to have needs, conflicts, and defenses similar to those of the opposite sex. Personality characteristics reflect the sex of rearing and a basic temperamental disposition. Children whose personalities are closer to the norms for the opposite sex may suffer anxiety about it, but if not pathologically extreme, it may be of advantage. The intuitive, empathic boy or the competitive, independent girl, if they also have characteristics appropriate to their sex, are often more creative than the more rigidly sex-typed personalities.

Girls who have a high need for achievement and who are not anxious about successfully achieving have little identification or perceived similarity with their mothers, low levels of guilt about expressing aggression toward authority figures, and little interest in being socially accepted. They are also able to criticize their mothers (Lansky, Crandall, Kagan, and Baker, 1961). These are the more atypical girls and they contrast strongly with the other teenage girls in the study who were high on sexual anxiety, affiliation needs, and restitutive responses to guilt. Boys were higher on aggression, independence, and autonomy. Boys in general were more aggressive than girls, and typical girls were more preoccupied with affiliation and sex anxiety. For boys, aggression tended to be an independent variable—this is a behavior which is accepted in boys, if not valued, and the aggressive boy may have other very diverse personality characteristics. But the correlations for aggression in the girl with other personality characteristics is high—the girl who is deviant in aggression is also likely to have correlated deviant characteristics. For example, the girl who is aggressive may also be searching for personal independence and competence and for an identity dependent in part upon achievement. These are goals more characteristic of boys, and the deviant girl who is successful in these attempts is likely to suffer rejection in the dating activities of adolescence.

When we look at studies of college students or older adults we find that men are still more aggressive than women, that they suffer less guilt about acting aggressively, that men and women may have similar hostile feelings but females do not express them, and that verbal measures of aggression show the least amount of sex difference.

As dependency was a stable personality trait for women in the 1962 Kagan and Moss study, aggression was a stable trait for men. While temper tantrums and aggressive behavior toward the mother in a 10-year-old boy were fairly good predictors of his ease of anger arousal as an adult, it was very difficult to predict adult aggressive behavior for women on the basis of childhood behaviors. Kagan and Moss suggest that this is due to the greater socialization of aggression in girls and the cultural ideal in which women suppress open forms of anger and aggression. Not only is overt aggression incongruent with the idealized norm, but "it is possible that the differential stability of dependency and aggression for males and females is the product of interaction in which constitutional variables find support in the behavioral rules promoted by the child's culture." One of the more recent popular experimental designs has the subject ostensibly or actually giving an electric shock to some hapless, innocent victim (Buss, 1963; Buss and Brock, 1963). In these experiments the men are significantly more aggressive than the women, female victims arouse more guilt than male victims, and women are significantly more guilty about giving shock.

The relationship between aggression and sex-role identity is the same in the older population as in the younger. Heilbrun (1964) found that women who had a feminine sex-role identity were less aggressive. Greater femininity was associated with greater anxiety about aggression for both males and females (Cosentino and Heilbrun, 1964). These psychologists found that a more feminine sex-role identity in either sex involved a real disposition to respond with anxiety to aggression cues. There are numerous studies we could cite, but the facts are getting too repetitive—men act on their aggression and tend not to feel guilty about it.

I happen to think that women are really much more hostile and aggressive than most experimental procedures reveal. The problem is that women feel guilty about expressing hostility and they are interpersonally dependent, so that in experiments where the subject and the experimenter are visible to each other, or where the aggressor and the victim are visible to each other, manifest hostility by women will be low. But what happens when the aggressor and victim cannot see each other? Rapoport and Chammah (1965) do game studies in which people can make real money depending upon whether they cooperate or not. There are variations but the basic game stems from "Prisoner's Dilemma." Two prisoners are accused of the same crime and are held incommunicado. Each has the choice of confessing to the crime or not, and this decision is made by each independently out of sight of the other. If both confess, both will be convicted. If neither confesses, they will both be acquitted because of a lack of evidence. If only one confesses, he not only goes free but also gets a reward for turning state's witness. In that event, the one who refused to confess gets a more severe sentence than if he had confessed in the first place. In the game and in terms of the monetary pay-off it is to each one's personal advantage to confess regardless of what the other does, but at the same time it is better for both of them not to confess than to confess. This is a problem of individual rationality (defection) versus collective rationality (cooperation).

The Rapoport and Chammah study used 70 pairs of males, 70 pairs of females, and 70 mixed pairs. Each pair played the game 300 times in succession, and each time a decision was reached the experimenter told the result to both members of the pair. No signaling or communication or visibility was possible between members of the pair. The most significant sex difference was the small amount of cooperation shown by the female pair in comparison with either the male pair or the mixed pair. Seventy percent of the male pairs locked into one response in the last 25 responses, and four times as many male pairs locked into the cooperation response as locked into the defection response. For the female pairs, half locked into a response, and twice as many of their pairs locked into the defection response. In the mixed pairs the performance was intermediate. Compared with the male pairs, the female pairs showed a significantly lower degree of cooperation. When faces are hidden and the game situation permits it, women are aggressive toward each other.

Let us return to Kagan and Moss's data and see one culturally sanctioned sublimation of aggression in girls. They found that achievement and recognition behaviors were stable for both sexes; this is not a surprising finding since middle-class parents tend to value success for their children of both sexes. (That is probably true until middle or late adolescence, when parents perceive the academic success of their daughter as a threat to her dating success.) Kagan and Moss found that boys who were fearful when they were children and girls who were bold between the ages of 10 and 14 aspired to intellectual mastery as adults. Boys who were quick to anger when they were 6 to 10 proved to be men who were quick to anger. Girls who were overtly aggressive at 6 to 10 proved to be intellectually competitive women with more masculine interests. In their sample it is clear that intellectual competitiveness evolved from quite different personalities in men and women; persons who were at variance with the cultural standard for their sex elected to use intellectual mastery for conflict resolution. Boys who were fearful of bodily injury and who failed in the daring, aggressive, physical competitions of boyhood turned to intellectual pursuits for status. For women, Kagan and Moss found one major cluster of intercorrelated variables that included competitiveness, achievement, intellectual mastery, masculine interests, low social anxiety, and a reluctance to withdraw from stressful situations. This seems to reveal a woman whose personality is in these aspects closer to the male model and who uses her intellectual or professional area as the place in which she can express her abilities, independence, and competitiveness with a lessened likelihood of alienating others.

Kagan and Moss, along with other psychologists, found that the daughters of well-educated parents tended to be less conforming with adults and more verbally aggressive with their peers than daughters of less well-educated parents. The parents with more education were able to tolerate deviation from the sex-role norms and this, of course, includes aggressive behavior. It seems to me that these daughters may be different from the daughters of critical mothers who achieve an early independence from their families and later use achievement and intellectual competition for sublimation. The parents who tolerate or even encourage aggression from their daughters present less of an obstacle to the girl, and in that case the independence is probably not quite so decisive. Highly educated parents are likely to value high levels of academic performance in their children of both sexes. I suspect that these girls achieve because they are motivated by affiliative needs and are conforming to parental expectations. In that case the motive to achieve, especially competitively, is probably not a core part of the personality. As a guess I would say that this is the rather polite and definitely predictable "B" female student that one sees in class all the time, who does well but not too well and who probably fears real success. In my experience, the really independent, aggressive, iconoclastic female student is rare.

While males and females may have similar aggressive needs (and females *may* have lower levels of aggression), males can express their aggressions much more directly than females and can do so without guilt. Females are more likely to feel guilt, to feel conflict, and are most likely to inhibit the direct expression of aggression.

To measure the true levels of aggression in males and females one must include verbal aggression, interpersonal rejection, academic competitiveness, gossip (especially against other girls), deviation from sexual standards, passive aggression, the manipulation of adults with power, withdrawal, tears, and somatic complaints—as well as fighting, hitting, and biting.

chapter 8
IDENTIFICATION

The term "identification" is used in psychology to explain everything from intense guilt about moral standards to the 2-year-old's imitation of hammering and sweeping. Basically, the term describes the incorporation of the model into oneself, in which there is no boundary between the self and the model. However, a person's *identity* is larger than the sum of his identifications.

CHILDREN IDENTIFY WITH TWO PARENTS

One of the studies I recently read reported that in a testing situation boys between the ages of 2 and 8 were more upset than girls of the same age when they were separated from their mothers. That made me wonder whether the affectional tie of the boy to the mother was greater and whether girls might not be more ambivalent in their relationships with their mothers—loving, aggressive, and a little independent. I was also reminded of other cultures where the training-discipline roles are held by the biological parents and the affectional-noncritical roles by aunts and uncles, and I wondered whether something similar might be happening here. Not only may the child be identifying with the parent of the same sex, but the like-sexed parent may be identifying with the child and assuming the responsibility for role training and the creation of role expectations in the child. Training necessarily requires some discipline, some frustration, and therefore some (mutual) aggression. The parent of the opposite sex, although not totally removed from disciplining (especially for personality qualities rather than role characteristics), is likely to act with less discipline and aggression and is therefore likely to be perceived by the child as the good guy, affectionate, supportive, and permissive. This will also affect the child's expectation that those of the opposite sex can love and be loved in a relatively unambivalent relationship and be trusted with intimacy. Indeed, if you think about it, "femininity" is really a relative term and is probably first learned by girls in their relationships with their fathers—as "masculinity" is a relative term and is probably first learned by boys in relationships with their mothers. The sex-linked differences in parental behaviors are not absolute. But later there will be reinforcement for the original percepts as boys scramble for peer dominance and compete aggressively, and the boy will see males as potentially hostile, thwarting, and competitive—as well as affectionate. These are the same ambivalent sentiments they have toward their fathers. A girl will have similar experiences. In the single-sex play groups prior to adolescence the ambivalence of a girl's relationship to her mother will be repeated in her experiences with girlfriends. (Of course the intrusion of sex into adolescent relationships will result in strong ambivalence to persons of the opposite sex, but there the goal will be the establishment of an honest, trusting, and mutually dependent relationship.)

In much of the literature the mother is described as *expressive*, which means she is primarily concerned with affects, with the establishment of warm, rather uncritical relationships with her children. The father is described as *instrumental*, largely preoccupied with the long-term goals and accomplishments of the family and the children in the world outside of the home. I think it is an error to view the mother as only expressive and not instrumental. Compared with the father, she is likely to be more expressive, but she is also likely to be rather instrumental toward her daughter and rather expressive toward her son. In terms of instrumental behavior she may discriminate little when compared with the father, but discrimination should increase as the children grow older and she no longer perceives them as babies. Dependency on the part of the children, especially daughters, which evoked expressive, affectionate, supportive behavior from her, should decrease as the children grow older. The father, in a like way, should be more instrumental than the mother in general—but more so to his son than to his daughter. Thus it may be normal and beneficial when children can perceive one parent as rather uncritical and unambivalent and the other as more directive. Of course it may also be dangerous to the sex identity of the child when the instrumental, critical parent is not expressive and supportive at all. In that case, the child may be drawn or driven to the parent of the opposite sex, with whom he may identify.

Although children receive both instrumental and expressive responses from both parents, I think that

1. The mother is more expressive than the father, but especially to her son;
2. The mother is less instrumental than the father, but more so to her daughter;
3. The father is more instrumental than the mother, but especially to his son;
4. The father is less expressive than the mother, but more so to his daughter.

Philip Slater (1961) has written a paper on identification which I thoroughly enjoy because he has returned warmth to the parent-child relationship and because he also feels that children must identify with both parents in order to be psychologically healthy. Slater distinguished between *personal* and *positional* identification. In personal identification, the child identifies with the role model and adopts the values, attitudes, and personality traits of the model. This kind of identification is motivated primarily by the child's love and admiration. Slater writes that the child is, in effect, saying: "I want to be like you. If I were, I would have you (and your virtues) with me all the time, and I would love myself as much as I love you. To achieve this I will incorporate your qualities and your values and ideals. I will view and judge myself through your eyes" (p. 113). This kind of identification is the result of parental warmth, affection, and support; it seems to be an intervening variable between a supportive relationship and the child's internalization of parental values.

In positional identification, the child identifies with the position or role of the model. Instead of an empathic personal relationship, there is a fantasied projection into the situation of the model and the role behavior of the model. Slater tells us that this child is saying: "I wish I were in your shoes. If I were, I would not be in the unpleasant position I am in now. If I wish hard enough and act like you do, I may after all achieve your more advantageous status" (p. 113). The motives involved are identification with the aggressor ("I will be strong, powerful, and menacing instead of weak, powerless and menaced") and the Oedipal wish ("Mother or Father will love me and not you"). In positional identification there is a wish for the destruction and replacement of the model by the identifier. Slater conceives of this kind of identification as a defensive reaction to the frustration of a lack of parental warmth, support, and affection. For children of both sexes, both kinds of identification will occur at the same time and, I would add, with both parents.

Insofar as the model commands because of positive qualities in his personality, the identification will be personal; if the model commands because of his role or status, the identification will be positional. "Positional identification, then, will occur insofar as personal identification has failed to occur" (Slater, p. 118). It should be clear that interaction is probable—even warm and supportive child relationships are ambivalent, and the parent is always in a more powerful status than the child. (And the child's percept of parental power is greater than the actual power the parent commands.)

I suggest that both parents are a source of love to children of both sexes, and they are also a source of rejection. The mother's relationship to the daughter, especially insofar as the female role is concerned, is largely instrumental; in Slater's terms, the identification is positional. But to the extent that the mother is also a nurturant, warm human being, the identification is simultaneously personal. Insofar as the mother pushes the daughter to the assumption of role responsibilities, she will be perceived as manipulative and powerful. The girl is also aware that she is expected to learn role behaviors and that she will receive reinforcement for learning. In the analytic model, she has an unconscious identification with the mother; she has a learning-theory identification with the mother insofar as she perceives similarities in personality between herself and her mother and insofar as she sees herself in the female role. She has a personal identification with the father because that relationship is warmer and less ambivalent than the relationship with the mother. She may also have a positional identification with the father because she perceives that his roles, especially economically, are sources of money, power, and prestige, which are generally valued by the culture. Thus the girl identifies with the personal qualities of the mother and with the role of the mother, and simultaneously, in a reciprocal role relationship, she identifies with the father because she loves him and because she is loved by him.

If the daughter rejects the maternal role, or if her mother is more rejecting than supportive, or if her relationship with her father is the only source of love and support, she may well identify with his role activities, especially because this culture values the achievements that come from successful competition in nonfeminine roles. These relationships may change over time so that, for example, the sexuality of the adolescent girl and her dating activity arouse anxiety in the father. He now becomes more restrictive and less supportive than the mother, who can identify with the daughter and enjoy her daughter's social successes. At that point, the identification with the mother may be less ambivalent than it had been, and the daughter can empathize with and desire the role and the femininity of the mother.

The psychoanalysts, especially Fenichel (1945), conceive of identification as an all-or-nothing proposition with only one parent. We are suggesting that identification is also a developmental process and involves both parents. Slater writes, "When measured independently and correlated (as they rarely are), paternal and maternal identification are strongly and positively related" (Slater, 1955, p. 119). One can identify with the roles of both parents, one can identify with the concept of the appropriate role, and one can personally identify with the model and reject the appropriate role. There are basic and unconscious core identifications, there are learned identifications that reflect one's age and status, there are identifications with one's own parents, and there are identifications with cultural models. There are internalized expectations and standards and there are reactions from others. All of these combine in complex ways and probably reflect the strengths and pressures in individual family situations as well as in general cultural patterns.

Rothbart and Maccoby (1966) have to some extent verified the cross-sex interaction that we have been describing. (That's very pleasing to me, of course, and doubly so because they didn't expect the results they got.) In a previous study (1957), Sears, Maccoby, and Levin[1] had found that mothers were tolerant of aggression from sons while fathers took the major responsibility for disciplining sons when both parents were at home. The 1966 study was designed to explore a rather traditional hypothesis: both parents would reinforce aggression in sons and dependency in daughters.

The experimenters taped the voice of a 4-year-old who made 12 statements like "Daddy, help me," or "I don't like this game . . . I'm gonna break it." Sixty mothers and 21 fathers were told that the voice was a girl's; 38 mothers and 11 fathers were told that it was a boy's. Contrary to expectations from Maccoby's original study, mothers tended to be more permissive when the voice was identified as a boy's, fathers when the voice was a girl's. Fathers showed more permissiveness and positive attention to their daughters, and allowed them more autonomy. Mothers were more restrictive and negative to their daughters. Confounding the sex-role stereotype, parents were not warm to girls and harsh to boys but showed cross-sexed responses.

Maccoby and Rothbart felt that these were unexpected results because in this study the sex of the parent was a better predictor of the response to a girl or boy than the sex-role stereotype. These authors suggested that parents shift their reinforcements of behavior as the children grow older—an idea we have also suggested.

The data are new enough so that we cannot be certain of the specific ways in which parents differentially respond to their children at any one age or of how these responses change as the children grow older. For example, Emmerich (1962) found that mothers were more nurturant and less restrictive than fathers, and the 306 parents in his study were neither more nurturant nor more restrictive toward the same-sex child than toward the opposite-sex child; but at the same time he found that with children aged

[1]Sears, R. R., E. E. Maccoby, and H. Levin 1957 *Patterns of Child Rearing,* Harper & Row, New York.

6 to 10 fathers exerted more power toward their sons while mothers exerted more power toward their daughters. Later research may spell out the details of the interactions.

Mussen and Rutherford (1963) suggest that the interactive variables which are usually omitted in studies of identification include the personality qualities of the parents and the general cultural sex-role values. They found that the feminization of daughters was dependent upon a warm relationship between the mother and daughter (personal identification). They also found that those mothers whose daughters were most feminine were not more feminine themselves, nor did they particularly encourage their daughters to participate in feminine activities, but were themselves clearly more self-accepting and self-confident. The fathers of very feminine girls tended to be masculine and tended to encourage their daughters to participate in feminine activities. They found that the mother's personality and interactions with the son tended to have little influence on his sex-role preference, but the father's personality and interest and his encouragement of his daughter's femininity were crucial in the girl's development of an appropriate sex-role preference. Feminization of the daughter depended upon a warm relationship with a mother who held herself in esteem and with a father who encouraged and responded to his daughter's emerging femininity.

Mussen and Rutherford feel that the family is more critically important in the daughter's sex-role socialization than the son's. The male role in this culture is more highly valued and more clearly defined, and for the son there is a consistency of role expectation over his lifetime and a consistency in the portrait of that role in the entire culture. Therefore the boy receives assistance, support, and criticism from all of the culture's socialization agents, while the girl does not. Indeed, because the feminine role is devalued, a daughter is likely to have a mother who is experiencing conflicts about her own femininity and who therefore cannot support her daughter's self-esteem or serve as a successful role model.

THE BISEXUAL IDENTIFICATION
OF MIDDLE-CLASS AMERICAN GIRLS

The culture values masculine roles, goals, and success. What effect does this have upon the female's identification? We find a peculiar state of affairs in which the roles of both parents are changing, girls are permitted (and sometimes encouraged) to succeed in traditionally masculine pursuits at least until adolescence, 38.5 percent of American women are working, and children still perceive the sex roles traditionally.

Many of the personality and identification studies have been done with very young children in nursery schools. This has led to the idea that, unlike fathers, mothers do not discriminate among their children in terms of any variable, including the sex of the child. This may be true with very young children who evoke nurturant, protective responses in the mother, and to a lesser extent, in the father.[2] As children grow older the instrumentality of both parents' responses would be expected to increase. Goodenough (1957) interviewed upper-status parents of nursery-school children about their ideas of masculinity and femininity and found that the mothers were not nearly so concerned with the appropriate sex-typing in their children as were the fathers. The fathers were already actively involved in the sex-typing of their children, and while the mothers were aware of what the fathers were doing they did not actively participate. "It almost seems as if sex-typing goes on in boys independent of maternal influence, and goes on in girls with very little effort from the mother to exclude masculine influence" (p. 312). That is not surprising if one recalls that as the son emerges from infancy his dependent behavior will be perceived by the father as effeminate and he will be pressured to behave in a more masculine, independent, or aggressive way. One should also anticipate that any perceived effeteness in the son arouses more anxiety in the father than in the mother. The masculine influences on the young girl probably have two components: one is reciprocal femininity in her relations with her father, in which he responds to her feminine qualities, and the other is permission to engage in competitive sports or competitive academics or leadership roles, which will *later* be associated with the male role or masculine traits. The girl's early participation and possible success in activities which will later be defined as masculine provide the underpinnings for what I call a "bisexual" identification. By that I mean that the normal girl will identify herself as female and perceive herself as feminine but she may have also learned that she is capable of achieving success and self-esteem in the competitive and aggressive modes of scholastic achievement or athletics that are precursors of professional achievement. Since the culture is essentially masculine and masculine activities are more valued than traditional feminine ones (Brown, 1958), and since females are permitted masculine-role participation, it is likely that a part of the girl's self-percept evolves in relation to the more highly valued activities. At the same time, since many of her peers are also engaged in these activities and since there are no negative repercussions, she can still feel unambivalently female. This apparent role contradiction

[2] I wonder if we can appreciate to what extent the father's role in rearing his children has changed in a single generation. There is a classic story in my husband's family about a family friend who went so far as to baby-sit with his infant for a few hours while his wife was shopping. When she returned the baby was in the buggy in front of an open window. "Clara," he said, "your baby smells." Contrast that with the suburban ideal in which the father spends most of his free time in the Little League and other child-centered activities. The father who does not take an important share in the rearing of his children, with the assumption that he enjoys it, is now considered abnormal. This reflects the extent to which we have become a child-centered culture. The value of *that* is debatable.

will not become important until adolescence, when achievement success can be seen as threatening affiliative (dating) success; at that time it will be an important conflict if the girl cannot gratify both her traditionally feminine needs and her achievement needs.

THE DEVELOPMENT OF SEXUAL IDENTITY

By the age of 3, children are able to tell you what sex they belong to and also which jobs are done by women and which by men. The 3-year-old generalizes to the sexes from his perception of his parents, and he imposes the traditional sex-role functions even though his mother may be working: mothers take care of the house and children, fathers work; mothers are "nicer" and fathers are more competent and punitive (Dubin and Dubin, 1965). When I look at my own children I think the imposition of the traditional roles is a cognitive simplification by young children who are uncertain of their status. The simplification is clearly aided by the content of children's books and television programs.

Young children are terribly pragmatic, literal, concrete. They are highly motivated to achieve some kind of stable self-definition, and one of the components of that self-definition is sex. One's sex is a "given," not subject to change as one grows older. From that point of view it is one of the few variables the child can grasp as a stable part of himself. Sex for 3-year-old children doesn't even involve the genitals (that comes when they are 5). My youngest daughter, wearing slacks, tells me that she knows another child is a girl "because she wears a dress." Their early interest in sex identity generally reveals curiosity about their future adult roles, but they have no uncertainty about their own sex. I don't think that sex identity, for girls, is an important part of self-esteem. The major tasks that children set for themselves are the mastery of cognitive, physical, verbal, and interpersonal skills, and in the early years age is the important variable, not sex. Whether behavior is appropriate, what goals the child sets for himself, the way he perceives himself, what parents expect of him, are more determined by age than by sex. Support for this idea is illustrated by Emmerich and Smoller's study (1964) of 4-year-olds which showed that parents respond primarily to the age of young children rather than to the sex.

But the pressure to become masculine, to grow up, begins early for boys, about the age of 5, and sex-identity becomes a crucial issue. By this time the boy has learned that he has to earn his masculinity. It is no longer given. By the time he reaches adolescence the psychologically healthy boy, helped by the power and the clarity of the male sex-role in the culture, will be certain of his masculinity and of his future role. Of course the new role-demands of adolescence will generate anxiety about whether he can be successful in his new responsibilities, but the bases of his male identity will have developed in the so-called latency years. The identification pressures on girls to become really feminine, to inhibit their freedom, and to inhibit masculine behaviors or personality traits do not occur until adolescence. Prepubertal girls are aware of their sex, they practice certain housekeeping roles, sometimes they baby-sit, and they can tell you what their future responsibilities as women will be. But this is all still playing, anticipating. When the pubertal development creates the extraordinary physical changes of the menstrual cycle and the secondary sex characteristics, the girl's status now depends upon her feminine desirability, and her psyche depends upon her acceptance of these happy and threatening changes. Anxiety can come from external parental or cultural pressures or from changes within oneself and one's own body. Early adolescence is probably the first critical identity period for girls. There is likely to be a somewhat dangerous consequence of this identity delay—the girl has had many years in which she has been permitted to participate in what will be perceived as masculine activities, and to the extent that success in these activities, especially individual competitive ones, form a core part of her self-esteem, it will be difficult for her to assume a clearly feminine sex-role identity and a preference for the feminine role. This ambiguity does not exist for boys, and in this sense their sex-role identity is both clearer and easier.

In adolescence the evaluative importance of parents probably diminishes proportionately to the increased importance of peer evaluation. The adolescent's behavior is guided by internalized values, responses of the parents, and the real or anticipated reactions of peers. Girls will be able to perceive themselves as feminine in spite of academic success or other male-associated activity, unless they are so tomboyish that they cannot interact with girls and the girls reject them, or unless they fail in the competition of adolescent dating, or, later on, unless they fail to marry and have a child. In other words, the more permissive identification process in girls allows them to perceive themselves as feminine even while they are competitive, verbally aggressive, or independent, if they are also able to succeed in the distinctly feminine tasks appropriate to their age. In that special sense the identification of girls is bisexual. (Life is not really so simple of course, and in adolescence a girl is likely to feel anxiety about ambitions or personality characteristics closer to the male model if her parents or peers react to such qualities as real or potential threats to success in the female role. For many girls the solution is a self-conscious deference to the male, a role played with tongue-in-cheek.) But the data in the preceding chapters give support to the idea that the majority of girls are not aggressive, active, or independent, and along with their feminine personality characteristics the physical changes of puberty and the joys of successful courtship will make their assumption of a feminine-role identity and feminine-role preference relatively easy. Most books on the subject written by women are by the achieving woman who is probably dissatisfied with the feminine role. Most of the studies are done on female college students who have competed successfully enough to get into college. The majority has been relatively silent and satisfied.

Since masculine behaviors are valued, since girls frequently say they envy boys, since masculine characteristics are highly rated by children and adults of both sexes, we may assert that the culture strongly motivates the boy to become masculine and rewards him when he does. The girl is not as highly motivated to become feminine, and when she does succeed she is not as highly rewarded. Even in very young children, the acceptable behaviors for boys are very clearly defined, and if a boy crosses the sex-line in behavior he is likely to be rejected by parents, friends, and teachers. Not so with girls. Unless they are grotesquely masculine in dress and play, they are permitted masculine activities (the number of tomboys is greater than the number of sissies). We might expect that the specific family of the girl is crucially important in inducing motivation for her to become feminine and in presenting behaviors acceptable as feminine. We might also expect a greater diversity in women, a wider range of feminine sex-role attributes and personality qualities than is true for the male in his sex-role, because the culture, by not defining the female role as rigidly as the male, permits greater variance. Female role expectations become more specific in adolescence, but by that time it is rather late to impose stringent criteria for acceptable personality traits and behaviors. Many personality qualities, motives, and behaviors are formed in childhood and latency, and the sudden pressure for the girl to conform to a rather specific sex-role stereotype is bound to induce some role-conflict and anxiety about her femininity. Fortunately, I think two things mitigate the new demands: In their relationships with boys, the girls use a self-conscious adaptation pattern of deference and seduction, and, as I indicated in Chapter 7, girls tend to be basically more passive, less active, less sexy, and more dependent than boys. There should be relatively little conflict, but for some percentage of girls conflict is probably inevitable. Lynn (1966) predicts that because girls are not punished as much for masculine behavior as boys are for feminine, and because the masculine role has more prestige, a higher proportion of American females will adopt aspects of the opposite sex:

Despite the overrepresentation of women in the boy's world and the concomitant shortage of male models a somewhat stereotyped and conventional masculine role is clearly spelled out for him, positively reinforced if he complies and negatively reinforced if he does not behave in a masculine-stereotyped fashion. Moreover, he is rewarded simply for being born male through countless privileges accorded males and not females. Thus, through the reinforcement of the culture's highly developed system of rewards and punishment, the boy's early learned identification with the mother eventually weakens and becomes more or less replaced by the later learned identification with a culturally defined, somewhat stereotyped masculine role. . . .

The development of the appropriate sex-role identification for the girl is converse that for the boy. She moves from a same-sex-oriented to an opposite-sex-oriented world. Upon leaving infancy she is, in a sense, punished for being female (does not benefit from the same advantages and privileges as the boy) nor is she given the degree of negative reinforcement for adopting certain aspects of the opposite-sex role. The result of these forces is a weakening of the girl's feminine identification. The girl learns to prefer the masculine role because of its many advantages and since while she is unmarried she is barred from playing her primary role of wife and mother she is unclear about what her role really is.

In a sense Lynn is repeating the phallocentric position, although he has shorn it of the psychoanalytic terms.

We know from simple observation as well as from complex psychological reasoning that the rewards of competitive success in the marketplace are status, money, power, self-esteem, heart attacks, and ulcers. We assume that women have internalized the same set of values, and in part they have. Realistically, most women participate in the success of men in their roles as wives, and for most women that appears to be enough. Simultaneously, women have also internalized a set of discretely feminine values which receive less public attention and reward. They conceive of their achievements differently than men, and they evaluate their success as women and as persons in terms of feminine criteria as well as the more obvious masculine values. Women do not perceive rearing children as a secondary accomplishment and they do perceive themselves as successful when they enjoy love (and power and status) from their husbands and children and when they give love and support. They conceive of this as their major function, and their success in affiliative relationships defines their personal success. Although we have a tendency to ignore it or claim that it is a defensive solution to frustrated masculine aspirations, the apparent truth is that this is the primary role and source of gratification for the majority of middle-class American women.

Feminism is not and actually never has been a widespread movement among American women, and the goals and values held by most women are gratified primarily in the traditional feminine activities. Given the extent of the preference in the culture for masculine activities, one must ask why this is so, why so few women are motivated to achieve professionally. Most women may never have developed a strong achievement motivation as children and adolescents, they may fear failure because they fear competition and the implications of public failure, and they may fear that success will make them less feminine.

We are rather glib in assuming that girls are second-class citizens; until a girl marries and has the responsibility of home and children she is more likely to be pampered. Indeed, if she has been successful as a female, she is courted. In these affluent times I think that there are very few privileges that middle-class girls are cheated of in comparison with their brothers. Only in terms of freedom does the adolescent girl feel a measure of sex-linked restriction, and little in her life prepares her for the restrictions she will encounter later as a mother, for the unending responsibility and the myriad of unfinished details that accompany raising children. This is a peculiar situation. If the woman is barren she is regarded and regards herself as a failure; on the other hand, having children does not bestow status. When we see women returning to work when their children are all in school, we see not so much a running *to* express oneself as much as a reaction *from* the closed and inhibiting world of small children. But identification remains feminine; in a primary sense and as a reaction to guilt the motive for the return to work is to increase the standard of living for the family. It is also my feeling that when women have achieved security in their relationships with their husbands, they can permit the reemergence of achievement motives they had as girls. I also think that women feel the need to perceive themselves as able and independent, although this need develops later than it does in men, and after awhile they reject their total dependency on their husbands and search for a more individual feeling of identity and a feeling of direct participation in the real world.[3] Because they are still expressive or nurturant or attuned to the well-being of people instead of abstract ideas, they may also find a real commitment to welfare or voluntary organizations very gratifying.

THE EFFECT OF WORKING MOTHERS ON CHILDREN'S IDENTITY

What are the effects upon the daughter's sex-role identity and aspirations when her mother works? Hartley (1960) found that not only do the children perceive the mother's role as an extension of her traditional responsibilities but most of the working mothers also perceived their work as an extension of their nurturant role. A very large percentage of American women work, but a real revolution would occur only if women worked not particularly to maximize the welfare of their families but to enhance their own self-esteem, to gratify their own ambitions. Most working mothers and their children continue to perceive the father as responsible for the economic support of the family, and the working mother is seen as adding this extra duty to all of her other role responsibilities. Hartley writes that the sex-role changes in American adults are more a matter of a change in form than function (the apparent change is an extension of the older responsibilities into another place); for this reason, and also because children do not perceive social changes that occur over a long time-span, the children of working mothers

---

[3] A clinician told me of a meeting at which a breast-feeding mother said, "Sometimes I feel as if the top of me is the baby's and the bottom is my husband's and nothing is left for me at all" (Mary McCaulley, personal communication, 1970).

do not perceive any real change in the sex roles. The professional women, the small minority of American women who work in order to use all of their potential and who need achievements for self-esteem, probably create a somewhat different picture for their children; even so, if we look closely at the families of these women, we find that the major responsibility for the home and the children is still assumed by the mother.

Hartley found that children of mothers who work tend to perceive their mothers as enjoying work and anticipate similar roles when they grow up. Hoffman (1961) found that working mothers were warmer, more helpful, supportive and mild, more relaxed and satisfied with themselves as people, than nonworking mothers. They are successful in the traditional mothering responsibilities and as active participants in the economy. This means that the working mother is a likelier model for personal identification. It is logical for daughters of these mothers to have an anticipatory self-concept that is both traditionally female and nontraditional. If the woman is successful in the basic female responsibilities, participation in a job does not necessarily mean a profound role conflict. Conflict in that case is only pragmatic and comes down to a question of which traditional female role-responsibilities need to be shared with other family members.

Since most working women are content with an agreeable job that makes limited demands, and since they are not striving for positions of economic power or large monetary success, there has not really been a radical reversal of the traditional sex-role functions in the United States. This is probably an evolutionary period. For some women with high achievement aspirations there is likely to be profound role conflict touching not only behaviors but acceptable personality traits, but these women are still in the minority. Most of the overt sex-typed responses that girls make require a response from someone else, and most children and adults expect more dependence, passivity, and nurturance from females than males. These expectations and responses and the personality qualities of most women make their job selections of nurse, secretary, teacher, pediatrician, and psychologist understandable.

IDENTIFICATION IN ADOLESCENCE

Between Simone de Beauvoir's *The Second Sex* and Betty Friedan's *The Feminine Mystique*, the college students who serve as subjects in psychological experiments, and the return of women to work after their children are in school we tend to forget that most adolescent girls are motivated to achieve within the traditional feminine role. One of the most interesting studies on sex differences in adolescence is Douvan and Adelson's *The Adolescent Experience* (1966). In 1955–1956 they interviewed in depth 1045 boys aged 14 through 16 and 2005 girls aged 11 through 18. Their major theoretical assumption was that as a result of the diffuse sexual impulses of the adolescent girl, her previous ego development, her high degree of compliance, and the controls imposed upon her from external sources, the development of internal controls would be less salient and pressing than for boys.[4] They therefore hypothesized that girls would show more compliant relationships with their parents, would identify with their parents' standards, would be less consciously concerned with the control of their impulses, and would tend not to differentiate between parental standards and controls and their own. In other words, adolescent girls would be less concerned with the development of personal values and internal controls of behavior than boys. A girl's sensitivity and skill in her interpersonal relationships are the critical variables in her personal adjustment, and in general the feminine character—in terms of personal standards, controls, and an individual sense of self—develops after adolescence. Adolescence is more dramatic and probably crucial for boys (Douvan, 1960). Insofar as the girl's self-percept is dependent upon reflected appraisals in interpersonal relationships, adolescence will be a critical period in her development too, but it will not result in an individual sense of identity.

What did Douvan and Adelson find in their interviews? During the ages of 14 through 16 boys consistently view their relations with their families as combative, with the major battles over independence, behavior control, and an individual sense of autonomy. In terms of the actual development of internal controls and values, the boys have developed much further than the girls. Boys think of their future in an instrumental way. Their plans are rather concrete, crystallized, and tied to reality, especially concerning their future vocation. A boy's hopes for adult status reflect his faith in himself, and the goal he chooses is realistic in terms of his talents and opportunities. He is highly motivated to be independent, and his identity and capacity for erotic ties depend upon autonomy and separation from the parents. To achieve status as an adult he particularly severs his ties with his father and clarifies (and achieves) his vocational goals. His vocational identity and his sexual identity are separate.

Douvan and Adelson found the adolescent girl very different: While boys rebel, girls remain compliant, continue dependency relationships with their parents, and do not express an intense internal need to break the old familial bonds. While the boy's preoccupation and development of internal standards allowed one to predict his ego strength, only the girl's interpersonal relationships related to her ego strength. In social relations girls are very much more mature than boys. The girl's identity is critically dependent upon the man she marries and the children she has. She perceives her major

[4]A follow-up study is in preparation and it will be interesting to see whether significant changes have occurred in these 15 years. Current data on college students do not suggest that the main ideas discussed here have altered significantly. On the other hand, college students seem more aware of role conflicts than my generation was in the 1950s.

task as assuring her acceptability as a person who will be loved, a person someone will marry.

The adolescent girls interviewed focused on the interpersonal aspects of their future life, on their roles as wives and mothers. They anticipated their future roles in fantasy, and this imagining allowed a clear concept of their adult femininity and goals. Up until the age of 18 (the oldest girls in this study), girls showed no urge to develop independent beliefs, standards, or controls. They were compliant, dependent upon authority, and progressing in all areas except those of achievement and moral autonomy. They used authority, especially parental, as a means of controlling their impulses and as a source of self-identity. (You may recall our suggestion that the impulse levels of girls are originally lower than those of boys and necessitate less control while, simultaneously, the culture permits female dependence upon adults for impulse control.) The quality of dependence changes over the years, becoming more rational and sophisticated. Thus the 11-year-old girl says that one obeys parental rules because it is expected and because the rules help kids, but the 18-year-old says that one obeys so as not to worry one's parents or because the rules reflect standards and guidelines for behavior (which, presumably, everyone should agree with).

For the adolescent girl, the interpersonal sphere is pivotal. Her sensitivity and skill in interpersonal relations express her developing eroticism, and her efforts to gain popularity express her erotic needs and her skills in winning and maintaining love. I believe that this takes a competitive form marked by a good deal of achievement motivation—that instead of an academic or vocational achievement goal, the adolescent girl has an affiliative achievement goal. What the boy achieves through separation and autonomy the girl achieves through intimate connections with others because her identity is defined through her attachments to others. Douvan and Adelson found that the girl's vocational identity and her sexual identity were interlaced, her vocational ideas were infused with sexual and sex-role themes, and her goals were closely tied to the objects she identified with. This served to continue her tendency to be dependent, compliant, and conformist. An independent sense of self is not accomplished without severance of old interpersonal ties, without the establishment of internal, individual criteria for achievement, without a sense of identity that is relatively independent of other people.

In a book like this there is an exaggeration of the differences between sexes and a minimizing of the differences within one sex. Obviously not all girls, adolescent or otherwise, are the same in traits or ambitions. In this context it is useful to briefly summarize the different types of female development that Douvan and Adelson found in their study.

Feminine patterns

   1. *Unambivalent, feminine girls.* Most thoroughly focused on the social

and personal aspects of reality. These girls gain self-esteem from help-ing others and being succorant. They show little motivation for per-sonal achievement and prefer security to success; they daydream about popularity, marriage, and family goals. Their educational goals are relatively low. They have a compliant, dependent relationship to their parents.

2. *Ambivalent, feminine girls.* While these girls are also concerned with marriage, motherhood, and social development, they are also inter-ested in personal achievements and individual development. They are interested in jobs and real (versus social) skills. They select as models masculine figures or women who are nonfamily figures. Their family milieu emphasizes autonomy, and their parents encourage self-reli-ance and independence to a greater extent than the parents of femi-nine, unambivalent girls.

Nonfeminine Patterns

1. *Achievement-oriented Girls.* These girls want to marry, but they do not make marriage and feminine goals central to their future plans. Their ideas about marriage are less detailed and less mature than those of the feminine girls. These girls are less socially developed, less mature in their attitudes about friendship, and less concerned with boys and popularity than the feminine girls. Their relationships with their par-ents are pleasant.

2. *Boyish Girls.* These girls emphasize current interests and boyish ac-tivities. They feel important and useful when they are in competitive sports and games. They have a more limited time-perspective and are worried about their current adolescent problems, but they do want to marry ultimately. While their parents are not unduly strict, these girls perceive their parents as very restrictive. This is felt to be a slow-developing group.

3. *Neutral Girls.* These girls are nonfeminine only in the sense that their future plans and their current activities are not focused on marriage or feminine roles. The authors also consider this group slow-develop-ing.

4. *Antifeminine Girls.* This group includes all the girls in the sample who said they did not want to marry. These girls showed psychological deviance and signs of severe pathology. They have little awareness of their internal selves, have limited fantasy, and give the impression of having constructed a wall about their internal world. They are all from large families and are often the first-born. Their parents tend to be traditional, restrictive, and punitive. All of these girls wish to be boys, and it is probably not accidental that they tend to menstruate later than the other girls.

Girls who scored high on measures of femininity were more explicitly interested in boys and popularity with boys and were preoccupied with thoughts of marriage and family life. Their concepts about marriage were more detailed and sophisticated than other girls. The feminine girl is not passive in the ordinary sense; she is passive only in interpersonal situations and only at the level of overt activity. She is active on a psychological level trying to handle problems and conflicts by absorbing some of these conflicts rather than using aggressive assertion. She has a love of social activity, an extended time-perspective, greater poise and social skill, more sources of self-esteem, and an integrated ego ideal (she can name an adult she would like to be like, while nonfeminine girls tend to reject all adults as models).

Douvan and Adelson found that the most typical pattern of identity formation was that of the unambivalent, feminine girl. In an adolescent girl this is the most functional for her future success as a wife and mother. Since the girl remains tied to others, she never really achieves a strong sense of identity with strong values and criteria, and this allows her to identify with the man she marries and adapt herself to the needs of the marriage relationship.

I have also found the unambivalent, feminine girl to be most typical, and agree that she will function successfully in the marital role, yet I find this a disquieting observation. I think it is dangerous for a woman's sense of worth to be enormously dependent upon her husband's reactions to her and to her contributions to his welfare. As husbands become more and more involved in their vocational efforts, as children grow and go to school and as they need to become independent, the value of the traditional female role declines. The return of women to the work force when children go to school can be a time of crisis. While the middle-class college-educated woman's adolescence is typically preoccupied with questions of feminine interpersonal achievement, she also has a secondary identity component which is related to vocational success. In a very real way, girls achieve identity when they marry and when they have children—but when their most important functions in that role dissolve, they have an identity crisis.

Adherence to the traditional sex-role behaviors is breaking down in the middle class and this is strongly correlated with educational levels. Perhaps the confidence which accrues from being well-educated with a high-status vocation allows one to relax about conforming to other persons' expectations, which would include role expectations. Rosenberg and Sutton-Smith (1960) found that girls in 1960 were more masculine in their game preferences than they had been 30 years before. But there are class differences in these patterns. Thus Rabban (1950) found that lower-class boys and girls had toy preferences much closer to the traditional sex-typed choices. Lower-class mothers encourage sex-typing more vigorously and consistently than middle-class mothers (Kohn, 1959), and the class difference in pressures is greater for girls (Rabban). Kagan and Moss (1962) found that the higher the educational level of the parents, the more a daughter is permitted to participate in masculine activities. Middle-class boys, like lower-class children of both sexes, are fairly restricted in sex-appropriate behaviors.

There are other differences which will prove to be important when we look at academic achievement as used for conflict resolution or as the preliminary for vocational success. While boys of both classes reject the effeminate boy, the middle-class boy accepts the academically studious boy. Both lower- and middle-class girls accept the academically serious girl. But the middle-class girl rejects the girl who displays an early and excessive interest in dating, while the lower-class girl accepts her. The lower-class girl who accepts the traditional sex-role earlier and with more enthusiasm than the middle-class girl is more concerned with dating, with personal attractiveness, and with her feminine success earlier than the middle-class girl. In terms of Douvan and Adelson's typology, I would anticipate that increasing numbers of middle-class girls can be characterized as ambivalent feminine girls or achievement-oriented girls. This is a logical evolution of their histories and does not indicate a rejection of femininity; it is normal and not pathological. To the extent that the girl does not perceive academic or vocational achievements as a route to independence and esteem, she will continue to depend upon the reactions of others to assure her that she is attractive and an object to love, and her personality qualities will conform to the traditional female model.

The feminine girl who is nonetheless achievement-oriented will have anxieties that the less ambitious girl does not have: fear that men may reject her for her intelligence, her competitiveness, or her success; anger over the dominance of men at work and anxiety about the place of women in the home; real conflicts between the demands of family and work upon her time and her psychological energy; ambivalence about when to marry or have children; some possible difficulty in accepting the general responsibilities of the female role; and possible difficulties in shifting from the interpersonal demands of her different roles as wife, mother, and professionally committed worker. She is not a man and she is still vulnerable to being rejected. Fear that she may lose love or guilt that she may fail her family will coexist with ambitions to succeed and fears of failing.

Komarovsky (1950) interviewed undergraduate women at Barnard College in the 1940s. They expressed a particular conflict: they found that there was a *sudden* reversal of the behaviors for which they were applauded and *suddenly* the standards of behavior seemed ambiguous. Whereas the girls had been compared favorably with their brothers and their parents were pleased with academic success, they were now being evaluated in terms of some abstract standard of femininity with an emphasis on marriage as the appropriate goal. We usually assume that this message comes down from the parents, but we ought not to ignore the fact that the peer-group has enormous influence at this time (Slote, 1962), and the pressure on the girl comes not only from the parents (whom she may relatively easily reject as "not understanding"), but from her girlfriends. The values of peers are not easily shrugged off. I don't know what it is called in other schools but at the University of Michigan we call it the "senior slump," and it refers to a great increase in the anxiety levels of senior girls who have not become engaged, pinned, or married. Most of the women who go to graduate school tend to express a feeling that not having found a husband their identities are not yet settled, and staying in school rather than working allows them to continue to slowly evolve a sense of self-identity. (It is no wonder that the woman in graduate school who is married tends to do better in academics—she has achieved an acknowledged love relationship, she has settled a sense of identity in terms of the man she married, and he has accepted her abilities and ambitions.) In my interviews with graduate-school students I find many of them consciously rejecting an identification with their mothers' traditional sex-role. When I ask them why they are going to graduate school many reply that they have looked at their mothers and at their mothers' lives, and while they do not really know what they want to do, they do not want to spend their lives as their mothers did. It is my impression that the mothers share these views and are in sympathy with their daughters.

Seward (1964) states the problem of the middle-class girl with more anger than I feel:

American core culture overtly offers its girls the same social role choices in the competitive status hierarchy as its boys, while covertly expecting them to decline the more challenging instrumental roles in favor of low-status domestic roles for which they are paradoxically both overqualified and untrained. Here is a case of cultural discontinuity, where preparation for adult participation in society is followed by regression to dependency upon husband and children. Her situation constitutes a double bind in which either alternative leads to frustration: if she accepts at face value the invitation to share all areas of responsibility with men, she does so at the cost of denying herself as a woman. If, on the other hand, she responds to the hidden message, leaving the broader social field for the protection of the home, it is too frequently at the cost of denying herself as a person.

Our women tend not to participate fully in activities outside of the traditional spheres. The critical question, which we will take up in a later chapter, is whether this is because they are not highly motivated to do so in the first place or because such motives are seen as destructive of their success as women.

chapter 9
THE EGO
AND SELF-ESTEEM

We have been discussing in a rather simplified way the personality qualities and ego skills of women as these characteristics derive from the models of identification. There has been an implicit assumption that femininity is a global or total characteristic, which is probably not true. The feminine woman has been described as passive, masochistic, nurturant, dependent, sensual, receptive, maternal, intuitive, emotional, labile, and empathic. But how generalized are these characteristics? Are feminine women high on all of these variables, in every situation? Or can a woman be "feminine" when she interacts with a man or her children and "nonfeminine" when she works? As they grow up, do psychologically healthy girls evolve personality skills that are not in the feminine model? Does competitive success result in important subidentities within the image of the self that do not relate to the traditional female role-model? Do feminine women react in feminine ways in all roles, or do some situations bring out nonfeminine traits?

The self acts as a point of stability, a frame of reference, the main organizing principle available in dealings with the social and physical worlds. The self is an object to oneself as well as to others, and one conceives of oneself in the terms that have been learned in interaction with others. The self is a source of action, of motivation, of direction. How one perceives the value of the self determines the level of self-esteem, and the lower a person's self-esteem the greater the anxiety and the greater the response to pressures to assume a role. Boys may opt for more self-utilization, perceiving themselves as using skills or attributes that are encouraged by society. Because of role expectations, girls may not want to develop all their abilities (such as scholastic excellence). They may then perceive themselves as not using their potential skills or attributes, and as not approximating their ideal selves. It is not only that the culture values the achievements of the masculine world—a girl who has internalized these values will have an idealized self-concept partially dependent upon achievement-oriented skills. And wide divergence from one's ideal self-concept leads to low self-esteem. Girls who combine roles and who act on their various skills and attributes, and girls who are motivated only within the feminine model, are likely to have high feelings of self-esteem. Girls who defensively utilize only certain aspects of their potential but who are motivated to gratify the achievement aspects of themselves in addition to the feminine aspects are likely to have low feelings of self-esteem. A critical factor would seem to be the range of important motives a girl has developed, the diversity of her subidentities, and the extent to which she gratifies diverse aspects of her self-identity. *Role conflict, or the frustration of aspects of the self, does not exist unless diverse and conflicting motives have evolved.* Because role conflict is more likely to exist in women, in particular situations and in general women have lower self-esteem than men.

The basic sense of the self as a separate entity probably begins to develop around the age of 2, when a child begins referring to himself as "I." Because this concept develops when the child is very young, I suspect that feelings of aloneness, separation, and powerlessness are always part of the core self-concept—as well as feelings of object constancy (the permanence of the self), sex identity, trust, love, and acceptance. The core sense of self becomes fixed early in life; it is the residue of primary social learning and probably the more psychoanalytic mechanisms of identification. It includes the body image and the feelings of the body, sexual identification, basic techniques for enhancement of the self and defense of the self, and feelings of volition and responsibility. *It is the basic identity and it limits the subidentities that can be acquired later.* The core self is general; it crosses specific roles and subidentities, and it is not a verbal self so much as a psychological concept. This aspect of the self probably changes slowly with age, and because it is structured it results in a limitation upon the degrees of freedom for potential alternative behaviors. There is probably some kind of critical stage or time limit within which normal people develop this core concept or basic feeling of identity. The core sexual identification is the primary sexual identity but it will interact with a range of subidentities or roles. The social world one is in will define the opportunities or subidentities available, and these will change over the life cycle. In psychological theory, however, basic motivations evolve in childhood. If the basic core motivations have not evolved early, then motives to participate in different roles or subidentities later, when opportunities are available, will not evolve. For example, if the core self-concept is really completely traditionally feminine, there will be no motivation to participate in achievement roles nor will there be a perception of the opportunity.

Subidentities are also rather stable. They are acquired later than the core self, and they are acquired continuously within the roles that the person performs. The subidentity is the product of the basic expectations the society holds about each role, unique characteristics the person brings to the role, the experiences he has in the role, and his perceptions of himself in the role. This means that role behaviors will reflect a standard social personality (such as the mother role) and will also be idiosyncratic, reflecting the characteristics of the person who is acting within the role. While the social role is external to the individual, the subidentity is internal, part of the person's perception of himself. The range of roles or subidentities is a function of both the sex and age of the individual. One can conceive of self-esteem as a function of how well one performs in each of the roles one participates in and the extent to which the range of roles and one's performance in them utilizes one's perceived capacity. For some women, the feeling that the traditional role does not permit them to use the range of their potential results in low feelings of self-esteem.

An independent sense of self develops later in women than in men. I think it possible that the core sense of self, the sense of female identity, develops relatively early. But the sense of self that evolves from role participations, from subidentities, develops later. Most of the critically important specifically feminine roles for women cannot be rehearsed—they must wait until the girl marries and has a child.

MOTIVES TO ACHIEVE AND TO AFFILIATE

Let us look at just two motives, the motive to achieve and the motive to affiliate. The achievement motive refers to the desire to do something, independent of others, according to some internal criteria of excellence. The affiliation motive refers to the need to acquire love and, perhaps, to give love. The role sources of self-esteem, which are critical in determining how one perceives and evaluates oneself, change for women over a period of time. Although there is a consistency in the personality and in the core roles, subidentities change and these changes are related to success in achieving or affiliating.

When children are very young their self-esteem is primarily related to their mastery of skills appropriate to their age, and the importance of their sex role is just beginning to become salient. Based upon a stable feeling that they are loved, I think their main preoccupations have to do with achievement. In prepuberty this is still true, but we begin to see girls anticipating adult sex roles by engaging in fantasies of dating, by discussing such matters as how many children they want to have, and by real behaviors such as cooking or baby-sitting. These anticipations are still in terms of achievement if the girl feels basically loved by her family and liked by her friends. Although she is deeply motivated to continue receiving familial love, anxiety about love or affiliation will increase significantly when she turns for love to people outside of her family—especially when that love will be earned in competition with others and is not the result of simply being a member of a family.

For middle-class girls there is likely to be continued pressure for achievement, especially in academics (which has now become a part of the ideal self), and a new pressure for affiliation where affiliation is also seen as achievement and as an affirmation of the self. In adolescence the question of one's identity is a core anxiety and one's self-esteem is vulnerable. Because of parental, societal, and peer pressure, the girl will begin to perceive heterosexual affiliation as the dominant source of self-esteem as well as anxiety. For basic feelings of esteem she must be certain that she can achieve affiliatively, and this will become the more important motive. In addition, the nearness in time of being able to actually participate in the adult sex role will increase her motivation to secure the love of a man so that she can participate in the role.

In college, girls as well as boys seem preoccupied with questions about their identity, about their relations with others, their worth, their abilities, their goals, power, morality, and about the direction their life is taking. Boys are preoccupied with achievement, and affiliation is an important but secondary motive. For girls, adult sex-role identity depends upon their affiliative success; therefore, affiliative motives are dominant and achievement motives are important but secondary. Girls perceive heterosexual affiliation as the critical achievement for self-esteem.

In the early years of marriage women are not yet secure in the stability of the affiliative relationship and are motivated to succeed in the relationship because it is the major source of their esteem. They are vulnerable to the discord inevitable in any such important relationship, and they defer to the male in many ways in order not to jeopardize the marriage. They find fulfillment as well as frustration in their relationships with their husbands and children, and slowly they evolve a self-concept of being successful in the establishment of their most important affiliations.

After some years (some of the data suggest it may be as long as fifteen) —when women are secure in the nuclear family relationships and have feelings of self-esteem as females, when their husbands are secure in their achievements and affiliative relationships, when the children are in school— they will increasingly be motivated to achieve in the world of work. When a woman can take her family and the affiliative relationship for granted as a stable part of her life, as she did with her family in childhood, then she can extend herself in other directions, to assume new roles and new subidentities. If she has been feeling that her potential was not being realized in the traditional role, and therefore her self-esteem is low, participation in an occupation will seem to be the most relevant means to utilize her skills and attributes, to come closer to an ideal self which was formed in early childhood. I think that if a woman has a feminine and normal core identity, failure in the feminine roles will preclude feelings of self-esteem. Normally, women will not participate in roles which threaten their affiliative needs, because these needs are critical in their basic concept of themselves.

In early puberty the girl, like the boy, will see the parents as inhibitors and as representatives of childhood. She will devalue the parents and seek a more independent self through identification with persons outside the family. Because of guilt, anxiety, and long-term dependency relations, her attempts at independence will not be as complete as the boy's. As she matures, she will transfer the dependent relation from her parents (especially her father) to her boyfriend, and then to her husband. Striving for some sense of independence, she will vacillate between independence and dependence. The greatest independent sense of self will be achieved when she has successfully realized her potential in the interdependent relationships of wife and mother.

Women continue to perceive the world in interpersonal terms and personalize the objective world in a way that men do not. Notwithstanding occupational achievements, they tend to esteem themselves only insofar as they are esteemed by those they love and respect. Unlike the man, who is considered successful when he has achieved within his occupation, the woman who achieves is generally not considered successful unless she also has a husband and children. Because of her needs and society's expectations, the woman who aims for career success assumes the responsibilities of two major roles. One wonders whether mores are changing. The college students I speak with at least voice a desire for a more equitable sharing of role responsibilities between the sexes. They view as offensive the image of the dependent woman whose self-esteem derives entirely from her familial commitment.

ROLE BEHAVIORS

It is probably clear by now that I believe the female's need to establish herself in a loving, intimate relationship, to love and be loved, is dominant. I also believe that the gratification of maternal needs are necessary for feelings of well-being. And I think that for most women in our society gratification of these needs, at home or at work (e.g., nursing, teaching), are dominant motives. I also think that for large groups of middle-class women, especially those who went to college or who learned that they are able to produce independently, gratification of the traditional needs is insufficient for a feeling of self-esteem. Their sense of identity is closely tied in with more traditional feminine needs, but the traditional feminine image—in which a sense of identity derives from an identification with a husband and from contributions to the welfare of a family—is inadequate.

Work is a situation to which many motives are brought and in which many gratifications are possible. So is maternity. The motives might be pregnancy, having someone to love who will love you and someone to nurture and protect, the generation of new life from the love relationship, and the certainty of successful femininity. Negative or aggressive motives are also brought to bear, and pregnancy and maternity can be a means of aggressing against the self, the husband, the parents, and the child. But no motives can prepare for the realities of housekeeping and child-rearing, the absorption of the husband in his roles, and the decreasing importance of the mother to her children as they grow and become more independent. If a woman's self-esteem rests on her feeling able, contributing, and creative, and if her self-esteem then depends entirely upon a role whose functions diminish, or a role which almost anyone may be able to perform, a role where creativity, excitement, and pleasure are low compared with the total of routinized activity, she is going to be frustrated. On the other hand, few middle-class American women are willing to give up the pleasure and responsibility of being with their children in the early formative years and let someone else nurture them. In addition, the marital stresses of the early years and the crises of parenthood preclude taking for granted the stability of the new family.

In the reality of today, I think that the pattern of compromise in which the woman works part-time, or works after children are in school, is both logical and least threatening. Or, to put it more positively, it is a more certain route to feelings of self-esteem and the utilization of one's potential —assuming that the woman does not need to be really preeminent in her career in order to feel fulfilled. The pattern of compromise means that the responsibilities of the traditional role are still most important and the commitment to work is secondary. For those very few women whose self-esteem derives predominantly from their independent achievements, the compromise pattern will be frustrating. For the majority of women whose primary commitment is to their feminine role, the compromise pattern will be satisfactory—especially if their work does not require personality qualities in strong opposition to characteristic feminine traits.

I am sometimes asked what is the effect upon the family when the wife returns to work. Good data on this topic are generally lacking. I think that the woman who is more secure in self-esteem does not need to demand reassurance from the family and make herself feel necessary by intruding into the lives of others. As a mother she is better able to let her children grow to independence and as a wife she is less psychologically demanding. The assignment of role behaviors alters somewhat from the clear traditional ones, but the assumption of most of the traditional roles still goes to the wife. Perhaps most difficult are the changes in subidentities as she goes from one role to another. Work creates new demands upon oneself, and the gratifications of work are proportionate to success and to the motives which led one to work in the first place.

If we go back to Douvan and Adelson's (1966) study of adolescents (see page 151) we read that the vocational plans and goals of girls were infused with the feminine needs of wanting to help others, to meet people, and to find some setting where they could meet husbands. In the same study, boys said that work and achievement made them feel important, while girls listed acceptance, popularity, and praise.

Girls in college are also greatly concerned with feminine goals and with the realization that their identity will be closely tied to the man they marry. But they are concerned in addition with the conflict between their individual aspirations and the culture's definition of femininity. Middle-class college girls who are successful in school think of themselves as students as well as members of a sex (Douvan and Gold, 1961). But the internalization of the culture's standards for femininity, the need to make identity certain, and the pressure from parents and peers serve to make affiliative needs critical for even the middle-class college girl.[1] For most women the need to gratify motives to achieve independently and occupationally can become important when affiliative gratification is certain and when feminine identity is achieved.

We might also mention here another idea which will be discussed in detail later. It is quite a different thing to develop self-esteem because of production in the competitive marketplace. As the self-esteem of most men is closely tied to their vocational achievements, so is the self-esteem of the working woman who is psychologically committed to achievement in her occupation. In work one is no longer applauded for who he is but for what he does. If a man fails in his achievement goals he fails publicly as well as

[1]Two of the questions I recently asked female college students were "What would make you happiest?" and "What makes you sad or angry?" It rather surprised me that in this highly educated group of women all of the responses were interpersonal and never abstract. Things that would make them happy were to marry, to have children, to make someone happy, or to enable someone else to realize his potential. Anger and sadness were responses to rejection from other people, the death or illness of someone, or unfair treatment of someone. In a time when the university population was preoccupied with Vietnam, interracial conflict, personal freedoms, and the definition of citizen responsibility, not one of these more abstract causes was cited. It was also illuminating that not one girl in the university referred to her academic or professional role as a source of joy or sadness.

in his private self-evaluation. Women who are motivated enough to enter the marketplace in spite of traditional role-demands and prejudiced expectations are putting themselves in a position where self-esteem may be lost instead of enhanced. It is probable that the motivation of these women to succeed is very high, especially because they have a lot to lose. This is psychologically quite different from the majority of the female working force who are content to take jobs with low ceilings of possible achievement, in which their responsibilities are clearly defined, and in which the tasks of the job are not very demanding.

It is common to see women, especially those who are college-educated, complaining when their children are young, looking forward to their return to the work force where they can "realize their potential." It is easy to talk but difficult to face potential failure and loss of self-esteem. As their children grow older and the possibility of entry into their profession becomes a reality, their interest declines. The logical and salient mechanism for prohibiting entrance into the occupational world is a new "accidental" pregnancy. Once again, sometimes complaining loudly, they are forced by the new baby to remain within the easier confines of the house. In this case achievement aspirations are dulled by a fear of failure.

I should like to point out a derivative observation. Although I have posited a normal physiologically linked maternal motive, it should be obvious that maternity is an overdetermined behavior. That means that many different motives within the same person are gratified through maternity, and it also means that different people's motives to have a child may also be quite different. All of the important behaviors, such as academic achievement, vocational efforts, pregnancy and maternity, are similarly overdetermined. One cannot simply look at the behavior and assume the relevant motives that have been brought to bear. As I noted in Chapter 4, the importance of the reproductive functions in the self-identity of women will make this system a frequent site for the gratification of many motives and the expression of diverse anxieties.

Motherhood, for example, is an opportunity for women to act out all of the affects from sentimental, tender, and loving to authoritarian, punitive, and aggressive. Since gender identity is a core part of the self-image it is also true that a threat to one's self-esteem can be perceived as a threat to one's masculinity or femininity. Adopting the behaviors of the sex-role *stereotype* allows one to ameliorate anxiety regarding femininity or masculinity.

Simplifying, we can say that there are basically four groups of adult women: women who are content within the traditional role; women who are willing to enter the labor force at some time in their lives but who are not really committed to professional achievement and who perceive the job as an extension of their traditional role; a minority who, having achieved success within the traditional role, maintain a core commitment to achievement in a vocation; and women who are not motivated to achieve the traditional role responsibilities, who shy from marriage and children, and who work in order to achieve occupational status. All of the data lend support to the hypothesis that women in this culture are highly motivated to achieve an affiliative relationship although they may have "masculine" achievement strivings as well.

In the reality of current socialization and expectations, I regard women who are not motivated to achieve the affiliative role with husband and children as not normal. The psychological needs that evolve from the body, the internalization of cultural expectation as part of the self-concept, and the pressure from parents and peers all converge to make marriage and children, love and nurturance, the most important of feminine psychological needs. When these needs are absent, denied, or defended against, my clinical observation is that there is evidence for pathological levels of anxiety, a distorted sex identity, and a neurotic solution.

Nevertheless, we can currently see that the population explosion may well result in a change in values where parents are rewarded for producing only two children, or even none. Literature on the psychological and role effects of childlessness is extremely limited and we do not know what psychological or role changes are likely to occur because of this possible widespread change in values. Part of the question is to what extent are needs for nurturance, maternity, and paternity part of our mammalian heritage.

We started this chapter asking the question whether femininity is a global characteristic. Like many answers in psychology, the answer is yes and no. When we compare women with men, we could say that women are generally more nurturant, dependent, passive, receptive, maternal, intuitive, empathic, and labile, and that these characteristics become stronger as girls become women. But we could also say that these characteristics are seen mostly in interactive situations, in relationships with other people. It is likely that women are most "feminine" when they interact with their husbands, boyfriends, and children. It is also likely that women are not "feminine" when they are working. In other words, personality qualities of femininity will be present or absent partly depending upon the role, and partly depending upon individual personality traits. Most women I know are less feminine when they interact with other women than when they interact with men. Women often are verbally aggressive directly towards other women, obviously towards their children, and more or less subtly towards their husbands. And a woman can be nonfeminine in her feminine activities. For example, she can take pleasure in giving elaborate dinner parties while really competing for achievement within that role.

Women are able to successfully compete in the masculine occupational world to the extent that they can bring "masculine" personality qualities to the role: objectivity and not subjectivity, assertion and not passivity, achievement motivation and not fears of success or commitment or ambition and drive. By temperament and socialization, relatively few women have these personality qualities. Success can be achieved by a greater number of women in less masculine occupations—those that professionalize interpersonal communication, subjectivity, empathy and nurturance—not simply because these are traditionally feminine fields but because the personality qualities women bring to these fields aid them in achieving.

EGO STYLES IN WOMEN

Women perceive the world differently from men; not only their skills but their interests and thought processes are in some ways different. Psychologically speaking, the easiest professions for women are those in which their interests, skills, and personality qualities are to their advantage, and this will minimize personality conflict within different roles. In terms of personality qualities, it is more difficult for most women to engage in vocations in which they need to be objective, aggressive, and independent. (These descriptions are, of course, simplistic. People are not simple and they develop personality qualities in diverse roles, and in different situations different aspects of the self will emerge.)

You may remember that in Chapter 6 we cited sex differences in infants and very young children. Let me briefly repeat them because they seem to be precursors of adult cognitive styles. Six-month-old girls have longer fixation times to visually presented stimuli, less motor activity, and larger magnitudes of cardiac deceleration—all correlates of a perceptual type that perceives similarities or relatedness. Girls show more attention to very complex stimuli, to social stimuli (faces), and to subtle differences in stimuli. These early differences between girls and boys seem to be constitutional; but whether or not they are genetic potentials, women develop attitudes based on perceptions that emphasize social cues, context, the subtle aspects of a situation, and the interpersonal expressions in the situation.

The way a person makes sense out of experience and develops his creative expression is called his "ego style." How ego style develops in adult women has been described in two papers by Gutmann (1965, 1968). "Various observers, whether psychologists, misanthropes, lovers or male chauvinists have noted a female tendency to leap to conclusions, to decide issues on emotional rather than rational grounds, and to disregard what men regard as the great necessities of existence" (1968).

Gutmann gave normal adult men and women the Thematic Apperception Test (TAT) in which the subject is asked to tell a story that describes the action in a picture.

I found that women were more erratic and personalizing in their handling of the TAT stimuli. Men tended to approach the cards as a task or as a puzzle, while women tended not to maintain such a rational perspective, such distance, and responded to the cards as if they actually were vivid, exciting or troubling events, rather than representations of such events. Women, for example, would be disturbed by situations which they first imparted to the cards and then experienced as an external reality. Thus, women would finish stories with, "I hope things turn out well for them," or, "A boy like that should get what he deserves!" Women vented their immediate emotional reactions to the cards, "This one's horrible!" or, "He has a mean expression!"—and would then elaborate and justify their impulsive response to the subsequent story. Accordingly, by contrast to the male approach, the female approach tended to lack those qualities which are presumably the keystones of the secondary processes of the ego—delay, objectivity, and especially boundary. That is, for women, the boundary between self and other, between the object and the emotion that pertained to that object, seemed more tenuous, or more permeable than was true of men. The world of women, as they mapped it on to the TAT, tended to be a metaphor, an extension of the affective reaction that it aroused in them. . . .

Most interesting was that women seemed to find this rather boundaryless mode congenial and perhaps even adaptive. Men who demonstrated an unbounded approach to the TAT showed up as neurotic by other, independent measures. But women who featured the unbounded TAT approach achieved higher scores on life satisfaction and morale than did their more contained and boundaried sisters. That is, the woman whose ego style resembled the normative male style was more apt than either the typical man *or* the typical woman to be anxious, depressed, neurotic. [1968]

Although men and women can and do agree on what is good and bad, possible and impossible, their experiences of self and other, space and time, constancy and change may be very different. Men live in an impersonal world, women, in their domestic role, live in a very personal world. The female world is *autocentric*, which Gutmann defines as one where the individual has recurrent experiences of being the focus, the center, of communal events and ties. In the *allocentric* world of men, the individual has the feeling that the centers and sources of organization, social bonds, and initiatives are separate from him. In the perceptual world of women there is the feeling that she is a part of all that is worth being a part of, and the sense of self includes all of those others that persistently evoke action and affect from oneself. Whereas for men success depends upon the ability to perceive the world objectively, women can personalize the world, perceiving it without boundary.

The home environment of the American woman can also be described as autocentric. It is built upon the comparatively predictable and controllable events of the family, home, and neighborhood and reflects the wishes of the woman who is central to its running and the children who were once part of the mother.

In such a world porous ego boundaries might be a necessary precondition for contentment; and so-called strong ego boundaries could lead to alienation, a rupture of empathic bonds with one's children, and with the pleasant, self-confirming cycles of domestic life. [Gutmann, 1968]

This is not to say that women have no potential capacity for detached rationality nor men no potential for warm responsiveness; rather, women's affectional and response style is the one most relevant to the autocentric situation. Thus, the tendency of women, observed in their TAT responses, to override boundaries and to experience their own affective states in the world does not imply primitiveness, or regressive solutions to id problems. Rather, this tendency reflects a developed style, with its own sophistications, its own logic, its own version of creativity—a style that develops out of and is harmonious with its psychological ecology. [Gutmann, 1965]

We would only add that the origins for this ego style seem to lie not only in an adaptiveness to the reality of the traditional female role but in an empathic, intuitive, person-oriented style of perception that had its origins in infantile styles of perceiving and in childhood reinforcements. It is not simply that women evaluate themselves in terms of others' appraisals—it is also that in a very real way their perceptual world is composed of their interactions with the subjective world of human relatedness. The subjective quality of feminine ego-functions is praised and valued in the warm mother-child and wife-husband relationships and in extensions of those relationships, such as nursing or voluntary activities in charities. But when this ego quality intrudes into the vocational sphere it is perceived negatively; in the more masculine world it is seen as dysfunctional (although, in fact, it may be functional). As the culture values vocational achievement and rewards ego styles more likely to result in that kind of success, the female may perceive her very personality qualities as second-rate.

The roles of men and women are traditionally different; the ego styles of men and women are also different. In their specific roles, some of the personality dispositions generally attributed to one sex or the other will make for greater success. Each sex has positive contributions to make to the welfare of both. But the pervasiveness of the masculine standards of excellence is so complete that we hardly notice its existence. McClelland (1965) has observed that women are perceived and defined as the opposite of men —and the adjectives describing men are all the positive ones. Both sexes describe men as "large," "strong," "hard," "heavy." The opposite adjectives, which characterize women, are "small," "weak," "soft," "light." The female image also includes the adjectives "dull," "peaceful," "relaxed," "cold," "rounded," "passive," and "slow." If male standards are esteemed, women seem inferior. The positive qualities and contributions which women make seem to be denied by men and women alike.

There is a school in psychology which feels that sex differences are attributable only to cultural molding and that as culture changes what we perceive as the more basic differences between the sexes could be eliminated or even reversed. There is another school, or, if you like, a variant of the first, which feels that there is an incompatibility between a person's sense of identity as a human being and his sexual identity (Cohen, 1966). I suggest that the origin of the sex differences lies in cultural molding of a constitutional-physiological disposition, and that the overwhelmingly vast majority of cultures have defined the roles of the sexes in terms of the given disposition. It is not that genetics and the body automatically define the adult personality; on the other hand, cultures are not molding "tabula rasa" either. Men and women differ in abilities and traits, in motives, in interactions, in ego styles, and in the perception of what stimuli are relevant. But an insistence that the sexes are unable to effectively cross sex-lines in behaviors, that they are suited only for the traditional divisions of responsibility, seems wrong. It seems to me that men who are most confident in their masculinity are those who find it easiest to be nurturant; women who are most confident in their femininity need not limit their behaviors to stereotyped dependence and passivity. An exaggerated conformity to the stereotype of the sex roles in behaviors and personality traits is probably indicative of anxiety about one's core masculinity or femininity. The feminine core seems to me unchanged, although aspects may become emphasized, or specific behaviors may alter in different cultures and in different periods of history. In American society today women can work and participate in the masculine-occupational sphere without the connotation of protest against feminine functions or expressing a fear of those functions.

In our masculine-oriented culture a person is worth the market value of his skills and personality. One's esteem depends not on the human qualities which one possesses but on success in the competitive marketplace. Failure in this competition produces anxiety in the individual because it is one's worth as a person that is threatened. The striving for success is the striving for self-esteem. The individual with a stable self-concept and a high sense of self-esteem is better able to face the unknown, the changing demands of the market. The person whose sense of self is not stable nor well-defined, who has not achieved self-esteem, will fear the unknown as potentially dangerous to the self-concept he has, and he will cling to old patterns of dependence. In our culture we would expect much anxiety to occur in the striving for individual competitive success. This is an area of anxiety which women are able to avoid insofar as they do not put themselves into the marketplace competition, deriving their sense of self and their self-esteem from the traditional relationships. But like men, some American women perceive competitive achievement as a route to self-affirmation and self-realization, despite its being anxiety provoking. In the next chapter we shall explore the psychological literature which will help us to understand why women who have a choice elect to participate in both the traditional female role and in the sphere of vocational competition.

chapter 10
THE MOTIVE
TO ACHIEVE

Psychologists assume that the motive to achieve is one of the major determinants of anyone's striving to succeed. We know that women underachieve in the occupations, but when we turn to the psychological data to find out why, we have trouble. A theoretically consistent body of data exists which enables us to predict achievement behavior as a function of the strength of the achievement motive, but it applies to men. The sparse data available about women is contradictory and inconsistent with the achievement theory for men. In Atkinson's *Motives in Fantasy, Action and Society* (1958), women occupy an entire footnote (the book is over 800 pages long) in which Atkinson says that the difference between the sexes is "perhaps the most persistent unresolved problem in research on need achievement."[1] I don't think the problem is all that difficult if we keep in mind that while men may develop a motive to achieve that remains consistent over their life spans,

[1]A probable source of the apparent contradiction in the data comes from the fact that most of the psychological studies are done on undergraduate college students. It is exactly at that time in her life that a woman is motivated to achieve and most anxious about achieving.

women experience both a desire to achieve and an anxiety related to achieving, the desire and anxiety occurring in different amounts at different times during their lives.

Although opportunity is there for the grasping, the outstandingly successful or really professionally committed woman is still an exception. Most of the talk about realizing one's potential in the work force comes from women who have been married for more than 10 years and who have in that decade devoted themselves entirely to their traditional roles. Sex discrimination in the marketplace is a fact, but a more cogent reason for the lack of women's work productivity is their unwillingness to assume a long-term professional commitment. Academically talented girls are less likely to enter college and complete the undergraduate degree than equally bright young men; they are less likely to take advanced degrees; they are less likely to use the PhD's they do take; and they are less productive than men even if they do take the PhD, remain unmarried, and continue to work full time (National Manpower Council, 1957; President's Commission on the Status of Women, 1963; Radcliffe Committee on Graduate Education for Women, 1956). In addition, girls underestimate their academic abilities and choose academic majors and jobs that are not challenging (National Manpower Council, 1957; Isaacson, 1964). Thus, during the period in their lives when it is traditional to make a professional commitment, girls are psychologically least able to do so. Since there are relatively few women who are really involved professionally, there are few role models for girls to identify with. The women faculty members at my university have been told that part of our contribution to our departments is that we are married, have children, and successfully achieve professionally, and therefore serve as role models for female students. Of course that assumes that the girls have already developed a strong motive to achieve.

THE NEED TO ACHIEVE AND THE NEED TO AFFILIATE

What is the motive to achieve? Atkinson (1964) and McClelland (1958) describe it as a motive to be competent in a situation in which there are standards of excellence. The person who is achievement motivated takes pride in his work when he is held responsible for his actions, when he is informed of his level of performance and there are criteria of performance, and when there is an element of risk involved (when he is not certain of success). The amount of effort that will be expended in the pursuit of achievement depends upon the person's stable level of achievement motivation, his expectancy of success in the specific task or area, and the value he places on success in that area. The person with a high achievement motive has developed an internal standard of excellence, is independent, persistent, undertakes realistic tasks, performs well academically, and has clearly understood goals. This model predicts the direction, magnitude, and persistence of achievement behaviors in male students. But not in females.

Most authors implicitly or explicitly assume that the need to achieve is an internalized motive, independent of the need to affiliate with others. Only when experimenters assess the need to achieve and the need to affiliate as potentially interactive do we see the hypothesis that achieving may be fused with affiliation, that is, the motive to achieve may depend on the expectation of praise, love, or rejection from others as they evaluate the achievement. The data on the two sexes differ on this very point and therefore so do definitions. Crandall, Katkovsky, and Preston (1960) write that "achievement behavior" (not "achievement motivation") is behavior "directed toward the attainment of approval or the avoidance of disapproval from oneself or from others, for competence of performance in situations where standards of excellence are applicable." McClelland (1953) gave this definition of the motive to achieve: "The child must begin to perceive performance in terms of standards of excellence and to experience pleasant or unpleasant feelings about meeting or failing to meet these standards." The origin of the need to achieve, for McClelland, is in those pleasant feelings that the child experiences when he first attempts independent mastery and when he does something a little harder or a little better than he did before. McClelland seems to assume that these mild self-demands come naturally to children but that a strong need to achieve requires standards of performance and demands of performance by parents and other members of the culture (1953; 1958a,b). Crandall, Preston, and Robson (1960) place the primary emphasis for the development of strong achievement needs on the rewards, demands and punishments meted out by parents, teachers, and other adults. They argue that if the child is going to value achievement activities as a potential source of satisfaction and security, direct social reinforcement is necessary. In their view, only later, and only for some children, will approval from others become unnecessary as a goal to good performance and will good feelings of pride and self-approval be sufficient to maintain or increase achievement behaviors.

The question of motive, then, becomes clear. Does a person strive to achieve because he has an internal standard of excellence, a self-image and feeling of self-esteem dependent on how he perceives himself performing—or does he achieve primarily in order to receive praise from others? Veroff (1969) suggests that for boys the achievement motive is easily cued by internal standards of excellence, but for girls external support is critically important.

Even in the definitions there is an interchange of motive and behavior that becomes confusing because motives often interact with each other and interact with situational determinants, and we assess motive partly by behavior. There also may be changes over time in the specific areas of accomplishment, the object of satisfaction, and the motives underlying behavior. Thus the young girl might seek parental applause for athletics, for coloring in her book, for memorizing, or for playing "nicely." Later she might gain parental approval, peer status, and even internal satisfaction through academic achievement, or good looks, or popularity. The dependence of achievement upon affiliation rewards (others' reactions) would seem to be only one aspect of the personality development of the individual, who is more or less either generally independent or dependent.

What are the experiences or the attributes that are likely to lead to general independence, or an internalized need to achieve? Why are boys more likely to achieve internalized standards of excellence, or motives to achieve an independent sense of self? The motive to achieve is only one motive in the integrated personality, and it should be consistent with the rest of the personality. Therefore, the immature boy might well have motives to achieve and feelings of self-esteem which are dependent upon others' reactions. When we find similar personality traits in girls is this also a sign of immaturity? The literature has consistently suggested that girls are generally more dependent, more conformist, more persuasible, and more vulnerable to interpersonal rejection than boys. I think that the atypical independent girl who has a high internalized need to achieve, and the dependent feminine girl who has fused achievement and affiliation rewards, represent the maturation of the two different personality models that are available in this culture, albeit unequally. For boys, only the independent personality model is sanctioned.

We must remember that achievement and independence are not the same thing; behaviorally, we can find achievement-striving either in response to an internalized standard or as a means of securing applause and affection. The young girl is rewarded for achievements—in school and in other areas that she shares with boys. But later she is rewarded for social success and all of the derivates of affiliative achievement. Generally, we think of achievement in terms of the marketplace; the traditional feminine-role accomplishments are not included. This is not just a cultural value-judgment external to the girl, but is something she internalizes. In the internalization of the cultural standard, the girl also learns to value accomplishment in marketplace terms and to denigrate the feminine accomplishments she desires, will be rewarded for, and is striving to achieve within the traditional role. According to her level of achievement motivation, she will add feminine-role activities to the usual academic grade-point or problem-solving kinds of activities. After leaving school, she may strive to be the best gourmet cook, the unique interior decorator, the mother of the smartest children, the wife of the most successful man, the initiator of a charity. In part this is an identification with her husband and children, and in large part it is achievement-motivated behavior merely transferred to another set of activities. By keeping within the traditional role women can avoid crashing failure or the equally threatening competitive, "male-castrating" success. This is a working solution for many, but it is not sufficiently gratifying for those women with high achievement motives that they define vocationally, in the real marketplace.

But achievement activity within the traditional role is not just an escape from vocational competition, it is also a positive turning toward achievements with others. Lipinski (1966) asked college women, "What kinds of things have you done in your life which you think of as accomplishments and achievements?" She found that the standard masculine categories of intellectual, athletic, mechanical, and artistic endeavors were insufficient. Her subjects added success in achieving a certain kind of relationship with family and friends, coping with problems, achieving maturity and independence, arriving at a personally acceptable philosophy of life, and serving in executive positions in social clubs and organizations. The emphasis in this list of accomplishments, as the young women themselves perceived it, was on interpersonal relationships and internal development. This is consistent with the strivings, rewards, and pressures that they have experienced, and which are critical during the college years. Definitions of achievement and measures of achievement always derive from the academic-vocational-masculine model, but this is not the only model which is relevant for women. At different times in their lives, the masculine model and the feminine internal-interpersonal model will be salient for women, while only one model will be acceptable for men.

Another rather basic question arises. Most theorists in this area feel that the development of the motive to achieve must occur in childhood, and if it has not developed by then it never will. Baruch (1966) has written that in the Thematic Apperception Test (in which people create stories to accompany illustrations) she and other investigators are finding that 10 to 15 years after marriage responses of women who had been college students indicate a development of or an increase in motives to achieve. At this time many women actually do return to school or work. One possible interpretation is that an internalized motive to achieve does develop in women, but many years later than in men. It might be that in women the motive to achieve and achieving behaviors need the security of fulfillment of affiliation needs that reduce anxiety about achieving; a stable marital relationship may permit the development of a secure and independent sense of self and the motive to achieve. It may also be true that the women Baruch speaks of had developed strong *motives* to achieve in childhood but suppressed achieving *behaviors* because of anxiety about failing or succeeding or alienating others; the stability of their long marriages would have reduced these anxieties and permitted them to respond to the Thematic Apperception Test (TAT) cards with achievement-related stories. There are then two possibilities: the later development of achievement needs in women, and the reemergence of a preexisting motive.

In part this is a technical problem of measurement. Psychologists measure a fairly stable and unconscious motive to achieve through the subject's telling a story about what is assumed to be unstructured pictures. But experimenters use different pictures that have different cues, and stories will differ according to the cues presented by the stimuli. There is another possibility in interpreting the Baruch data: Women who find themselves frustrated by the apparent limits of the traditional role, especially those who have been in college, may perceive the vocational world as the antithesis of the world of minutiae which they feel they inhabit. In that case one would expect them to be preoccupied with the possibilities that the vocational world offers, and a whole range of achieving motives would be hidden beneath the frequency of vocational-achievement stories. That is, women who fantasy from a grass-is-greener kind of syndrome, and women who are deeply committed professionally and simply waiting for their responsibilities to change so that they can enter the labor force, might, on a TAT, look very similar.

In women one must look at the relationship between affiliation and achievement motives and consider to what extent achieving behaviors derive from achievement or other motives and whether achieving is perceived as a probable threat to affiliation.

I think we should underscore the point that we are not discussing those women who enter the labor force before they marry and stay in until their first child is born, and who reenter the labor force later in order to increase the family income—all motivated to earn enough money to live better, but satisfied with relatively limited jobs. We are discussing the motive to achieve and to succeed, and that motive may emerge in work or it may emerge within the traditional activities. The essential characteristic is the commitment to a high quality of effort, a necessary high standard of performance, and a drive to excel—which characterizes some percentage of the female population.

ACHIEVEMENT MOTIVES IN CHILDREN

We know from the studies of older children, adolescents, and the ubiquitous college freshmen that the sexes usually differ on measures of achievement need, achieving behavior, and anxiety. Do young children show similar differences? If not, at what age, in what ways, in what contexts do they diverge? Do the differences seem to change when we measure achievement motives in fantasy, in behavior, under neutral or arousal conditions? Do the sex differences in achievement motives and behavior relate to differences in self-confidence, independence, aggression, affiliation, compliance?

Crandall, Preston, and Robson (1960), Sears and Levin (1957), Tyler, Rafferty, and Tyler (1962), and McClelland (1958a,b) all report finding individual differences in the frequency and persistence with which pre-school children attempt tasks requiring skill and effort and attempt to get recognition for achieving. These studies indicate that differences in needs to achieve have already developed by this time, but just when they begin is uncertain. Children in the first through third grades try harder in selectively different activities requiring physical, intellectual, artistic, or mechanical skills. We can already observe in these young children differences in achievement striving, and we can also observe that one child will strive differently in different areas. Talent or ability and previous experience have already made certain areas especially relevant for success or failure by the time children are 6 to 8 years old.

But studies of children in nursery school seem less concerned with achievement motives per se than with the relationship between the motive and other personality characteristics. For example, Crandall and Robson (1960) studied children who were 3 to 5 and 6 to 8. They found that the sexes differed on all variables *except* achievement efforts, but the girls lacked confidence in their work and looked for help and approval from adults. One interesting difference was that as the boys grew older they chose to return to tasks at which they had previously failed, but the girls tended to withdraw from the possibility of repeating failures.

Sontag, Baker, and Nelson (1958) rated children's behavior in nursery and elementary schools and at home, and found that children whose IQ's increased (not a measure of achievement needs) were independent of adults and competitive with peers; the girls in this group were less "feminine" in their behavior and better able to delay gratification. During the elementary-school years, these "ascenders" were competitive, independent, and took the initiative in overcoming obstacles.

Crandall, Katkovsky, and Preston (1962) studied children in the first to third grades and found no sex differences in thematic measures of achievement motives or in competition in intellectual or play activities. But the girls valued intellectual accomplishment over other areas more than boys did (for whom I suspect mechanical, athletic, and aggressive skills are at least as salient). The girls lacked confidence, they expected to fail whereas the boys expected to succeed, and the girls took the blame for intellectual failure while the boys projected the blame. The brighter the girl, the less expectation she had of being successful on intellectual tasks (duller girls had higher expectations). The boys were not only more realistic in their expectations, they had higher standards and a feeling that they, rather than fate or other people, determined whether they eventually succeeded or failed.

Sears (1962) found that affiliation rather than achievement needs of girls correlated with academic success. Tyler, Rafferty, and Tyler (1962) found that the girls in nursery school who tried to get recognition for achievement also made more attempts to get love and affection. Girls in elementary school who tried hardest to achieve were also more eager to gain approval. These relationships were not true for boys.

Thus, young girls are using achievement as a primary means of securing love and approval from others. Why don't boys have similar responses? I think it likely that all children explore their abilities and attempt to master skills when they are very young. As they become more aware of parental reactions and of their own feelings of well-being that derive from parental approval, they will naturally use any available technique to increase parental approval. One perceptually prominent way for children to secure attention and applause is through achievement. I think this is not sex-linked in the very early years. Seldom do we hear parents say that a child walks early "for a girl" or talks early "for a boy." Although there *are* sex differences, most parents are not aware of them. Praise is given for the acquisition of a new skill, which assures parents that the child is bright; they also enjoy the child's own pleasure in his new skills—the child's pleasure from his parents' response to his skills is a merging of the motive to achieve and the motive to affiliate. But at about the age of 2½, the boy begins to be pressured to give up infantile dependency, to strive for independence, to compete— and he begins to regard the parents as a less than absolutely certain source of approval. If a boy develops a need to achieve it can therefore become relatively independent of external sources of reinforcement. The general tendency for girls is different: they continue to achieve for self-approval but always for approval from others too. There is one exception, and that is the girl who, like most boys, is significantly independent of her parents and is therefore more likely to develop an autonomous motive to achieve. It should not surprise us to find that highly developed, autonomous achievement motives in girls tend to be associated with alienation from parents, especially mothers.[2]

Most theorists feel that the motive to achieve begins to develop in early childhood, with a critical stage at perhaps 4 or 5 years. Veroff (1965) has suggested that at this point in development the child is not yet able to clearly distinguish exactly which behaviors have led to the reward of praise and affection, and different behaviors will be perceptually fused and rewarded. In other words, many general types of behaviors would be seen by the child as leading to rewards. If the parents press for mastery or independence in performing certain tasks before the child is capable of achieving them, he will probably feel frustrated and will later have a general disposition to avoid tasks that require mastery or independence. On the other hand, if the parents wait beyond the optimal time, the child is able to

----

[2]The special importance of independence from the mother is understandable if my identification model is correct. In that model the girl's father is normally likely to be generally nurturant and supportive. If the girl's mother is predominantly expressive and supportive, neither parent is likely to push their daughter to develop an independent sense of self or a motive to achieve divorced from affiliation cues. When a child is primarily supported, especially by both parents, the tendency to evaluate the self in terms of parental (and other) responses continues. While this can be true for boys, it is more typical of girls.

distinguish specific behaviors and situations that led to rewards and he will concentrate on achieving in those specific areas. But the need to achieve is conceived of as a more general tendency, with the highly motivated person disposed to extend his efforts to many areas. In the young child the motive to achieve results from a combination of affectionate responses and the child's own awareness of his growing capabilities. While the interpersonal rewards remain salient for girls, internalized criteria of achievement and personal satisfaction become more important for boys.

Sears (1963) found that girls who conformed to adult demands when they were 4 and 5 had mothers who tolerated dependent behavior and discouraged aggression. Bronfenbrenner (1961a,b) has suggested that girls may be "oversocialized," receiving too much care and support, never really learning to stand on their own two feet without help. Kagan and Moss (1962) found that girls who were overprotected through the age of 3 became "typical" passive females. Crandall et al. (1964) studied children in grades 2 through 4 and found that girls who were high achievers had mothers who were less affectionate and nurturant. These authors found that it was not the mother's emphasis on independence or mastery but her emotional relationship with the child that was crucial. When the mother had a nurturing attitude toward her son and a hostile attitude toward her daughter during their preschool years, both the son and the daughter had high achievement motives when they were adults.

I think that the explanation for the apparent sex discrepancy in these data can be made in terms of the cross-sex affectionate support model I have hypothesized before (see page 139). While the boy is pressured by his father to become independent and to achieve, optimally he is affectionately supported by his mother. She tends to love him for who he is rather than for what he does, which makes the demands by the father less crushing. The mother's support encourages the development of enough self-confidence for the son to extend himself in somewhat risky achievement attempts. Similarly, in this model, the girl is emotionally supported primarily by the father while her mother demands and evaluates her achievements. But if neither the mother nor the father pressures the daughter to achieve, she will not develop a motive to achieve or a sense of independence derived from the experiences of achieving. While girls can learn to achieve in order to get affiliative rewards, an independent motive to achieve probably requires that the child of either sex realize that he is being rewarded for achievement and punished for failure and that he is not being rewarded merely for existing, especially by the parent of the same sex. It is not direct training for independence that is crucial in motivating the child to develop an independent sense of self, but his realization that he will not be consistently rewarded. He will then learn to make his own judgment of his achievements in order to make himself less vulnerable to parental rejection. For children, achievement is a means of securing parental affection—but it is also a most important way to reward themselves, to enhance their individual sense of self-esteem.

It might be appropriate to note at this point that I am not equating the demanding parent with the rejecting parent. Parents who basically aggress against their children and rarely reward them are likely to produce dependent, neurotic children. Parents who maximize achievement and independence in their children do so by rewarding individual achievement in a generally affectionate milieu.

The question has come up whether girls need to be independent of or even alienated from the mother in order to develop a high need to achieve. It seems that it is insufficient for parents simply to value achievement in order for girls to become high achievers. Veroff (1969) feels that the development of achievement motives in girls requires a somewhat rejecting attitude by the mother when the girl is young, an appropriate timing of stress and mastery when she is in middle childhood, her acceptance of the appropriateness of female achievement, and a female role-model who is not too strong and domineering. She should also not have experienced too strong an emphasis on interpersonal gratification during early childhood.

But since mothers tend to be warm and affectionate, since mastery of skills is perceived as less critical for girls than boys, since female achievement is controversial, and since the importance of interpersonal gratification is constantly emphasized in the lives of most girls, we should expect relatively few girls to have developed a strong need to achieve. Moreover, if these data are consistent with other personality information, we should expect to find that girls tend to fuse the need to achieve with the need to affiliate, using achievement as a means of securing acceptance and love.

Additional data also indicate that it might take considerable maternal rejection, if not hostility, for girls to develop a high need to achieve. But I am not completely convinced that this is really true. For example, very bright girls are possibly more likely to follow more masculine kinds of achievement development without maternal rejection, especially if they are simply not thwarted. A girl who really excels is usually very acceptable to middle-class parents; it is only in adolescence that parents might become anxious about an ambitious and achieving daughter. In any event, there seems to be an asymmetrical hypothesis; similar maternal treatment yields different results in the two sexes.

Other early sex differences, the continued reinforcement of childhood types of relationships, and a general lack of self-confidence probably make it difficult—even exceptional—for girls to develop a strong motive to achieve. But it is important to remember that as girls are doing well in school —in grammar, or spelling, or reading vocabulary—they are also learning that they are capable of achieving or even excelling in academics. A part of their self-concept will be an awareness of an ability to achieve. While they may later give up achieving efforts in academics or vocational areas in order to secure the traditional role, the self-concept still includes an achievement factor.[3]

ACHIEVEMENT MOTIVES IN ADOLESCENCE

In adolescence the nature of the academic demand changes and there is an increased pressure for more independent or creative work, which boys tend to do better. Boys seem to achieve enough maturity by the age of 12 or so to make enormous strides in their academic efforts. They tend to become involved in specific content areas and begin to see academic achieving as part of their masculine role and their vocational identity. Girls, on the other hand, may begin at this time to fear seeming unfeminine or too aggressive. At any rate, they do not become committed to a vocational identity. I don't know whether there is an actual decrement in girls' academic achievements at adolescence or whether there is a comparative decline so that girls stay at their previous level while boys accelerate. But a relative change in performance occurs, and many girls may well be giving up efforts to achieve.

Our information on the achievement motive is distorted by the practice of using college and high-school students for testing. Girls who go to college are more likely to have high achievement needs, and girls who are not motivated for academic achievement are less likely to be represented in the experimental groups. (Percentages are unknown for the three basic groups: girls who never develop a high need to achieve, the larger group who merge achievement and affiliation motives, and the small group with an autonomous need to achieve.) High-school-age girls are in a contradictory period —after a lifetime of experiencing reward for achievement, they simultaneously and suddenly find achievement actually threatening to their affiliative needs. It is a time when they are encouraged to do well but not to make a real commitment to vocational success. The girl who persists in successful academic competition has in some way decided that the reward is great enough for her to gamble with peer acceptance. For the majority of girls, excelling in academics gets to be threatening to social prestige. Some girls will strive to succeed so long as most of their friends do not know how well they are doing. It is the public quality of the success which is probably most threatening. In addition to fears of being rejected by their peers, when girls perceive that successful competition is based on aggression, a personality

[3]From the *University Record,* University of Michigan: "Senior women, as a group, achieved the highest grade-point average in the fall term, according to a scholarship report prepared by the Office of the Registrar. In fact, of 20 groupings of undergraduates by sex, housing, and year, women were in the top 6. Senior women had a GPA of 3.13, followed by women's cooperative housing, 2.99; general sororities, 2.97; junior women, 2.96; all women, 2.92; independent women, 2.92; senior men, 2.86; women's residence halls, 2.84; sophomore women, 2.82; and the average for all men and women undergraduates, 2.82. The lowest group was freshmen men, with a GPA of 2.65. Freshmen women ranked 12th at 2.75." (March 27, 1969)

quality identified with boys, their feminine self-percept may be jeopardized if they continue their efforts to achieve.

There are girls who have high needs to achieve, there are also girls who define achievement only in terms of affiliation (like Douvan and Adelson's most feminine girls?), and there are girls who achieve academically in order to receive affiliative rewards. Even for girls who fuse motives for achievement and affiliation, who worry because achievement success may threaten their popularity, achieving is rewarded to the extent that they really do successfully achieve. In that case achieving is likely to develop as an ambivalent but autonomous motive, and the motive to achieve is likely to be resurrected later in life when affiliative anxieties and achievement gratifications are both minimal.

It would be useful to be able to predict achievement behaviors, but unfortunately it is rather difficult. The girl who never develops a high motive to achieve or who has had little achievement success in academics or work is likely never to become highly motivated to achieve in the work force; she is likely to be happiest within traditional role behaviors. The girl who fuses achievement and affiliative needs will probably be motivated to return to the work force 10 to 15 years after marriage. The girl who develops high and autonomous achievement needs is hardest to make predictions for. While one might think that these girls are so dependent upon achievement for self-esteem that they cannot give it up, they are also likely to be girls who are more competitive, aggressive, independent—in short, least "feminine." Their consequent greater anxiety about femininity and greater vulnerability in their sex-role identity may actually cause them to give up achievement efforts altogether.

To recapitulate, many girls experience achievement success in school and develop a motive to achieve and a self-concept dependent upon achieving. This kind of achievement is perceived by girls, as by boys, in terms of vocation. But simultaneously, girls remain dependent upon the reactions of others for feelings of esteem, and they use achievement as a means of securing affection. Not until the physical changes of puberty occur, with the concomitant increased stress on social success, does academic success begin to become less important as a verification of self-esteem. This shift continues until academic-vocational achievement is perceived as a threat to the more important social success.

THE FEAR OF SUCCESS

When we study achievement motives in college women, we must keep in mind that sex-role identity and sex-role conflict are crucially relevant variables. If we turn to studies of achievement motives, behaviors, and anxieties, we find that we cannot predict achievement behavior in female subjects as we can in male subjects. We also know that females have consistently higher anxiety scores, which have been assumed to reflect a fear of failure. Matina Horner, whose approach will be discussed in some detail below, would explain it differently:

1. The achievement situation is competitive.
2. Competition may be viewed as a "sublimated" form of aggressive behavior.
3. "Any" type of aggressive behavior is negatively sanctioned by society as unfeminine.
4. Therefore, a female who is successful in achievement situations outside the home, especially against male competitors, finds herself in a position considered unfeminine (and "masculine").
5. This creates conflict for the female, evidenced by her higher anxiety level which is in turn reflected in her behavior.
6. Rather than fearing *failure*, women are motivated by a fear of *success*.

Rostow (1964) quotes Margaret Mead, who has suggested that in our culture boys are unsexed by failure and girls by success. Mead suggests that girls actually "quest for failure" in the working world of men as their adaptation to the conflicts involved in combining a career with marriage and motherhood. Rostow feels that the ambition to do well at a job in the masculine world is not probably a strong emotional need for most educated young women although "concededly subordinate to the demands of her primary goal." I suppose that a "fear of success" sounds strange, but it is very logical, especially for girls who have not yet established their feminine identity within marriage.[4] While the fear of failure may be a critical anxiety in men, at least during the college years women may fear success as well as failure. It is hard to imagine a situation where men are penalized for success, whereas penalties for failure in women are relatively mild. In the following pages I am going to expand on what led Matina Horner to feel that a fear of success is an important motive for women.

Horner described the evolution of this idea in an unpublished paper written in 1965:

An explanation for some of these problems in terms of differential defense reactions seemed possible to me when I turned my attention to the problem of achievement-related anxiety in women. If, for the reasons to be discussed below, competitive achievement behavior is anxiety-provoking for women, especially those who value intellectual achievement, then it is quite possible that in order

---

[4] I have noticed that many of my male colleagues find it difficult to accept the idea that girls are afraid to succeed. Let me recall my own undergraduate days. Purdue University, where I earned my B. S. degree, used to publish the names of all students who earned an "A" average during the previous semester. The first time my name was listed I was enraged, told the newspaper office "they had a nerve," and in general carried on outrageously and the reason, which I was fully aware of, was my fear that now the girls would dislike me and the boys would be afraid of me. In other words, my academic success would shoot my social life down. I think this fear is maximized during the college years, but that in itself is important. If a girl's fear of success precludes a professional commitment she may give up her major opportunity for later vocational efforts and success.

to reduce their anxiety they defensively project their motivation (1) into less conflictful situations such as homemaking for females or (2) into intellectual achievement situations with male figures.

Perhaps the most consistent result with sex differences has been that women get higher anxiety scores than men on the typical measures of Test Anxiety.

Females may in fact be more anxious than males in achievement-oriented testing situations because for them not only are there negative consequences and hence anxiety associated with failure but also with success. Since the measuring devices don't distinguish sources of anxiety, it is quite possible that the anxiety scores for men and women have different meanings and it would no longer be surprising to find that the anxiety scores relate differently to performance for the two sexes in a number of cases.

This idea, that success in competitive-achievement activity has negative consequences and is hence anxiety-provoking seemed at first a bit remote and far-fetched, especially since involvement in mastery of academic skills is considered appropriate and encouraged for both sexes and sex role standards don't *directly* dictate strong inhibition of intellectual mastery for either sex.

I kept at this notion of anxiety about success for a number of reasons, among which was the consistent evidence that girls' academic performance is superior to boys' during early school years but gradually gets inferior during late adolescence and adulthood, even though what I said would imply a behavorial continuity between childhood and adolescence for both sexes. The chief reasons offered for this developmental shift is that in late adolescence academic proficiency gets linked to vocational success and therefore the boy's achievement motivation becomes stronger than it was during the early years of school and is reflected in his higher performance. The argument continues that positive achievement motivation for women is decreasing because at this time her sex-role identity is more dependent on her ability to attract and maintain a love relationship and academic or competitive proficiency is irrelevant if not in fact detrimental to this goal. It seems to me that this latter argument might have some validity for those women who do not value academic success for themselves but not for those who do value it and whose positive motivation remains high. It seems more reasonable to me to argue that the expression of their achievement motivation is being inhibited by the conflict and anxiety aroused by the fact that intense intellectual striving can be and is viewed as competitively aggressive behavior and aggressive behavior is not feminine behavior even in such sublimated forms, especially if the competition is against males.

Kagan and Moss [1962] say that "the typical female has greater anxiety over aggressive and competitive behavior than the male. She, therefore, experiences greater conflict over intellectual competition which in turn leads to inhibition of intense strivings for academic excellence.

Horner is arguing that in addition to the obvious and overt social rejection that a competitively achieving girl may experience, there is also an internal anxiety, a fear about one's femininity. If anxiety about success, that is, anxiety about competitiveness and its aggressive overtones, is a major determining factor of sex differences in achievement-related research, then the differences should be maximized in competitive as opposed to noncompetitive situations, especially those in which competition is against men. A fear of success will be strongest for those women who have high motives to achieve and who value success. Women whose achievement motivation is low in the first place will have no conflict because they do not initially value success. A fear of success in men is probably both rare and negligible.

Horner feels that women are threatened by success because outstanding academic or other competitive achievement activities are consciously or unconsciously equated with a loss of femininity as well as leading to real social rejection.[5] Maccoby (1963) has written that "the girl who maintains qualities of independence and active striving (achievement orientation) necessary for intellectual mastery defies the conventions of sex-appropriate behavior and must pay 'a price in anxiety'." In a recent paper (1968), Horner has reported the results of a study in which she hypothesized that the motive to avoid success is more characteristic of women than men and is more characteristic of women who have high motives to achieve along with the ability to succeed in competitive achievement. The fear of success should be higher in competitive rather than noncompetitive situations, and it should be higher when women are competing against men. It should also be higher in areas outside of the traditional female roles, or closer to traditionally masculine activities. This means that high-achieving women may fear academic or vocational success and therefore turn to competition within the traditional role (i.e., the best cook or hostess, the mother of the most successful children, the best dressed, the most popular socially, etc.).[6]

Using 90 female and 88 male freshman and sophomore college-students as subjects, Horner devised two story cues. The women were asked to write a story to the cue, "After first-term finals, Anne finds herself at the top of her medical-school class." The men were given the cue, "After first-term finals, John finds himself at the top of his medical-school class."

Three main kinds of responses emerged from the women's stories. The most frequent showed affiliative concerns such as the fear of being socially

[5] I am not certain that it is *necessary* to assume an unconscious anxiety about femininity. Since the girl's core identity has not yet stabilized and she still assesses her qualities largely in terms of reflected appraisals, social rejection alone would be enough to make her anxious about her femininity. In any event, on the behavioral level, we could predict that the academically able girl who values and is successful in academic achievement would be likely to fear success and would not compete to the level of her ability especially in public competition, and particularly against men.

[6] The frequency of this kind of competition is obvious—so obvious that we may not notice it. I was reminded of it recently when someone told me why she no longer played "social" bridge with the ladies. This woman had been invited to play bridge at 8:30 in the evening, after dinner. As soon as everyone started to play, the hostess began to bring out trays of elaborate food. The food parade continued for the entire evening and culminated in an even more elaborate buffet. The food preparation had clearly taken three days, and the hostess remarked, "That's nothing, you should see what Mrs. X gives!" This also reminds us that women tend to direct their competitive strivings and aggressions toward other women, although they may take such subtle forms as competitive hostessing.

rejected, of losing friends, of losing dating or marriageable qualities, the fear of isolation as the result of success, and a desire to keep the success a secret by pretending that it had nothing to do with intelligence.

In the second type of response the fears were not related to affiliation and were not linked to whether or not anyone found out about the success. This group of stories showed guilt, doubts about one's femininity, despair about the success, and anxiety about one's normality.

The third group of stories used denial of different kinds—denying the situation given by the cue, changing the content, denying that the cue was possible, and denying any effort or responsibility for the success. These are examples of stories using denial:

"Anne is a code name for a nonexistent person created by a group of med students. They take turns taking exams and writing papers for her."

"Anne is really happy she's on top, though Tom is higher than she—though that's as it should be. Anne doesn't mind Tom winning."

"Anne is talking to her counselor. Counselor says she will make a fine nurse. She will continue her med-school courses. She will study very hard and find she can and will become a good nurse."

Some of the stories were bizarre:

She starts proclaiming her surprise and joy. Her fellow classmates are so disgusted with her behavior that they jump on her in a body and beat her. She is maimed for life."

Here is another story, not so obviously bizarre, but the level of anxiety that the cue aroused is very clear:

Anne is an acne-faced bookworm. She runs to the bulletin board and finds she's at the top. "As usual," she smarts off. A chorus of groans is the rest of the class's reply. Anne was always praised for her initiative and study habits— mainly because these were the only things one could praise her for. She studies 12 hours a day, and lives at home to save money. She rents her books. 'Well it certainly paid off. All the Friday and Saturday nights with my books, who needs dates, fun—I'll be the best woman doctor alive!' And yet, a twinge of sadness comes through—she wonders what she really has. But, as is her habit, she promptly erases the thought, and goes off reciting aloud the 231 bones in her wrist."

As Horner had predicted, the response of the fear of success was significantly more common for the women. Of the 90 women in the study, 59 presented stories reflecting this fear; of the 88 men, only 8 responded with fear.

Here is a story that is characteristic of the male response:

John is a conscientious young man who worked hard. He is pleased with himself. John has always wanted to go into medicine and is very dedicated. His hard work has paid off. He is thinking that he must not let up now, but must work even harder than he did before. His good marks have encouraged him. (He may even consider going into research now.) While others with good first-term marks slough off, John continues working hard and eventually graduates at the top of his class. (Specializing in neurology.)

The characteristic female story expresses all of the anxiety and ambivalence we have been describing. The contrast between the two stories speaks for itself.

Anne has a boyfriend Carl in the same class and they are quite serious. Anne met Carl at college and they started dating around their soph years in undergraduate school. Anne is rather upset and so is Carl. She wants him to be higher scholastically than she is. Anne will deliberately lower her academic standing the next term, while she does all she subtly can to help Carl. His grades come up and Anne soon drops out of med school. They marry and he goes on in school while she raises their family.

In another part of the same study, Horner tried to see whether fear of success was aroused by the aggressive overtones of competition, especially against men. Subjects did tasks in competitive and noncompetitive situations. More than two-thirds of the men did best under competition, as against less than one-third of the women. Of women who were high in the motive to avoid success, 77 percent did significantly better in the noncompetitive situation; of those who were *low* in the motive to avoid success, 93 percent behaved like the men, performing at a significantly higher level in the competitive situation. "The results suggest that women, especially those high in the motive to avoid success, will explore their intellectual potential to full measure only when they are in a noncompetitive setting and least of all when competing against men" (1968, p. 11).

We know that predicting women's achievement behavior is more difficult than predicting men's. In addition to the level of the motive to achieve, and a fear of failure, we also have to account for a significant fear of success. And there is another variable, one we have mentioned before—although we expect the motive to achieve in men to be internalized, independent of other motives, in women we may find a fused motive of affiliation and achievement. Not only can achievement be designed to secure affection and approval from others, but the content area may be one in which women can be nurturant and fairly noncompetitive, as in nursing and education. The reasons that the majority of middle-class women have entered these traditionally acceptable occupations are becoming clear.

MOTIVATION AND THE CHOICE OF CAREER

Sundheim (1963) reports that the highest motives to achieve were found in women majoring in the atypical and difficult choice of science. College women majoring in language had a medium achievement score and those in education had the lowest score. The affiliation-need scores for women majoring in education were highest. According to the National Manpower Council Report of 1957, 54 percent of American college women take a degree in education, and another 20 percent take a degree in nursing. Highly achievement-motivated students who are least anxious are better able to select more difficult and atypical curricula. Women who are most anxious or least achievement-motivated may not complete a degree at all, but certain fields obviously lend themselves to a less ambivalent success than others. The woman who succeeds in an atypical vocation is anxious about her success and is, in addition, particularly vulnerable to competitive vocational failure, to social rejection, and to anxieties about her femininity.

In a 1964 study Taylor reviewed the literature about students who underachieved. Although there was no differentiation between the sexes in the study, the results are illuminating. Taylor found seven major differences between achieving and underachieving students: (1) While the underachiever suffers from a vague, nondirected anxiety and feels "helpless," the achiever directs his tensions to the task. (2) Underachievers fluctuate between very high and low self-concepts, while the stable achievers are generally self-confident. (3) Compared with underachievers, achievers place less emphasis on their social life. (4) The achiever seems to be generally accepted by peers and authorities while the underachiever is in conflict with parents, usually about demands for independence. (5) Achievers are concerned with their scholastic interests, accomplishing their work well and on time, while the underachievers are indecisive about their course work, their academic major, and are preoccupied with social goals. (6) While the achiever sets realistic goals, the underachiever has vague or unrealistic goals or is indecisive about risks. (7) The achievers impress others by their seriousness of purpose, while underachievers seem to be overly influenced by the opinions of others.

It is not hard to see that the achiever seems to fit the male stereotype while the underachiever bears a distinct resemblance to the typical female stereotype. The underachiever is preoccupied with social achievements, is susceptible to interpersonal judgments, has unrealistic conceptions of goals and abilities, does not have a clear idea of the relationship between self-identity and vocational success, does not seem to have an internalized standard of excellence, and reviews achievements and the self in terms of others' reactions. Like most girls, underachievers are dependent upon reflected appraisals for feelings of self-esteem. This brings up the question whether most females are underachievers. I suppose I am opening a hornet's nest when I suggest that while education and nursing careers are not intellectually demanding they do permit the typical girl to safely satisfy internal and external demands for achievement and affiliation. But it is also clear that she is not going to be first in her medical-school class.

Davis and Olsen (1965) decided to investigate the "professionalizing effect" of all the years that girls spend in a university working toward a nursing degree. They asked students to evaluate statements supporting what they called the "orthodox view" and the "reform view." The reform view was represented by statements such as: "Radical alterations in the division of labor in the family ought to be made so that women can make their full contribution to social progress." "If society did not make women feel so guilty about outside agencies helping them in the care and upbringing of their children, more women would want to work and neither they nor their children would suffer for it." Statements representing the orthodox view included: "Regardless of her worldly accomplishment a woman who never marries is more to be pitied than emulated." "There is something unnatural and unattractive about women who seem to be more preoccupied with their work and careers than they are with their homes." The responses of the female students to these statements were measured when they entered school and again at graduation. Davis and Olsen found, to their apparent disappointment, that most of the students at both times took the orthodox stand, saying that the woman's primary role is at home. The three years in school did not change their initial attitudes.

The investigators then circulated a second set of statements. The students were asked to rank, from 1 to 4, four different attributes commonly associated with the adult female role. The directions read:

Here are four kinds of womanly qualities admired in America today. Ideally, if you could arrange your life, which quality would you choose to emphasize most, which second, which third, and which last? (1) Great attractiveness to men, dresses stunningly, has charm and sophistication. (2) Devoted to her family, manages her home with great interest, cares well for her husband and children, enriches their lives. (3) Active in community affairs and performs good works which give her a position of leadership in the community. (4) Dedicated to work and career, believes that her work is significant in its own right, and is respected in her field.

Again the students at both time-points disappointed the authors. Over 87 percent ranked "home and family" in first place. There was no increase in the number of girls from school entry to graduation who "at least" gave a second place to work and career. In one group of students 82 percent selected work and career in second place when they entered school, but at graduation this percentage was reduced to 61.

Despite the previous "negative results," the authors tried a third study in which they thought that the years in school might increase the quality of the students' professional commitment even though they did not value work and career as much as other goals. In this study they asked the students to evaluate five vocational items (e.g., good pay, regular hours) and four professional items (e.g., to be a spokesman in the field, to follow through on those things in the field that are of interest). From entry to graduation there was some increase in vocational interest, but not only was there no increase in professional involvement, there was actually some deterioration. For the majority of girls, a career is what you do between the time you graduate from college and the time you get married.[7]

A study of former Vassar students (Sanford, 1962) found that most young alumnae seemed happy to attune their lives to those of their husbands. The family unit and their husband's career took precedence over any ambitions they might have had. Rather than feelings of suffering as second-class citizens, the alumnae indicated unambivalent adjustment with a minimum of conflict. Those with strong professional commitments were ready to stay home when their children were small and were prepared to reenter the labor force when the children were older. The great majority were not at all concerned with what their roles would be 15 or 20 years later; they were preoccupied with short-term goals and activities, and they gave the investigators the impression that they felt the future would take care of itself. The Vassar study and similar studies suggest that most college women are adequate students without any marked intellectual predisposition who have reasonably active social lives and who anticipate fairly early marriages. Whether because of a low achievement motive, a high affiliation motive, a fear of failure, or a fear of success, they are defining their identities in terms of the traditional female role.

But there is another kind of female college student, closer to the masculine model, who has had a long-standing interest in academic competition and is achieving successfully. Either because experimenters are not tapping the right variables or because she actually represents a very small part of the female population, there are few studies in which this type of student emerges in important percentages. My own hunch is that there are few middle-class American college women who have internalized a really independent motive to achieve and who *will* achieve, social success be damned.

Some of the young women whom I see as seniors going on to graduate school seem to represent a new intermediate type of student. These students are motivated to do very well academically; they expect to take the graduate degree and to work at their professions. The content of the commitment of

---

[7]Last year 14 female graduate students who were enrolled in a seminar I was teaching came over to my home and sat around talking about why they were in graduate school, about their personal histories and aspirations, in an attempt to find some core motivation common to the group. We found none. The motive to succeed in academics or professionally is not single or simple. Most studies suggest that the early relationships with parents had some problematic aspect with tensions generated and channeled into scholastic achievement. I think the critical factor is the development of an independent self and an independent motive to achieve. Alienation from parents is probably insufficient by itself to account for the achievement motive, and we certainly are all familiar with people who are alienated from one or both parents and who are not motivated to achieve. The women who are most professionally committed have a feeling of independence, internalized criteria for esteem, and enough social alienation to be able to defer marriage until they have prepared themselves for their future vocations.

the psychology majors that I see tends to be directed toward the more nurturant aspects of the field (clinical psychology, child psychology, work with underprivileged community groups, etc.), but the achievement levels they demand of themselves are very high. The women are obviously feminine in appearance and both they and the men in class accept their professional commitment. In discussions, a common theme emerges and that is their perception of the futility or emptiness of their mothers' lives, especially after the children are grown and gone. There is some lack of reality in their goal aspirations since they all expect to marry and have children and work and none have any idea of the difficulties involved. But they also expect, individually, to settle those problems—which they regard as concrete and pragmatic. In other words, the problem of combining marriage and careers is not seen by them as a conflict in aspects of the personality or as a conflict between the partners in a marriage, or as a threat to their femininity—just a problem in baby-sitters, cleaning help, and so on. Perhaps, in a microcosm, I am beginning to see a new feminine pattern emerging in which interpersonal success and traditional behaviors remain important while the achievement success becomes equally important.

chapter 11

CHANGES IN MOTIVES
AND ROLES
DURING DIFFERENT
STAGES IN LIFE

One of the important differences in the lives of men and women is the difference in consistency of their major role responsibilities. Unlike the major occupational role responsibility of men, the traditional feminine responsibilities increase and decrease with the birth and the maturation of children. Most women do not seem to understand the profundity of these changes, not comprehending that they may find themselves at a relatively young age without meaningful work or purpose. And neither the adolescent girl nor her parents seem aware of the pervasive effect upon her future when she is encouraged to view the love of a man and the raising of children as the self-defining, self-esteeming achievement, limiting achievement to traditional tasks and the need to affiliate.

For the girl who is bright enough to do well, school achievement is a large and important part of her self-identity, at least until puberty. Before puberty, interest in and anxiety about femininity is not crucial. At adolescence, the criteria for self-approval change. As the pressure to attract boys becomes competitively more important and crucial to feelings of self-esteem, affiliation needs generally become more important. At this point the academically successful girl still has a "bisexual" identification. She perceives herself as a feminine girl who is able to compete successfully academically, but she also becomes increasingly aware that public competitive success or qualities of aggression threaten social success. She knows this by peer reactions, by parental expectations, and by her own internal criteria of femininity (femininity is now not a natural attribute of her sex, it is a quality of personality to be earned and an area of considerable anxiety). In terms of her own needs, self-definitions, and behaviors, she begins to define herself primarily in terms of the gratification of affiliative motives, with achievement needs becoming subsidiary.

Even when the middle-class female college student is successfully preparing for a professional career, she is likely to marry shortly after graduation or even before. If she goes on to graduate school she is likely to be a married graduate student, keeping house, earning grades, and swallowing oral contraceptives. She may work and she may compete academically, but her primary goals are feminine—traditionally feminine. She will create a home, please her husband, develop sexual skills, cook like a chef, and have children. More anxious about her femininity, which is established within the traditional role (at least in the first years of marriage), she will tend to defer to her husband, projecting a quality of authority to him even if he doesn't come so equipped.

The only way to achieve a feminine sense of identity, if one has internalized the general norms, is to succeed in the roles of wife, helpmate, and mother —and this takes years. But when self-esteem within the traditional roles has been won, we may perceive a switch to an internalized sense of self and sense of confidence. As a man's self-esteem is linked to his appraisal of his masculinity, apparently a woman's self-esteem is similarly linked to her feelings of femininity. The difference between them is that the goal of esteem and identity is achieved much later in life by women and is primarily achieved in the traditional, intense, and important relationships rather than in occupational achievements.

Assuming that the woman is successful in marriage, I think that anxieties about femininity and affiliation will decline. Ten to 15 years after marriage, achievement motives which had evolved much earlier may reemerge—not only because affiliation needs are gratified but because the traditional role-demands are also declining. But at this stage in life relatively few college-educated women go back to the professional positions they previously held or trained for. Very bright and successful women may have been afraid of "masculinizing" success while they were in college; now they may realistically be afraid of failure.

THE RETURN TO WORK

Most women, even those with an undergraduate degree, work for only a few years before their children are born. The jobs that one gets just out of college are not high in pay, status, or demands on ability. As a result, the work experience of those years does not leave one with very marketable skills. After the first child is born, one is immersed in the demands of motherhood —and that role makes few contributions to professional skills. For the next 10 to 15 years the demands on one's time are enormous and the world of work can be perceived as a sort of never-never land where no one grows old or has dishpan hands. While the vast majority of educated women may define their *femininity* in terms of achieving marriage and motherhood, their *self-percept* is very likely to include needs for independent achievement. The traditional role offers few opportunities for gratification of this secondary component of the self, especially since the culture does not esteem the traditional role as either independent or achieving. This is an extraordinary, widespread, ambivalent situation. When a woman is finally in a position to achieve feelings of self-esteem that come from successful femininity she is simultaneously losing esteem because neither she nor the general culture really value the role! Yet the traditional role is conceived as essential to normality.

Fifteen years is a long time in which to allow skills to lie fallow and to avoid competition. Esteem in the world of work derives from one's individual contributions within a competitive framework. When a woman *can* go back to school or back to work she realizes that she will be competing in school with youngsters who have never left the school system, or entering the work force in some lesser, low-status capacity. She will be risking her self-esteem, and that is frightening.

Why don't women achieve? Some, because they have never developed a very strong motive to achieve. Others, who have a high motive to achieve, because they fear success as well as failure at the very time when commitment to a profession is necessary. For many, their exit from the labor force and their total involvement in feminine activities allows them to develop a self-definition totally within the traditional female model. For those with a high need to achieve, the lapse of time until reentry into the professions brings with it a real possibility of failure; this means that the slowly developed sense of self and self-esteem can be jeopardized by a return to work. No wonder most women take jobs instead of entering professions, or put their energies and abilities into volunteer activities.

There is loud dissatisfaction with the slow progress of women in the United States, but progress is assumed. Actually, the proportion of American women in the professions has steadily declined since World War II, while the number of women in jobs has increased.

For example, Parrish (1962) has noted:

... in general, the percentage of women PhD's has declined from 15 percent during 1920–1940 to about 10 percent currently. Except for growth in the fields of psychology and education, top-level training of women in this country has shown little or no growth in the last 25 years despite unprecedented opportunities to acquire and utilize top training. ... If the last 25 years serve as a guide to the future, women will likely play a very small role and probably a declining one in the nation's intellectual efforts.

I think that part of the expressed desire of many women to enter the labor force stems less from the need to find personal fulfillment than the wish to remove themselves from the routine of housewifing. Fulfillment in work requires enormous effort (especially if one needs to succeed) and self-discipline—it means putting oneself on the line and being open to failure. And why should American women give up their security? But some do.

Close to half of the female population in this country works, and some of us have the impression that the pattern of working and not-working follows a pattern determined by the amount of traditional role responsibilities. Most women work after they graduate from high school or college and continue to work after marriage, leaving the labor force a month or two before their first child is born. Some reenter the labor force when their youngest child enters the school system; but many do not. The question that interests us is whether any evidence exists linking the return to the labor force and the motive to achieve, especially for women whose husbands earn enough money so that they have a choice about whether or not to return to work. I suspect that the decision to work depends in part upon the mores of the specific community of the individual.

In the college community in which I live, a return to school or work is not common enough to pass unnoticed but is not rare enough to evoke much comment. The general community sentiment would seem to favor a return to work, especially when that work is at the professional level, although there are subpopulations in the community in which a return to work might invoke a loss of status. That is, taking on a job for clearly economic reasons implies that the husband is not successful, but entering a profession suggests personal fulfillment, in which, almost as an aside, one gets a paycheck. It is open to speculation whether the return to school or work is not also influenced by one's specific friends. The problem of happily filling the hours when one's children are in school can be solved in diverse ways, most of which are less demanding or threatening than returning to the competition of school or work. My friends and I are aware that we are serving as models for our adult friends as well as the college women whom we teach. Our homes, the behavior of our children, and the stability of our marriages are examined, and I sometimes have the feeling that if we were in domestic trouble the local labor force might lose some of its new employees. Experience suggests that professional commitment is easiest when husbands are confident enough in their own achievements not to be threatened by their wives' successes.

Baruch's 1966 report is the most relevant study I know of relating the motive to achieve and the cyclical return to work. Using a sample of women who had been at Radcliffe, she found a significant relationship between the number of years a woman had been out of college, the level of the motive to achieve, and a return to work. For the women out of college for 10 years and whose children were very young, there was a decline in the need to achieve as measured with TAT-like cards. The motive to achieve rose for women who had been out of college for 15 years; in this group no more children were planned. While these mothers actually had the largest number of children younger than 8 years and may still have been preoccupied with the reality of child-rearing, Baruch felt that in fantasy they were beginning to be engrossed with achieving. The achievement motive was stable and high in the population who had left school 20 and 25 years previously. Once the nuclear family was stable, those women who had a high need to achieve returned to their careers. The women who had returned responded positively to pictures of women with achievement-related themes. Women who responded only to pictures of men with such themes seemed to feel that achievement was only appropriate for men, and these women had not returned to the labor force.

Even in the sample of the very atypical women who had attended Radcliffe College, Baruch found a moratorium on achievement striving 5 to 10 years after leaving the school. The motive to achieve returned by the time the women had been out of school for 15 years, on at least a fantasy level, but in general the women were not working. Among the group who had left school 20 years before and who had the highest measured motive to achieve, there was a return to paid employment. Since the Baruch data were taken on samples of students who had left the college 5 to 25 years before and the study was not longitudinal, we have no way of knowing whether the motive to achieve decreases and then increases in individual women over the life span.

I suppose that 15 years represents the length of time it takes to have all of the children in school, followed by a year or so of freedom from responsibility. It is difficult for people who have no children or whose children are grown to imagine or recall what it feels like to have the unending 24-hour-a-day responsibility of caring for young children. So it seems likely, especially when the family economy permits it, that mothers will be glad to enjoy the relative leisure that the first grade brings. For women whose motive to achieve was never high, or whose fear of failure is high, there is likely to be an increase in social or charitable activities but not a resumption of a career. For women whose need to achieve is high and whose fear in college was of success, not challenging their abilities in a demanding profession may be perceived by them as failure. Although some may criticize the values of an achievement-oriented society, most people in this culture have internalized the achievement-derived criteria of success and fulfillment. Women who do attempt to resume interrupted careers are probably not too frightened of success or failure—their feminine identity includes achieving as an important aspect. As we will see, this is a small part of the population.[1]

Baruch cites two additional studies which suggest that 15 years after women leave college is a critical time. A survey by the Women's Bureau (U.S. Department of Labor, 1962) found that women who had left college 15 years previously were expressing dissatisfaction with the limitations of the traditional female role-activities and were eager to resume their careers. Similarly, Friedan (1963) studied 200 classmates from Smith College and found that 15 years after graduation the women were looking for "something more than" husband, children, and home.

Smith and Radcliffe are among the most prestigious women's colleges in this country, and one can wonder how generalized the motive to make a professional commitment is in the entire population. Baruch took a sample of 763 women representative of the national population who had participated in a study done by the Survey Research Center (Gurin, Veroff, and Field, 1960). She considered four variables: work status, education, need to achieve, and age. There was some association between the achievement motive and age, but in general the pattern she had observed in the Radcliffe sample was not repeated in the more general sample. What she found instead was a decline in the motive to achieve as the women grew older, especially for women over 55.

In the national sample, the time pattern of achievement motive in college-educated women resembled but did not duplicate the pattern that Baruch had found in the Radcliffe sample. In the national sample the college women had not necessarily graduated, and some of them had only one year of college. Nonetheless, the pattern of an increase in the achievement motive was found in the group, with women aged 35–39 most likely to have a high need to achieve. Baruch reports a study by Dawson (1965) of 1569 married women graduates of the University of Sydney in Australia, which was very consistent with her own finding. Differences between the college women and women in the general population were very similar to the American pattern. The Australian women who returned to work gave as their reason an interest in their field and the desire to use their abilities and education. These are achievement-related rather than economic motives. Another

---

[1] The data do not permit us to determine whether the women who reenter the labor force have an independent motive to achieve, or whether there is a fusion of achievement and affiliation needs. One could speculate that women who had achieved in order to be rewarded with affiliative success might develop an independent motive to achieve when affiliation motives were gratified. I know of no studies bearing on that question.

study, of 898 applicants for the Minnesota Plan for Continuing Education of Women (University of Minnesota Newsletter, 1963, cited by Baruch) seems to conform to the temporal pattern of achievement striving. In the Minnesota population, women who had left school 15 to 19 years before were most likely to apply for entrance. This would seem again to be a behavioral response to an increase in the achievement motive, or the re-arousal of a previously developed high need to achieve.

This pattern seems limited to women who have had at least some college experience. In the national American sample, women who had a high-school education had highest achievement-motivation scores in the young-est age group (21–24), while those aged 30–39 had a decrease in the achievement motive followed by a slight rise. For those women who had had less than 12 years of schooling, there was a steady decline in the motive to achieve. The statistics published in 1962 by the Women's Bureau indicate that the more education a woman has, the greater the probability that she is working. Twenty-eight percent of the married women with an elemen-tary-school education were working, 34 percent of the high-school gradu-ates, and 43 percent of the college-educated women. That is probably especially revealing if one assumes that college-educated women married men with higher education and that the economic pressure to work is less critical for them than for the less-educated groups.

Motherhood is a role with different phases which make different demands and provide different gratifications at different times. A good mother must respond to the changing needs of her children—letting them go, permitting them to grow up, encouraging their independence. In the early years of children's lives motherhood lends itself to feelings of achievement, mastery, or competence. In these years the dependence of the children makes the mother's role a source of gratification for achievement, affiliation, and nur-turance (as well as power). In a very real way mothers extend themselves completely and contribute to the realization of the potential of their chil-dren and their husbands. But the demands of the role change and the gratifications that can be forthcoming change also. That the motive to achieve seems to be evidenced only in the college population of women whose children are grown suggests that only achievement-motivated women go to college in the first place, or the experience of higher education encourages college women to develop a self-concept that includes achiev-ing, or both.

Motherhood is also an ambivalent role, and lately this culture seems intent on denying that ambivalence, which, unfortunately, makes mothers who are aware of their hostility and ambivalence feel very guilty. This tends to create a dishonesty in the parent-child relationship where parental ag-gression takes subtle forms, especially in acts of omission. I was reminded of this very recently as I listened to an acquaintance bore a large group of trapped people with dreary anecdotes of toilet training and shoe sizes. What we were hearing was the subtle insistence by a resentful mother that she was preoccupied with the children and therefore a devoted mother. Without being permitted some public acknowledgment of ambivalence, the mother tends to find alternative roles more appealing. In any event, it is difficult to make motherhood a career unless one keeps having children every two-and-a-half years until the menopause.

Mothering is the single most demanding and rewarding aspect of the traditional role. But it is a role which, when done best, atrophies. The reasons that women do not return to work are clear, but the inevitable and interminable "empty nest" syndrome is a period of loneliness and stagnation for many.

Now we can see that many variables are interactively operating in determining whether women make a professional commitment—and we are probably still ignorant of some. What are the levels of the motive to achieve, the fear of failure, and the fear of success? What are the experiences of achieving? And how is achieving defined? Is it part of the self-concept? What are the levels of independence, self-confidence, and aggression? Has there been an early independence from the mother, a role identification with the father, a self-confident husband, a subculture that encourages reentry into the work force? What is the family's economic level, what are the ages of the children, what is the woman's educational level, and what are her skills? What kind of profession, traditionally derived or deviant, does she want to commit herself to? What is the availability of jobs, and what sacrifices would the family make if she went back to a profession?

THE NEW FEMINISM

I have tried to stay out of the feminist fight in these pages, partly because I think the data fall where they fall and partly because I personally don't think that work is the route to all good things for all women, just as I don't feel that a total immersion into Kinder, Kirche and Küche, barefoot in the summer and pregnant in the winter, is ego-enhancing for all women. But I think the inclusion of a more passionate position might be enlightening, and I am going to quote from two different articles. The first article, "Training the Woman to Know Her Place,"[2] was written by the psychologists Daryl and Sandra Bem in 1967.

It will be recalled that contempt has often been America's attitude toward the unable or unmotivated Black American; hopefully, now that attitude is being replaced by one of indignation, an indignation at the social conditions that cripple his ability and dampen his motivation to seek any career beyond the role that society has assigned to him solely because of his black skin. But where is our parallel reaction to the American woman who lacks either the ability or the

[2]Excerpts reprinted by permission of the authors. A revised version of this article appears in Daryl J. Bem, *Beliefs, Attitudes, and Human Affairs,* Brooks/Cole, Belmont, Calif., 1970.

motivation to seek any career beyond the housewife role that society has assigned to her solely because of her sex? Indeed, we appear to have no reaction whatever; even the question seems peculiar. But why? Because this description characterizes nearly every woman in our society. Just as the fish has no reaction to the water around him because he has never been exposed to anything else, so, too, we have no reaction to the woman who is unable or unmotivated to seek a career beyond the home and nursery.

The important point here is *not* that the role of full-time housewife and mother is inferior to other roles, rather, it is that our society is managing somehow to assign large segments of its population to a particular role solely on the basis of sex just as inexorably as it has consigned the individual with the black skin to the role of janitor and domestic. And yet, one hears no cry of moral outrage either from the liberals, who claim to be committed to the ideal of a fully equalitarian society, or from the full-time housewife, who comprises the majority of America's married women. . . . Her sigh of relief is almost audible when she marries and retires from the outside world of novel and unsolved problems.

Most Americans are not alarmed at this retirement, however. After all, they reason, a twenty-one year old woman is perfectly free to choose a career if she cares to do so; society is not standing in her way. But Americans overlook the fact that the society that has spent twenty years carefully marking the woman's ballot has nothing to lose in that twenty-first year by pretending to let her cast it for the alternative of her choice. Society has controlled not her alternatives, but her motivation to choose but one of these alternatives. The so-called "freedom to choose" is illusory and cannot be invoked to justify the society that controls the motivation to choose.

A second argument is often raised. Its proponents admit that women do end up as full-time housewives by virtue of their sex, and, in that sense, they exemplify a failure of our society to raise girls as unique individuals. But, they point out, the American women's position is *not* inferior to that of the man's career; it is complementary, but equal. This is particularly so, we are told, for the role of the mother. Raising children is not only as time-consuming as a professional career, it is also as satisfying and challenging. We should not despair, therefore, simply because so many women end up as full-time housewives and mothers. . . .

[Here the authors present data which show that the years of motherhood are a small part of a woman's productive life-span.]

In 1954, the U.S. Supreme Court declared officially what most Americans had known for years, namely, that a cruel fraud and hoax lay behind the slogan, "Separate But Equal." No Supreme Court is likely to do the same for the more subtle motto that successfully keeps the woman in her place: "Complementary But Equal."

Not all women arrive at adulthood devoid of career aspirations, and not all Americans are happy with the present role of the American married woman . . . . The following hypothetical example is taken from the academic world, but marriages just like it are becoming a reality for couples in many occupational groups.

Both the husband and wife earned Ph.D. degrees in their respective disciplines. The husband turned down a superior academic post in Oregon and accepted a slightly less desirable position in Pennsylvania, where his wife could obtain a part-time teaching job and do research at one of the several other colleges in the area. Although the husband would have preferred to live in a suburb, they purchased a home near the wife's college so that she could have an office at home where she would be when the children came home from school. Because the wife earns a good salary, she can easily afford to pay a maid to do her major household chores. The husband and wife share all other tasks around the house equally. For example, she cooks the meals, but the husband does the laundry for her and helps with many of her other household tasks.

Without questioning the basic happiness of such a marriage nor its appropriateness for many couples, one can nevertheless legitimately ask if such a marriage is, in fact, an instance of interpersonal equality. Have all the hidden assumptions and prejudices about the woman's "natural" role really been eliminated? There is a very simple test. If the marriage is truly equalitarian, then its description should retain the same flavor and tone even if the roles of the husband and wife were to be reversed. Thusly:

Both the wife and husband earned Ph.D. degrees in their respective disciplines. The wife turned down a superior academic post in Oregon and accepted a slightly less desirable position in Pennsylvania, where her husband could obtain a part-time teaching job and do research at one of the several other colleges in the area. Although the wife would have preferred to live in a suburb, they purchased a home near the husband's college so that he could have an office at home where he would be when the children came home from school. Because the husband earns a good salary, he can easily afford to pay a maid to do his major household chores. The wife and husband share all other tasks around the house equally. For example, he cooks the meals, but the wife does the laundry for him and helps with many of his other household tasks.

It seems unlikely that many men or women in our society would consider the marriage described in the last paragraph as either equalitarian or desirable, and thus it becomes apparent that the hidden prejudices and assumptions about the woman's "natural" role permeates the entire fabric of such quasi-equalitarian marriages . . .

The important point is not that such marriages are bad or that their basic assumptions of inequality produce unhappy frustrated women. Quite the contrary. It is the very happiness of the wives in such marriages that reveals society's smashing success at socializing its women. It is a measure of the distance our society must yet traverse toward self-fulfillment and interpersonal equality that such marriages are widely characterized as utopian and fully equalitarian. It is a mark of how well the woman has been kept in her place that the husband in such a marriage is often adulated by women, including his wife, for "permitting" her to squeeze a career into the interstices of their marriage as long as his own career is not unduly inconvenienced. Thus is the white man blessed for exercising his power benignly while his "natural" right to that power remains unquestioned.

I am going to reserve comments until I have quoted from the second article, but it is clear that the Bems make Betty Friedan look like an apologist. The second article is called "The New American Female—Demi-feminism Takes Over,"[3] and was written by Marion Sanders in 1965.

Why an unoppressed minority of the most-discussed sex do not feel sorry for themselves—and wish their self-appointed champions would find something else to fret about.

Mesdames McGuinley and Friedan have both made best-sellers of their conflicting theses, which suggests a certain schizophrenia among female book-buyers. On the other hand, this odd ambivalence may mean that a good many women are trying to plot a middle course between the two extreme positions, that they are seeking—in the style of Ladybird Johnson—to combine the functions of wife and mother with purposeful work outside their homes, which may or may not involve a professional job.

This posture—which might be called demi-feminism—is by no means a mass movement. The vast majority of American women are not even fractionally feminists and never were. This is why the Suffragists of yore had trouble recruiting doorbell ringers to circulate their petitions and marchers for their parades.

The average woman is otherwise occupied—chiefly in finding a man to support her and thereafter in keeping him reasonably content with his usually tedious job by baking pies and darning his socks when he comes home. Such are still the average female's prime concerns.

This fact has been disguised by the tidings that some twenty-three million American women are currently in the "work force" and that three out of five of them are married. This much-touted statistic creates the illusion of a nation of brisk career women who stack the breakfast dishes, park their children in nursery schools, and charge off each morning to "challenging" jobs.

Who then are the twenty-three million? Footnotes to the statistical tables disclose—to those who trouble to read them—that a mere three million are in occupations classified as "technical or professional." Another six million work only intermittently. And most of the remaining fourteen million are in lowly, ill-paid clerical, factory, sales, or service jobs. Of those who are also mothers of young children a dismaying proportion are Negro women. . . .

[The author interviewed eight well-educated young mothers and what follows is part of the interview with one of the women.]

"Are you afflicted with the Friedan Syndrome?" I asked.

"I am terribly sorry," she said, "But I don't have time to do much reading outside of my field, which is urban planning. So I have plenty of problems but they all have names. For instance, I am chairman of this committee against discrimination in housing. Some of my best neighbors are bigots. They are also good Democrats and I am Democratic Precinct Chairman. So I have a conflict of roles. What is worse, my husband says I am beginning to talk like one of those girls in the Feiffer cartoons."

The telephone rang at this point and I eavesdropped on a dialogue about setting up a nursery school for culturally deprived children and how to go about getting a subsidy from Operation Head Start to enable their culturally deprived mothers to spend a day a week at the school.

. . . Jane returned to our conference and launched into a discourse on what might be called the value system of the demi-feminist. Economically, it has a strong patriarchal base. Jane is convinced that when a man stops bringing home the bacon, marriage collapses. She believes also that marriage—with all its flaws —is the best arrangement yet invented for the rearing of a family.

Since her husband's job is arduous, she feels he is entitled to something better than a TV dinner when he gets home. Besides, she likes cooking. As for his duties as a father? "I don't go for this business of demanding that he change the baby and wash dishes," she said. "I think that's *sick* feminism. Why shouldn't he do something pleasant with the children? And I'd rather have him put up shelves in the basement than putter around my kitchen when he's in a domestic mood. Of course, he baby-sits for me when I'm out working."

. . . Jane has concluded that while the two-job family can work very well (whether or not the wife is paid for her extramural labors), the two-ambition family cannot.

The author interviewed another woman, a psychologist with three children, who has a part-time job and had just refused a higher paying, prestigeful position. The woman is quoted as saying: "I don't want to be away from home eight hours a day while the children are so young. And I don't want the kind of high-pressure work that will be on my mind all the time, even when I'm home." This mother feels she can do a better job with her children than anyone she might hire, and in any event, because she wanted—and enjoys—the experience of rearing them. As a result she has opted for a career of limited ambitions.

Demi-feminism, of course, makes sense only in a society where it is fun to be a wife. This takes a special and highly adaptable kind of husband—a breed produced in far greater abundance in this country than in most parts of the world. In nations afflicted with socially underdeveloped and spiritually overbearing males, such as Japan, wives badly need a Lucretia Mott to rescue them from their dreary housemaid–concubine status. This is true not only in Asian countries, but also in many parts of Europe where husbands tend to be tightfisted about money and demanding in the home, despite the political "emancipation" of women. Even in Sweden—where because of a labor shortage women are exhorted to take up plumbing, bus driving, and TV repairing—there is a great deal of discussion about "sex roles."

. . . On a visit to Stockholm last spring, I found bright young women hotly insisting that men share more in "the work of the home." I was puzzled at first as to why such an obvious point should be so belabored. The reason became clearer after I dined in a middle-class Swedish home where the daughters of the family waited on table and ate in the kitchen while the sons—and of course the hostess and pater-familias—graced the festive board.

Now we see that in addition to all of the psychological variables that we have been discussing, there are still additional reasons why American women do not participate fully in the professions. For one thing, and that is also so pervasive that we tend not to notice it, American industry has been developing for almost 200 years. We are not an underdeveloped nation that must make the great leap forward in some small fraction of a century. The nations that encourage professional participation (as well as job holding) by their women, and who institutionalize aids like nurseries for children, are those nations whose populations are too small for their industrial capacity, who were devastated by war, or who need all available talent in an enormous economic effort. During World War II this nation had nurseries; after the war, the nurseries closed. So on the one hand we do not have the same pressing need for professional skills that women can contribute, and, on the other hand we do not institutionalize facilities that would make a professional commitment by women relatively easy.

I keep discriminating between a job and a professional career because I think the difference is very important. By a "job" I mean some position where you work some 35 to 40 hours a week, and when you leave the employment premises the job is over until you return. A professional commitment is something else again. The successful man devotes as much time as is necessary to his career, and as much energy as he can muster, and the same expenditure of oneself is necessary for the woman who would succeed in the professions. That's very hard. In the reality of contemporary America where men link their self-esteem to achievement-related success, a disproportionate amount of their lives is spent in competitive, arduous striving. The professionally committed woman accepts that kind of pressure, and participation in such a role makes it difficult to muster either energy or interest in child-rearing, homemaking, or housewifing. *It is not two jobs, but two large ambitions that have trouble living together in a home with young children.*

There are other derivatives for the woman who makes the choice of a professional commitment. Most of my friends and I work, spend time with our families, and spend some small part of our time in social life. We have neither the time nor the energy to participate in clubs, volunteer agencies, community politics, or expeditions to stores. The decision to pursue ambition means that certain pleasures and community responsibilities are given up. For the most part we have added the demands of a career to those of the housewife-mother. Both the need to achieve and the pleasure in achieving must be very high for the mother of school-aged children (much less younger children) to *elect* the professional commitment.

Most of the professional women I know work part-time in their field when the children are young. As their maternal responsibilities decline, they increase the extent of their commitment. In other words, although they have made a professional commitment, they have compromised on the extent of that commitment. If one's self-esteem is not defined solely by professional success and the need to achieve, then this compromise seems to offer more satisfaction and less frustration than either withdrawing to the confines of the picket-fence or militantly demanding to be chairman of the board. Obviously this is a role-conflict resolution relevant only for those women who are motivated to achieve in the first place—and there is nothing to prevent a woman from increasing her professional activities as the traditional role-responsibilities decrease. The demifeminist often extends herself enormously in community service, and that is also achievement gratification —if she so defines it. One of the reasons for grief among women is that achievement usually is defined occupationally and professionally. A major source of women's anger and low self-esteem is their own criteria for success, which does not include traditionally feminine activities.

A loss of identity and esteem accompanies the loss of one's major role. The transition from mistress to mother is not so great as that from mother to not-mother. When the children leave home the major role-responsibility ends. And women can wonder, once again, who they are. They can also wonder how to fill the hours. But that is not role conflict. Role conflict means the desire to commit yourself to both your vocation *and* your family role simultaneously. Since most American women make their primary commitment to their feminine role, content to resume a career at some later time, if at all (women's magazines notwithstanding), role conflict has not been a widespread problem.

There is another reason why many women do not feel that they are wasting their talents or knowledge. While many feminists conceive of the vocational achievement-oriented society as an ideal, other ideals are possible. There is rather an implicit assumption that the charitable and community-directed efforts of women are a poor second choice, since they are rewarded with little status, no money, and no power. That is true if you assume that the "natural" goals are status, money, and power. We have already indicated that in addition to the goals and values of the masculine achievement model, women also value intrapsychic development and their contributions to others, their help in improving the welfare of others. In a real and immediate way many volunteer activities right wrongs and improve conditions in the cause that women are most concerned with—other people. These activities are logical extensions outside of the home of women's interests, traditional functions, and personality qualities. Gratifications from these efforts, as in professional efforts, are proportionate to the commitment.

I should emphasize here that I am not advocating women's leaving the professions. Women who have a high motive to achieve and who are committed to a particular area must satisfy those ambitions in the vocational world. I am suggesting that there is more than one kind of achievement, and one can make different contributions to the society in which one lives. It seems to me preferable for everyone to have interests outside of the nuclear family, to feel part of the mainstream of the culture, to make individual contributions to society—but there is more than one route. It is self-destructive for women to perceive and evaluate their qualities and their responsibilities as second-rate. It is similarly self-destructive when women invest their achievement efforts and self-esteem overwhelmingly in maternity which, if done well, is a role that disappears with the development of independent children.

WOMEN AND CREATIVITY

A woman with ideas and the ability to express them is something of a social embarrassment, like an unhousebroken pet. [Mannes, 1963]

Examining the life styles of educated women in Eli Ginzberg's study of women who held fellowships at Columbia University (from 1945 to 1951) nothing emerges as clearly as the lack of style. Having left behind them an undergraduate culture with its mannerisms or pseudo styles, these women go forth from Morningside Heights to become white-collar workers in government and academic bureaucracies, or to become suburban matrons committed to *Kinder*, CORE and gourmet Küche. Occasionally they surface, protesting against discrimination in hiring and promotion, the lack of domestic help and the disappearance of the extended family, bemoaning nepotism rules and the distances between home and library. But the overall impression is of a group of women who are intelligent, rarely intellectual; competent, rarely creative; performing necessary and useful services, rarely critical. Not a Beatrice Webb or a Simone de Beauvoir, not a Hannah Arendt or a Simone Weil among them. They are in every sense of the word—socially, intellectually and economically—underemployed. [McCormack, 1967]

Theses have been written supporting the idea that when a women has a child her artistic creativity ceases, or that preoccupation with household tasks results in an inability to abstract the self and therefore creativity is impossible, or that the biological creativity of pregnancy becomes the artistic creativity of child-rearing. These may be contributing factors to the lack of feminine creative productivity, but I don't think they are the core factors. Sex differences in personality and differences in the sex roles seem more salient.

It is difficult to define creativity, but let us say that it involves originality and skill. It is an ability which allows one to originate, to invent, to make, to perceive uniquely. Guilford (1967) reports that creative people are higher in fluency and flexibility of thinking, in sensitivity to problems, in elaboration, in their ability to concentrate and work long hours, in their ability to break set. In addition they are bolder, freer, more spontaneous, integrated, self-accepting, and open (as opposed to psychologically rigid—Maslow, 1954). They are not defensive, and evaluate themselves by internal criteria (Smith, 1961). They are emotionally stable, self-confident, self-critical and less anxious, and they are less interpersonally concerned and more experimental (Getzels, 1964). They are less dogmatic, and are interested in, and prefer, complexity. The creative person seems flexible, confident, and able to resist the pressures to conform.

The motive underlying creative production seems to be a drive for competence, development, and intellectual mastery, an urge to do something different, the preference for the complex (Guilford, 1967). Barron (1955) found that originality was related to independence of judgment, self-assertion, and dominance. Haimowitz and Haimowitz (1966) feel that the creative individual has to have enough of a feeling of security to be able to risk venturing beyond the social norms. Similarly, Hilgarde (1962) suggests that masculine problem-solving and social nonconformity are related to creative productivity.

Many of the skills and personality qualities that relate to creativity also relate to sex differences. We have already learned that boys are superior in breaking a set, in restructuring problems, and in logical thinking, and that girls are more afraid of failure, are more conforming, rule-obeying, dependent, and less confident. Female thinking is less analytic, more global and more perseverative (Maccoby, 1963). But the stereotyped male, like the stereotyped female, is not creative. While independence and autonomy are perceived as masculine characteristics, a high degree of sensitivity is feminine. Many studies now conclude that the really creative individual combines "masculine" and "feminine" personality qualities. That is, a high degree of bisexuality exists in those who are truly creative. Alternately we may say that the creative individual is open and can know wide-ranging experiences. The creative person resists pressure to be limited and conform to the sex-role stereotype.

Hammer (1964) studied male high-school students who had won art scholarships and found that the variables which distinguished the really creative from the merely facile were: high feminine characteristics or bisexuality, a high degree of confidence, determination, ambition, and power. For the boy, reinforcement for creativity in adolescence should derive from successful achieving, while achieving brings ambivalent rewards to girls. Helson (1966) found that creative female college students were characterized by impulsiveness, rebelliousness, an enduring interest in imaginative and artistic activity, a mistrust of personal relationships, an investment in inner life, an independence of judgment, and originality. Cashdan (1966) found that the creative adolescent and adult are similar in their independence, nonconformity, and their desire for change and variety. "There is more difference between high and low creatives than there is between female high-creatives and male high-creatives."

Similarly, Getzels (1964) found less difference between the male and female art students at the Art Institute in Chicago than between art students and other college students. The art students were more socially reserved, avoided close personal contacts, scored high in radicalism (they were more inclined to experiment and less inclined to moralize), the females were more dominant than college women in general, while the males were more timid and sensitive. The creative individual does not conform and feels less of a need to adhere to the stereotyped cultural norms than other people. Here, too, we would expect to find a sex difference: at least in adolescence and early adulthood females conform and determine their self-identity in adherence to the female model. Nonconformity to the sex role suggests a high level of self-confidence, and nonconformity in perception and thought seem necessary attributes for creative productivity.

Helson (1966) says that the reason why women are not creative is that they lack the masculine characteristics of assertiveness, initiative, independence, and expression in analytical and logical thinking. Creative women with imagination and artistic interests are less passive, less field-dependent, and have a high need for achievement. Like the creative male, the creative female must have bisexual qualities—the perceptual and analytic skills, the independence, ambition, and self-discipline that will allow for creativity and productivity, which are generally thought of as masculine. "It is in the fusion of the feminine and the masculine that part of the gift of creative individuals lies" (Hammer, 1964).

Generally we evaluate creativity in terms of a product—the original contribution must have gone beyond the incubation period and have been brought to fruition. If the achievement motive is low, the probability of realizing any potential talent is also low. In other words, women might be equally talented in terms of potential but differ in the extent of the work commitment. Some of the personality qualities that differentiate the sexes suggest that boys are likely to be potentially creative more frequently than girls. We really do not know whether that is true, especially since girls conform to others' expectations in their early years.

There have been some attempts to relate creativity differences to more biological differences. Erikson's study of sex differences in children's play and drawings found that girls were more static, peaceful, preoccupied with inner space. Greenacre (1960) would add that the boy's muscular activity leads to a concern with external responses and actions, whereas the girl turns toward imaginative fantasies and less experimentation. These tendencies result in a difference in the capacity to bring to an external form the conceptions that derive from creative ability.

For whatever reasons, and there seem to be many, women are less creatively productive than men. Original dispositions in temperament or in body-relatedness, interacting with strong social norms, result in low levels of the motive to achieve, the courage to be different, the self-confidence to have a divergent idea, the commitment to work, the aggression to succeed, and the self-discipline to produce. If for no other reason than the loss of pleasure in creative productivity, I find this pitiable.

Masculinity always has to be earned and is always in a state of being earned. Today women have problems not only in achieving femininity but even in defining it. This problem is not eased but is rather multiplied, because there are multiple routes to feminine success. Alternative roles represent a freedom of choice, but this freedom invokes the burden of increased self-responsibility. Only those women who have developed an independent sense of self and positive self-esteem will be able to elect their roles and enjoy their freedom of choice.

chapter 12

A SUMMING UP
AND SOME CONCLUDING
REMARKS

Many of the themes that have been developed in this book can be described in terms of a series of crises that are the process of growing up. A crisis is an unsettled time, a period of stress, in which anxiety about one's esteem, abilities, or identity increases. These normal developmental crises—periods of stress which occur to most or all members of a culture—are also opportunities for growth in psychological health and maturity when they are resolved. At times, males and females may experience similar crises but, overall, the nature and the timing of their sex-linked crises will tend to differ. The development of one's identity is inextricably linked with the development of one's masculinity and femininity, and the crises experienced will be interwoven with the tasks of one's sex-role—its challenges, gratifications and frustrations.

We have suggested that the behavior of infants seems largely an unfolding of personal qualities some of which may be sex-linked, having origins partly in endocrine and central-nervous-system differences. The importance of these qualities and differences is that they enable children to cope more or less well with the tasks appropriate to their ages. Girls seem initially better equipped than boys to perceive cues from people, to appraise responses accurately, to respond verbally—in short, to be "good." The internal qualities of the boy, his greater size, activity level, impulsiveness, genital sexuality, and externalized aggression in conjunction with the norms of socialization, especially the expectations of parents, result in an earlier stress—on boys who are more likely to be "bad."

I believe that sex is simply a verbal label to a young child. Sex is one of the few attributes which children do not earn, and which does not change as they succeed or fail, as they are good or bad. As a result, in the beginning, one's sex is one of the attributes that children are not anxious about. This changes when masculinity or femininity are defined by qualities that children develop or have to learn, and anxiety about one's "sex identity" begins. Because the cultural criteria for masculinity involve giving up dependency behaviors which are normal to young children of both sexes and because the boy's impulsive aggressive and sexual responses are likely to lead him into trouble, socialization for masculinity and being "good" makes sex identity a crisis and a task much earlier for boys; that is, the range of acceptable behaviors narrows earlier for boys than for girls. While dependent behaviors are perceived as sissyish and motoric aggression is perceived as destructive, the boy is pushed to conform to criteria of goodness and masculinity that force him to adopt styles of behavior that are significantly different from those tendencies he starts with. Compared with boys, until adolescence girls continue to be rewarded by significant adults just as they were rewarded in early childhood, and their natural responses are acceptable or even desirable. Dependence is acceptable, as is independence. Verbal girls use acceptable forms of aggression that do not threaten the authority of adults and, similarly, they do not invoke rejection from adults because of obvious sexual behaviors. We are suggesting that the general tendencies of girls are not likely to lead them into serious confrontations with adults, and simultaneously, that the range of acceptable behaviors, from tomboy to lady, is much wider for girls than for boys. Because girls are more rewarded by adults they have less need to look within themselves for rewards or esteem, and they continue to depend upon others for feelings of esteem. Compared with boys, there is a delay in the girl's development of an independent sense of self.

Thus, at about the age of 2 to 2½ boys begin to be pressured to give up their babyish characteristics, notably their dependency and passivity. Simultaneously, they are punished for acting out impulsive, aggressive, and sexual behaviors. At the age of 5 boys typically experience castration fears and know the anxiety that comes from Oedipal wishes. In contrast, I do not believe that young girls typically experience important feelings of rejection, castration, Oedipal jealousies and rages, or genital sexuality.

The differential stresses upon the sexes continue with their entrance into school. The beginning of school is more likely to be a crisis for the boy because he is not as adept as the girl at verbal and cognitive skills and because the school demands inhibition of muscular impulsivity and aggression. Compared with girls, the boys are immature, less able to cope with the demands of this institution. For boys the early years of school may be perceived as a feminine world, negative and threatening, a place where girls do better, a place where one's masculinity is threatened. The verbally adept girl—neither impulsive nor motorically aggressive, skillfully cued into accurately perceiving the responses of others, modifying her behavior with ease in order to be liked—conforms to expectations and is rewarded with affection and cognitive success. Compared with boys, girls know few crises in the early years of childhood, but of the few the most important are concerned with efforts to secure esteem from others. In many ways we can describe the development of a girl's self-esteem and identity in terms of her interpersonal successes and failures. Does she succeed in interpersonal relationships and evolve a capacity to interact as a confident and autonomous human being? Or does she fail to develop an independent sense of self and thus remain vulnerable in her need to be liked, esteemed, loved by others?

In school, both sexes learn criteria of self-evaluation that are related to mastering tasks. For some years the nature of the tasks—comprehension, memorization, verbal fluency—favor girls. Girls are also likely to be rewarded by their female teachers for their likability and good behavior at a time when one of the important sources of self-esteem is becoming linked to achievement in academics. While the preadolescent boy is becoming involved in needs to lead, to assert himself, to sublimate aggression, girls are occupied with the establishment of peer friendships. To the extent that girls are able to feel assured about the esteem in which they are held by their parents and their teachers, they can turn to peers for new sources of esteem. Dyadic and triadic friendships are characteristic for girls in the preadolescent years of latency, and rejection by friends is cyclic, predictable, and personal. The academically able girl is simultaneously evolving some personal concept of esteem that is based upon objective criteria of achievement at the same time that she is dependent on others and is aware that achievement results in approval from others. My feeling is that compared with boys, girls are not significantly stressed nor pressured until puberty and there is a critical delay in the establishment of an independent concept of the self and internalized criteria of self-esteem.

During latency and on into puberty the boy is unambivalently and increasingly preoccupied with defining himself as masculine. He is rewarded for developing qualities of masculinity and his anxieties are linked to the possibility of failure rather than to negative feelings about becoming a man. Despite stresses, unambivalently, boys value men and want to be men. In strong contrast, prepuberty and especially puberty are likely to be very ambivalent periods in the life of the girl. While the boy may experience puberty as a genital-sexual and vocational crisis, the girl must come to terms with ambivalence inherent in the value of being female. Thus girls may simultaneously enjoy and dislike their femininity, their rewarded qualities of passivity and dependency, their sexual bodies and reproductive functions, and their future traditional role. Despite the lack of stress, girls may not want to become women.

What are the most important crises normal to the adolescent girl? The physical changes of puberty are frightening in their link with blood and pain, and in their future link with pregnancy and childbirth. Simultaneously, these body changes are an assurance of normality and become the cues by which adults and peers perceive that she is no longer a child and is a potential sexual object. Success in affiliative relationships, notably heterosexual relationships, evolves as a more and more important source of esteem (or rejection), and the need to be chosen and loved renders the girl vulnerable to rejection and susceptible to ambivalently experienced sex play. Not experiencing high levels of genital arousal, fearful of pregnancy, aware of internalized moral standards, she is simultaneously responsible for seduction and inhibition. (We can see this conflict most clearly in the unusually lovely adolescent girl who fears that she is esteemed only as a sex object and, frankly, is.) At the same time girls are receiving cues that achievement in school is the preparation for adult professions, and while it is desirable to do well it is preferable not to do "too well." The awareness of competition and its relationship to aggression, and the fear of peer (and parental) rejection for outstanding academics, makes success in school both a source of esteem and a source of fear. Simultaneously the physical and emotional variability that derive from the menstrual cycle, the emphasis on the competitive-cosmetic body, and unresolved repressed fears about the reproductive body render a girl ambivalent about her body, while her body is critically important in terms of her self-esteem and future role responsibilities. Thus we can sometimes see in adolescent girls the beginning of psychosomatic symptoms, especially in the reproductive system.

When we observe girls in high school and in college, we find they have typically evolved different goals from boys and their perceived crises are notably linked to the interpersonal. The concept of the feminine self has become defined by the girls in terms of relationships with men, with the assumption that the primary role tasks will be the nurturant and supportive tasks characteristic of the traditional role. Other sources of esteem derive from peers, parents, and teachers—all of whom support this concept. Intimacy issues, the capacity to establish and sustain meaningful, important, nondestructive intimate relationships become the major goal and the most important crisis during adolescence and the college years.

By adolescence one's sex-role has become an important part of the search for identity for both males and females. The male role is traditionally defined largely vocationally, but the specifics of the role are open to choice; there is the explicit assumption that no matter what else girls do, they will assume the traditional responsibilities and they will have failed in the task of achieving femininity if they do not succeed in the traditional tasks. Women have a choice between working and not working and men do not. But women do not have the psychological freedom of not marrying while men (to some extent) do.

But internalizing this normative female goal may itself be a crisis. Girls who are in college today do not make the assumption that marriage and motherhood mean giving up their professional aspirations—although it may work out that way. The essence of the conflict is not at the behavioral level; it is internal and psychological. We reward achievement, successful competitiveness, leadership, innovativeness, productivity—and girls know that. To the extent that a girl does not have these qualities or to the extent that she masks them, she really does see herself, her abilities, her potential, her role, as second rate. But simultaneously she does value the traditional qualities and roles and these are part of her own internal criteria of normal achieved femininity. Femininity, when it is defined by the traditional role behaviors and attributes, continues to be an identity that is evaluated by other people and is conceived of in terms of others' responses. Thus, perhaps even more than they did as children, women are motivated to search for esteem that comes from others' evaluations.

When adolescent and college-age girls withdraw from competitive achievement because of fears of failure and because of fears of success, they ensure that their self-esteem will continue to depend upon reflected appraisals and this makes them perceptually attuned to others, empathic but vulnerable. On the other hand, a good, strong affiliative commitment is also their route to feelings of esteem, a sense of self, achieved femininity.

The *1969 Handbook of Women Workers,* released by the Women's Bureau of the Labor Department, reports that by the end of 1969 there were 31.4 million women workers. This statistic obviously reveals that very large numbers of American women are fulfilling work responsibilities in addition to their traditional ones. But while they work, few are attempting professional-level careers. (Another recent statistic, compiled by the National Register of Scientific and Technical Personnel, reported that in 1968 only 9 percent of American scientists were women.) One reason for American women's lack of professional participation is the critical salience of affiliative motivations which makes the establishment of marriage the most critical task for girls during their late adolescence and through their twenties. This contrasts strongly with the vocational-achievement goals more typical of boys.

Marriage is the resolution of one identity crisis and the beginning of another. While men are also invested in the development of healthy intimacy, of a strong marriage, they are simultaneously invested in their vocational commitment. The order of priorities is reversed for women; they are overwhelmingly invested in the creation and maintenance of the relationship with far less involvement in professions. Marriage is an enormous commitment, an unmasking of self, a relationship where rejection is searing. Because of their investment in the relationship, because of their history of assessing themselves by others' responses, and because they really do perceive reality in interpersonal terms, they overwhelmingly define and evaluate identity and femininity within the context of this relationship. And it is very difficult. Girls assume the female role-responsibilities without preparation—happy, excited, frightened, and apprehensive. While girls perceive that they are normal, selected, and lovable, they also perceive that they are no longer becoming intellectual, professional, independent. While the establishment of a stable marriage is the most frequent route to self-esteem for the majority of women, in the short run the critical question is whether her husband will support and love her. Simultaneously a source of esteem and identity, marriage also increases needs for reassurance of love.

I believe that, more than any of the preceding developmental tasks, the birth of the first child is ultimately the greatest crisis. A child is a real threat to the marriage partners, not just because of time, fatigue, and money problems, or the incurring of new responsibilities and the loss of some real freedoms, but because of the psychological investment in the child. Parents identify with the child and there is normally a change in the hierarchy of values such that the infant's welfare becomes the first concern; and the infant makes enormous demands. I am impressed by the swift identification of the parents with their child, their delight in the child's achievements and triumphs, and their extraordinary pain when the child is injured. Overall, both parents relate to the child but probably the mother's investment is greater. The birth of the first child means that the wife-mother shifts her psychological needs for emotional gratification from the interpersonal relationship with the husband to the interpersonal but nonetheless more objective relationship with the child. Creating a child is a real achievement and its value does not depend on others' responses.

I think that descriptions of the rewards of early maternity miss the essence of the experience. These are extremely difficult emotions to describe and those who have been there will understand and the rest will think me sentimental. Having a child means that you have created a human being. The words are banal but the emotions experienced are, I think, the most profound one ever knows (with the possible exception of the loss that accompanies death). When laymen talk about motives for conceiving they say things like, "That's what it's all about." The referent is to life. Observations of my peers, my professionally involved friends, reveal that during the infancy and early years of their children's lives these professionally ambitious and successful women experience the same change in priorities, the same enormous investment in the child. My hunch, and it is no more than that, is that there is a phylogenetic inheritance that makes maternity the most fulfilling role for women, at least when children are young. Pregnancy and early maternity may be "peak" experiences, the emotion felt toward the child, largely joy.

For most women maternity looms as a critical life task because the internalized values of the culture have defined it as the most important task and symbol of normality and maturity, because it gives them a feeling of having achieved adult status and of having joined the community of adult women, because it is a criterion for self-esteem, and because it is one route to identity and a lifetime of defined behaviors. Ideally, children are conceived in love and are perceived as a commitment to the marriage. Though the reality is often different, this stereotype is widespread.

But maternity is also an ambivalent role. In addition to real curtailments on one's style of life, on freedom and the ability to be spontaneous, child-rearing is a role that we are invested in and one gauges success by the success of the children. Living for children means living through children, potentially crippling the children and failing in the task. While evaluative pressures from society to be a good parent have increased enormously (pathologically?) since World War II, publicized criteria for parental behavior have become too idealistic. It is common to find guilt and anxiety because of presumed parental inadequacy. We also have a tendency to deny the unpleasantness of child-rearing and the psychological cost to the parent.

For the woman who has evolved a self-percept which includes being involved with the outer world, the new small, self-contained, and withdrawn world with young children may be threatening to her self-esteem. She may ask what she has become, who she is, what has she done with her potential. Motherhood is not only a source of esteem and role definition, it can also be a threat to esteem and self-definition. Frequently, mothers are now, in the small nuclear family, dependent upon the husband for some feeling of participation in the real world. This leads to demands for a feeling of participation or an increase in the need to feel important to the husband that he typically cannot fulfill. This is the potential beginning of the wife's romanticism about the world of work—romanticized because she cannot or does not participate in it. Other women will be threatened because their image of themselves was as sophisticated, achievement-oriented, able, outer-directed, independent women. They can become unhappy simply because they are content with the baby within their home.

The particular importance of parenthood for women is that it is simultaneously the gratification of some of their most important needs, an extraordinary source of self-esteem, and a further commitment to the very important marital relationship. It is success within the traditional role and the fulfillment of femininity. It is a most important source of confidence that can enhance those directions begun with the successful establishment of an important intimate relationship. At the same time, while maternity gratifies affiliative motives, the time-consuming, energy-draining, emotionally invested responsibility of the child-rearing role usually precludes the development of occupational-professional skills. This situation can be satisfactory if achievement-vocational motives are not strong, or while there is a natural redirection of investment from the outside world to the child and to the self, so long as achievement is perceived within traditional nurturing responsibilities. But this total investment in mothering is psychologically dangerous for that part of the population of women who are invested in professional achieving, who perceive traditional activities as second rate, who view themselves as less than perfect parents, who are aware that children become independent and leave home for school, or who are aware that their husbands are increasingly preoccupied with their achievements and there is a psychological separation between man and wife which will become more important when the children are grown. Women can redirect their search for affiliative rewards from their husband to their children, but this maintains their vulnerability—their self-esteem still is based on appreciation from other people.

When role definitions for women are no longer clear or restricted, then freedom of choice can be costly to individual women who are no longer certain of the cultural norms or their own normality. Educated women frequently leave their professions when their children are young and then suffer anxiety because they feel that they are losing their professional-intellectual abilities, because they have ceased developing their potentials, because they feel that their daily housework is repetitive and unimportant. On the other hand, the woman who elects to participate simultaneously in the traditional mothering role and in her professional capacity often feels guilty because her working evokes obvious, surface changes in the family. I mean very simply that she is busy and does not undertake the leadership of the PTA or become a girl-scout leader or take part in other activities that her children and the community perceive as her normal responsibilities. On another level, the dually committed mother can feel anxious about whether she is injuring her children because she is not solely preoccupied with them, whether she is placing stress on her husband, whether her independence, her achievement-oriented self-concept, her professional success, are evidence of her lack of femininity. This is especially likely to be true if she is uncertain about her femininity, if she achieves as well as her husband, or if her profession is atypical for women.

The breakup of a marriage always seems to be a devastating experience to both partners. This seems to be true even when divorce is clearly better than continuing the marriage. Divorce is a personal failure; if there are children there is usually much guilt; there is an economic crisis; and there is the resurgence of the threat of dating with its potential of new rejections. Divorce evokes tragic feelings of aloneness. Divorce is also the failure of "affiliation achievement," characteristically a woman's most important source of esteem. Divorce is likely to rearouse basic questions of identity because marriage has become one's reference point, the major definition of self. For the woman who never really confronted questions of her own identity, who went from the role-identity of daughter to that of wife, divorce may be the first time, in her aloneness and failure, that she confronts the issue of her values, her needs, her goals. The delay in the evolution of a sense of identity in women, which seems characteristic for women in this culture, makes it plausible and common for identity to be defined by interpersonal roles, notably those of daughter and then of wife and mother. Failure within these relationships or the feeling that the relationships are no longer rewarding enough is most likely to lead to low feelings of esteem and a search for new relationships where critically important rewards will again be forthcoming—or it may lead to giving up and withdrawing from the painful fears of new relationships.

In some ways the years of the thirties can often be perceived as dependent upon the important decisions, commitments, and responsibilities that were made during the twenties. The woman in her thirties is likely to feel that she is going on the momentum of previous decisions and that alternatives, role freedoms, are closing in. There can be conflict if she perceives the reality of her responsibilities and feels that she is the sum of her obligations. Simultaneously, in the decade of the thirties she frequently finds that the time-consuming routine demands of the previous decade have declined and the possibility for new commitments, of expansion, are increasing. The change in responsibilities invites new psychological evaluations, a development that continues into the forties. While on the one hand there are new freedoms, on the other hand there can be a fear of freedom as one realizes the restrictions one has evolved as a consequence of previous commitments. What then, are the consequences of having acted only within one traditional role for so long? Characteristically, women can be afraid because they lack the skills, the confidence, the self-concept that could enable them to participate in the competitive, impersonal, outer-directed, achievement-oriented world of work. Twenty years out of school. Twenty years out of the office. Free of old time-consuming responsibilities, motivated to achieve, to be creative, to find fulfillment, it is an act of courage when these women return to school or profession.

Involved here is not simply a question of filling time, but a question of what it means to grow older. The realization that half of one's life is likely to be over, that one's physical desirability is declining, may force a very new appraisal of values and life patterns. For many the thirties and the forties may be a time when one feels it is imperative to gratify one's needs now because otherwise one may never do so. Statistics tell us that some percentage of women resolve this identity question and take advantage of new freedoms by entering into professions, jobs, volunteer activities, or school. For others, there is the real possibility of participation in love affairs, possible divorce, and remarriage.

If the 30- to 40-year-old woman has a good marriage, it is likely to be about fifteen years old. If it is a good relationship, both partners have evolved a marvelous feeling of basic trust—a kind of trust that does not evolve with anyone else. But the marriage has tended to evolve into routines of living and relating, tied up with the realities of coping or the minutiae of tasks. Characteristically, while they may love, they don't feel acutely loving. The crisis of the thirties may become the need to recapture the passions remembered from adolescence and the twenties. Contributing to this development may be the mother's identification with her adolescent children and her envy of their passions. Participation in a love affair can be an attempt to reaffirm one's general lovability, one's sexual desirability, and one's youthfulness. It is simultaneously an attempt to recapture a feeling of being alive, of being aware of feelings. That is, participating in this new relationship, which has the potential for happiness and love, and grief and rejection, is also an attempt to recreate excitements that decline within any routinized experience.

If being loved is the major route not only for self-esteem but for feeling that one exists, then self-esteem is jeopardized when the other participants in these important relationships are invested in themselves, in their tasks, in their accomplishments. In a routinized relationship one can be taken for granted. Similarly, sex within a routinized relationship is not only likely to have become routinized itself, it is also likely to lack that quality of communicating love because the relationship takes that for granted.

In brief, it might be said:

I love and I am alive.
I am alive and therefore I love.
I am lovable; I can love; I am a woman.
I am not yet middle-aged.

I might add that I think similar motives impel men. Probably more men than women engage in affairs earlier in the marriage because sexuality for men is less likely to be tied to crises in life-stages. That is, sexual motives for men are more closely linked to sex *qua* sex and questions of masculinity and potency, while sex for women is more fused with issues of love, femininity, and identity. This is a matter of degree rather than a significant difference in kind. It is also plausible to hypothesize that investment in new sex-love affairs may occur characteristically later for men than for women because men may be invested professionally during their thirties and because threats to their self-esteem that emerge from changes in their bodies may be more critical in their forties. The establishment of a new heterosexual relationship may, in sum, be a major route for both sexes to reaffirm worth, lovability, and identity.

When parents are in their forties most children are grown and leave home, marry, and establish their own nuclear families. This not only invokes questions about one's identity, it can also cause a separation trauma similar to the mourning process. Some women become widows, and for others the specter of a lonely and empty future becomes perceived as a threatening possibility. Both parents, but especially mothers, are forced to ascertain who they are when they are no longer parents, before they are grandparents. Women experience menopause with its physical symptoms and the psychological implications of the loss of fertility, youth, and, for some, femininity. For some women, new goals and new capacities for self-realization may emerge at this time. For others the loss of identity as mother or wife is the loss of self. For both men and women, the loss of important sources of self-esteem and criteria of identity have to be replaced and new tasks evolved in order to experience a feeling of growing, living, being.

In some ways the data in this book raise questions about the extent of human variability. Endocrine data from animal studies, observations of infants, the longitudinal studies of human beings, and the implications of the endocrine-related effects in adult woman all lend support to the idea that there are differences between the sexes that have, as one origin, differences in the endocrine systems and possible differences in the central nervous system. The existence of these differences implies that there are modal differences in response potentials between the sexes and it further implies that there are likely to be other differences of which we are not yet aware. To the extent that there are physical contributions to the psychological development of human beings, there is likely to be a limit upon changes in the characteristic distribution of traits that can be wrought by different socialization practices. Neither the extent of the physical contribution nor the variability that socialization can effect are presently known. Thus far in history the overwhelming majority of cultures have socialized their children in such a way that original differences between the sexes are maximized. Simultaneously it is obvious that cultures have needed the products resulting from activity directed outward, of achievements resulting in things, and have rewarded those who possess these qualities and increase these contributions. De facto this means that both the personality qualities and the activities that are characteristically and traditionally male have been held in the highest esteem. The derivative of this has been that both the qualities and the activities characteristic of females have been denigrated.

If the self-esteem of women is to be enhanced, either the socialization of girls will alter so that they will be more likely to have "masculine" qualities of independence, activity, and assertiveness, or the values of cultures will change so that "feminine" humanistic goals—the enhancement of empathy, nurturance and sensitivity—will become esteemed. Or both.

From a psychologist's point of view, many of the problems besetting women can be understood as internal phenomena—motives, anxieties, guilts, fears, low self-esteem. But many of these negative feelings result from society's preference for and reward of occupational achievement and its inhibition of women through legislation, hiring practices, differential pay and prestige, the lack of child-care facilities, and so on. This inevitably leads to anger, especially among aware and educated women. Although I do not expect really radical changes in occupational and familial role-responsibilities (assuming we will not have a major crisis that would make women's professional contributions essential to the economy), large numbers of dissatisfied or angry women can exert pressure simply because of their numbers. It would seem that while revolution is not probable, compromise is inevitable. The extreme proponents of women's liberation movements are a small part of the population, but their extreme position establishes a new frame of reference for the rest of the population. Changes in role allocation that seemed extreme five years ago do not seem so extreme today.

It seems obvious that a society cannot educate large segments of its population to want to and to be able to participate in the larger culture and then effectively prohibit their participation without discontent. The formalization of adult sex-roles not only enhances differences between the sexes, it also goes, in stereotyped form, beyond what is necessary or desirable. I don't believe that one is a human being independent of one's masculinity or femininity but it is equally wrong to ascribe characteristics and limit goals solely in terms of sex. While the sexes appear to have characteristic qualities which are more or less functional in different activities, traditional role divisions have been far too restrictive for both sexes.

I hope that this generation of women will be better able to understand the origins for their motives, the sources of their anxieties, the reasons for their conflicts, and the time perspective of their lives. Then they may be better able to approach nurturance with more confidence, with self-esteem, with the capacity to empathize, protect and enhance—as the result of choice, as a means of realizing more of their potential. And similarly, they may attempt nontraditional achievements, from choice, relieved of anxiety about femininity or normality.

Women have role freedoms that men do not have and restrictions that men do not experience. I do not see that any one pattern of life-style will enable women as a group to achieve happiness. Some women will need to achieve within the occupational-professional sphere; others may feel fulfilled when they transfer their highly developed, active, interpersonal skills of relating, empathy, and nurturance to people outside of their nuclear family relationships. As with work, those typically voluntary activities are likely to be a source of self-esteem proportionate to one's investment in the task.

As is too often true, happiness is often an elusive goal that exists in some hoped-for future and is the property only of a role one is prevented from participating in. In reality there are no unambivalent roles. But to the extent that members of society feel that their capacities have been severely limited, feelings of resentment, emptiness, and futility pervade.

This generation of college students may be rejecting the traditional middle-class assumption that only occupational achieving is the route to success and self-esteem. Many of my students seem to perceive that their mothers' sole investment in child-rearing was futile—equalled only by the emptiness of their fathers' preoccupation with work. This is an affluent generation which takes money and economic security for granted. Perhaps this sociologic development is limited to the affluent members of a society and will persist as long as affluence does.

But I am equally impressed with the large numbers of 30- to 40-year-old professional men who seem to have achieved success in their occupational goals and who now, in an era of employment opportunities, are changing professions in search of new goals. It is possible that the contemporary women's revolution may be reflecting a larger sociological change wherein everyone is asking himself why he is doing what he is doing. New goals seem to be developing, and they seem to be personal, interpersonal, and humanistic: happiness, creativity, fulfillment, expansion, and personal growth. In order to achieve these goals one needs a fusion of what have been "masculine" and "feminine" qualities. It is not impossible that the women's revolution is the forerunner of a larger revolution in which men and women will experience both role freedom and the responsibility that always accompanies freedom.

REFERENCES

CHAPTER 1 PSYCHOANALYTIC THEORY

Bonaparte, Marie 1962 *Female sexuality.* Grove Press, New York.

Bosselman, Beulah Chamberlain 1960 Castration anxiety and phallus envy: A reformulation. *Psychiatric Quarterly* 34:252–259.

Erikson, E. H. 1964 Inner and outer space: Reflections on womanhood. *Daedalus,* 93(2): 582–606.

Freud, S. 1932 Female sexuality. *International Journal of Psychoanalysis* 13:281–297.

Freud, S. 1933 The psychology of women. In *New introductory lectures on psychoanalysis,* trans. W. J. H. Sprott. Norton, New York, pp. 153–185.

Freud, S. 1927 Some psychological consequences of the anatomical distinction between the sexes. *International Journal of Psychoanalysis* 8:133–142.

Horney, Karen 1924 On the genesis of the castration complex in women. *International Journal of Psychoanalysis* 5:50–65.

Horney, Karen 1926 The flight from womanhood. *International Journal of Psychoanalysis* 7:324–339.

Kestenberg, Judith S. 1956 On the development of maternal feelings in early childhood. *Psychoanalytic Study of the Child,* vol. 11. International Universities Press, New York, pp. 257–291.

Masters, W. H., and Virginia E. Johnson   1966   *Human sexual response.* Little, Brown, Boston.

Riesman, D.   1953   *The lonely crowd.* Knopf, New York.

Thompson, Clara   1961   Femininity. In Ellis, A., and A. Abarbanel, *The encyclopedia of sexual behavior.* Hawthorn, New York, p. 422.

Thompson, Clara   1942   Cultural pressures in the psychology of women. In Green, Maurice R. (ed.), *Interpersonal Psychoanalysis.* Basic Books, New York, pp. 229–242.

Zilboorg, G.   1944   Masculine and feminine. *Psychiatry* 7(2):257–296.

CHAPTER 2   THE EFFECT OF BODY STATES ON THE PSYCHE

August, G. P., M. Tkachuk, and M. M. Grumbach   1969   Plasma testosterone-binding affinity and testosterone in umbilical cord plasma, late pregnancy, prepubertal children, and adults. *The Journal of Clinical Endocrinology and Metabolism* 29:891–899.

Bardwick, Judith M.   1967   Need for individual assessment of Ss in psychosomatic research. *Psychological Reports* 21:81–86.

Bardwick, Judith M.   1968   Physiological contributions to the personality development of women. Paper presented at the symposium "New Contributions toward a Psychology of Women," American Psychological Association, August 1968, San Francisco.

Behrman, S. J.   1969   Which "pill" to choose? *Hospital Practice* 4(5):34–39.

Behrman, S. J., and J. R. G. Gosling   1959   *Fundamentals of gynecology.* Oxford, New York, pp. 87–97.

Benedek, Therese F.   1952   Psychosexual functions in women. Ronald Press, New York.

Benedek, Therese F.   1959   Sexual functions in women and their disturbance. In Arieti, S., *American handbook of psychiatry.* Basic Books, New York, pp. 727–748.

Benedek, Therese F., and B. Rubenstein   1942   *The sexual cycle in women: The relation between ovarian function and psychodynamic processes.* National Research Council, Washington, D. C.

Coppen, A., and N. Kessel   1963   Menstruation and personality. *British Journal of Psychiatry* 109:711–721.

Dalton, K.   1966   The influence of mother's menstruation on her child. *Proceedings of the Royal Society for Medicine* 59:1014.

Dalton. K   1964   *The premenstrual syndrome.* C. C. Thomas, Springfield, Ill.

Deutsch, Helene   1945   *The psychology of women,* vol. 2. Grune and Stratton, New York.

Frank, R. T.   1931   The hormonal causes of premenstrual tension. *Archives of Neurology and Psychiatry* 26:1053.

Gold, J. J.   1968   Endocrine laboratory procedures and available tests. In Gold, J. J. (ed.), *Textbook of gynecologic endocrinology.* Harper & Row, New York, pp. 643–666.

Goldberg, Minnie   1959   Medical management of the menopause. Modern Medical Monographs. Grune and Stratton, New York.

Greenblatt, R.   1955   Metabolic and psychosomatic disorders in menopausal women. *Geriatrics* 10:165.

Gottschalk, L. A., K. Springer, and Goldine D. Gleser   1961   Experiments with a method of assessing the variations in intensity of certain psychological states occurring during two psychotherapeutic interviews. In Gottschalk, L. A. (ed.), *Comparative psycholinguistic analysis of two psychotherapeutic interviews.* International Universities Press, New York.

Gottschalk, L. A., S. Kaplan, Goldine D. Gleser, and Carolyn M. Winget   1962   Variations in magnitude of emotion: A method applied to anxiety and hostility during phases of the menstrual cycle. *Psychosomatic Medicine* 24:300–311.

Gottschalk, L. A., and Goldine D. Gleser   1969   *The measurement of psychological states through the content analysis of verbal behavior.* University of California Press, Berkeley, Calif.

Green, R., and K. Dalton   1953   The premenstrual syndrome. *British Medical Journal* 1:1007–1013.

Hamblen, E. C.   1962   Benefits of steroid-induced pseudopregnancy. *Consultant,* February, p. 4.

Housman, H.   1955   A psychological study of menstruation. Ph.D. dissertation, The University of Michigan, unpublished.

Idestrom, C. M.   1966   Reaction to Noreshisterone withdrawal. *Lancet* 1:718.

Ivey, Melville E., and Judith M. Bardwick   1968   Patterns of affective fluctuation in the menstrual cycle. *Psychosomatic Medicine* 30:336–345.

Jaffe, R. B., G. Pérez-Palacios, and G. Serra   1969   The reproductive cycle in women. In Lednicer, D. (ed.), *Contraception: The chemical control of fertility.* Marcel Dekker, Inc., New York, pp. 1–22.

Janowsky, D. S., R. Gorney, and B. Kelly   1966   The curse: I. Vicissitudes and variations of the female fertility cycle. *Psychosomatics* 7:242–246.

Janowsky, D. S., R. Gorney, and A. J. Mandell   1967   The menstrual cycle. *Archives of General Psychiatry* 17 (Oct.):459–469.

Kane, J. F., R. J. Daly, M. H. Wallach, and M. H. Keeler   1966   Amelioration of premenstrual mood disturbance with a progestational agent (Enovid). *Diseases of the Nervous System* 27:339–342.

Kane, J. F., and M. H. Keeler   1965   Use of Enovid in post-partum mental disorders. *Southern Medical Journal* 58:1089–1092.

Kantor, H. I., Carmen M. Michael, S. H. Boulas, H. Shore, and H. W. Ludvigson   1966   The administration of estrogens to older women, a psychometric evaluation. Seventh International Congress of Gerontology Proceedings, June 1966.

Keeler, M. H., J. F. Kane, and R. J. Daly   1964   An acute schizophrenic episode following abrupt withdrawal of Enovid in a patient with previous post-partum psychiatric disorder. *American Journal of Psychiatry* 120:1123–1124.

Kestenberg, J. S.   1956   On the development of maternal feelings in early childhood. In *Psychoanalytic study of the child,* vol 11. International Universities Press, New York, pp. 257–291.

Kinsey, A. C., W. B. Pomeroy, C. E. Martin, and P. H. Gebhard   1953   *Sexual behavior in the human female.* Saunders, Philadelphia.

Kupperman, H. S.   1961   Sex hormones. In Ellis, S., and A. Abarbanel (eds.), *The encyclopedia of sexual behavior.* Hawthorn, New York, pp. 494–502.

Lee, P.   1965–1966   The vulnerability to trauma of women in relation to periodic stress. In *Medical commission of accident prevention: second annual report.* The Royal College of Surgeons of England, London.

Levy, D. M.   1956   Psychosomatic studies of some aspects of maternal behavior. In Kluckhorn, C., H. A. Murray, and D. M. Schneider, *Personality.* Knopf, New York, p. 104.

Mandell, A., and M. Mandell   1967   Suicide and the menstrual cycle. *Journal of American Medical Association* 200:792.

Masters, W. H., and M. H. Grody   1953   Estrogen-androgen substitution therapy in the aged female: II. Clinical response. *Obstetrics and Gynecology* 2:139–147.

Masters, W. H., and Virginia E. Johnson   1961   The artificial vagina: Anatomic, physiologic, psychosexual function. *Western Journal of Surgery, Obstetrics, and Gynecology* 69:192–212.

Money, J.   1961   The hormones and mating behavior. In Young, W. C., *Sex and internal secretions*, vol. 2, 3rd ed. Williams and Wilkins, Baltimore, Md.

Moos, R.   1968   Psychological aspects of oral contraceptives. *Archives of General Psychiatry* 19:87–94.

Moos, R.   1968   The development of a menstrual distress questionnaire. *Psychosomatic Medicine* 30:853–867.

Neugarten, Bernice L., and Ruth J. Kraines   1965   Menopausal symptoms in women of various ages. *Psychosomatic Medicine* 27(3):266–273.

Paige, Karen E.   1969   The effects of oral contraceptives on affective fluctuations associated with the menstrual cycle. Ph.D. dissertation, The University of Michigan, unpublished.

Persky, H.   1970   Personal communication, 25 February 1970.

Persky, H., G. K. Basu, K. D. Smith, and M. Zuckerman   1969   Testosterone production and aggression in man. Paper presented at the Society for the Study of Population, 9 September 1969, Davis, Calif.

Pincus, G.   1965   Physiological effects of cyclic administration of progestin-oestrogen combinations. In *Recent advances in ovarian and synthetic steroids and the control of ovarian function: proceedings of a symposium.* Globe Commercial Party Ltd., Sydney, Australia.

Ryan, K. J.   1963   Synthesis of hormones in the ovary. In *The ovary.* International Academy of Pathology Monographs (Grady, H. G., and D. E. Smith, eds.), Williams and Wilkins, Baltimore, Md.

Salhanick, H. A., and R. H. Margulis   1968   Hormonal physiology of the ovary. In Gold, J. J. (ed.), *Textbook of gynecologic endocrinology.* Harper and Row, New York, pp. 67–94.

Schwartz, Neena B.   1968   New concepts of gonadotropin and steroid feedback control mechanisms. In Gold, J. J. (ed.), *Textbook of gynecologic endocrinology.* Harper & Row, New York, pp. 33–50.

Shainess, Natalie   1961   A re-evaluation of some aspects of femininity through a study of menstruation: A preliminary report. *Comprehensive Psychiatry* 2:20–26.

Sherfey, Mary Jane   1966   The evolution and nature of female sexuality in relation to psychoanalytic theory. *Journal of the American Psychoanalytic Association* 14(1):28–128.

Southam, A. L., and F. P. Gonzoga   1965   Systemic changes during the menstrual cycle. *American Journal of Obstetrics and Gynecology* 91:142–165.

Sutherland, H., and I. Stewart   1965   A critical analysis of the premenstrual syndrome. *Lancet* 1:1180–1183.

Swanson, D. W., A. Barron, A. Floren, and J. A. Smith   1964   The use of norethynodrel in psychotic females. *American Journal of Psychiatry* 120:1101–1103.

Wilson, R.   1966   *Feminine forever.* M. Evans and Company, New York.

Wilson, R., and Thelma Wilson   1963   The non-treated postmenopausal woman. *American Geriatrics Society* 11:347.

Wiseman, W.   1965   Four years' experience with ovulation inhibitors in clinical trial and routine use. In *Recent advances in ovarian and synthetic steroids and the control of ovarian function: Proceedings of a symposium.* Globe Commercial Party Ltd., Sydney, Australia.

CHAPTER 3   PSYCHOLOGY AND THE SEXUAL BODY

Bardwick, Judith M.   1968   Physiological contributions to the personality development of women. Paper presented at the symposium "New Contributions toward a Psychology of Women," American Psychological Association, August 1968, San Francisco.

Benedek, Therese   1959   Sexual functions in women and their disturbance. In Arieti, S. (ed.), *American handbook of psychiatry,* vol 1. Basic Books, New York, pp. 727–748.

Deutsch, Helene   1944   *Psychology of women,* vol, 1. Grune and Stratton, New York.

Ehrmann, W.   1959   *Premarital dating behavior.* Holt, Rinehart and Winston, Inc., New York.

Fluhmann, C. F.   1956   Management of menstrual disorders. Saunders, Philadelphia.

Friedman, L. J.   1962   *Virgin wives: A study of unconsummated marriages.* Tavistock Publications, London.

Kinsey, A. C., W. B. Pomeroy, C. E. Martin, and P. H. Gebhard   1953   *Sexual behavior in the human female.* Saunders, Philadelphia.

Maslow, A.   1954   *Motivation and personality.* Harper and Row, New York.

Masters, W. H., and Virginia E. Johnson   1966   *Human sexual response.* Little, Brown, Boston.

Masters W. H., and Virginia E. Johnson   1965   The sexual response cycles of the human male and female: Comparative anatomy and physiology. In Beach, F. A. (eds.), *Sex and behavior.* Wiley, New York.

Masters, W. H., and Virginia E. Johnson   1965   The sexual response cycle of the human female: 1. Gross anatomic considerations. 2. The clitoris: Anatomic and clinical considerations. In Money, J. (ed.), *Sex Research: new developments.* Holt, Rinehart and Winston, Inc., New York.

Masters, W. H., and Virginia E. Johnson   1962   The sexual response cycle of the human female: 3. The clitoris: Anatomic and clinical considerations. *Western Journal of Surgery, Obstetrics, and Gynecology* 70:248–257.

Masters, W. H., and Virginia E. Johnson   1961   The artificial vagina: Anatomic, physiologic, psychosexual function. *Western Journal of Surgery, Obstetrics, and Gynecology* 69:192–212.

Masters, W. H., and Virginia E. Johnson   1961   The physiology of the vaginal reproductive function. *Western Journal of Surgery, Obstetrics, and Gynecology* 69:105–120.

Masters, W. H., and Virginia E. Johnson   1961   Orgasm, anatomy of the female. In Ellis, A., and A. Abarbanel (eds.), *Encyclopedia of sexual behavior.* Hawthorn, New York.

Moore, B. E.   1961   Panel report: Frigidity in women. *Journal of the American Psychoanalytic Association* 9:571–584.

Schaefer, Leah   1964   Sexual experiences and reactions of 30 women. Ph.D. dissertation, Columbia University, unpublished.

Shainess, Natalie   1961   A re-evaluation of some aspects of femininity through a study of menstruation: A preliminary report. *Comprehensive Psychiatry* 2:20–26.

Sherfey, Mary Jane   1966   The evolution and nature of female sexuality in relation to psychoanalytic theory. *Journal of the American Psychoanalytic Association* 14(1):28–128.

Wallin, P.   1960   A study of orgasm as a condition of woman's enjoyment of intercourse. *Journal of Social Psychology* 51:191–198.

Whalen, R. E.   1966   Sexual motivation. *Psychological review* (2):151–163.

CHAPTER 4   PSYCHOLOGICALLY MOTIVATED DYSFUNCTION OF THE REPRODUCTIVE SYSTEM

Adams, A. B.   1959   Choice of infant feeding technique as a function of maternal personality. *Journal of Consulting Psychology* 23:143–146.

Bardwick, Judith M., and S. J. Behrman   1967   Investigation into the effects of anxiety, sexual arousal, and menstrual cycle phase on uterine contractions. *Psychosomatic Medicine* 29(5):468–482.

Davids, A., S. DeVault, and M. Talmedge   1961   Anxiety, pregnancy and childbirth abnormalities. *Journal of Consulting Psychology* 25:74–77.

Davids, A., and S. DeVault   1962   Maternal anxiety during pregnancy and childbirth abnormalities. *Psychosomatic Medicine* 24(5):464–470.

Engstrom, L., G. Geijerstam, N. Holmberg, and K. Uhrus   1964   A prospective study of the relationship between psycho-social factors and course of pregnancy and delivery. *Journal of Psychosomatic Research* 8(2):151–155.

Ferreira, A.   1965   Emotional factors in the prenatal environment. *Journal of Nervous and Mental Disease* 141(1):108–118.

Fisher, S.   1964   Sex differences in body perception. *Psychology Monographs* 78(591).

Grace, W. J., and D. T. Graham   1952   Relationships of specific attitudes and emotions to certain bodily diseases. *Psychosomatic Medicine* 14:243.

Graham, D. T., and F. K. Graham   1964   Specific relations of attitudes to physiological change. The University of Wisconsin School of Medicine, unpublished progress report, 1 July 1961. Cited in Williams, R., and A. G. Krasnoff, *Psychosomatic Medicine* 26(6):701–709.

Grimm, Elaine R. 1961 Psychological tension in pregnancy. *Psychosomatic Medicine* 23:520–527.

Hetzel, B. S., Brigid Bruer, and L. Poidevin 1961 A survey of the relation between certain common antenatal complications in primiparae and stressful life situations during pregnancy. *Journal of Psychosomatic Research* 5:175–182.

Ibor, J. J. Lopez 1960 Current problems in psychosomatic medicine. *Acta Psychosomatica* no. 3, pp. 9–51.

Kapp, F. T., S. Horstein, and V. T. Graham 1963 Some psychological factors in prolonged labor due to inefficient uterine action. *Comprehensive Psychiatry* 4(1):9–18.

McDonald, R. L. 1965 Personality characteristics in patients with three obstetric complications. *Psychosomatic Medicine* 27(4):383–390.

Newton, N., and M. Newton 1967 Psychologic aspects of lactation. *The New England Journal of Medicine* 277(22):1179–1188.

Newton, N. 1968 Breast feeding. *Psychology Today* 2(1):34.

Salber, E. J., P. G. Stitt, and J. G. Babbott 1959 Patterns of breast feeding in family health clinics: II. Duration of feeding and reasons for weaning. *New England Journal of Medicine* 260:31–35.

Sears, R. R., Eleanor E. Maccoby, and H. Levin 1957 Patterns of child rearing. Row, Peterson, and Company, Evanston, Ill.

Seward, Georgene H., and H. L. Myerhoff 1965 The question of psychophysiologic infertility: Some negative answers. In *Proceedings of the 73rd annual convention of the American Psychological Association*, pp. 269–270.

Vanden Bergh, R. L., E. S. Taylor, and Vera Drose 1966 Emotional illness in habitual aborters following suturing of the incompetent cervical os. *Psychosomatic Medicine* 28(3):257–263.

Williams, R., and A. G. Krasnoff 1964 Body image and physiological patterns in patients with peptic ulcer and rheumatoid arthritis. *Psychosomatic Medicine* 26(6):701–709.

Zuckerman, M., J. Nurnberger, S. Gardiner, J. Vandiveer, B. Barrett, and A. den Breeijen 1963 Psychological correlates of somatic complaints in pregnancy and difficulty in childbirth. *Journal of Consulting Psychology* 27(4):324–329.

READINGS NOT CITED IN TEXT

Benedek, Therese 1959 Sexual functions in women and their disturbance. In Arieti, S. (ed.), *American handbook of psychiatry*, vol. 1. Basic Books, New York, pp. 727–748.

Berle, B. B., and C. T. Javert 1954 Stress and habitual abortion. *Obstetrics and Gynecology* 3:298.

Bressler, B., P. Nyhus, and F. Magnussen 1958 Pregnancy fantasies in psychosomatic illness and symptom formation. *Psychosomatic Medicine* 21:187.

Biven, G. D., and M. P. Klinger 1937 *Pseudocyesis*. Principia Press, Bloomington, Ind.

Chertok, L., M. L. Mondzin, and M. Bonnaud 1963 Vomiting and the wish to have a child. *Psychosomatic Medicine* 25(1):13–18.

Davids, A., and W. Rosengren 1962 Social stability and psychological adjustment during pregnancy. *Psychosomatic Medicine* 24:579–583.

Deutsch, Helene   1945   *The psychology of women*, vol. 2. Grune and Stratton, New York.

Draw, F. L.   1961   The epidemiology of secondary amenorrhea. *Journal of Chronic Diseases* 14:396.

Dunbar, H. F.   1954   *Emotions and bodily changes*, 4th ed. Columbia University Press, New York.

Engels, W. D., C. J. Pattee, and E. D. Wittkower   1964   Emotional settings of functional amenorrhea. *Psychosomatic Medicine* 26(6):682–699.

Erickson, Marilyn T.   1965   Relationship between psychological attitudes during pregnancy and complications of pregnancy, labor and delivery. In *Proceedings of the 73rd annual convention of the American Psychological Association*, pp. 213–214.

Fisher, I. C.   1962   *Hypothalamic amenorrhea: Psuedocyesis*. In Kroger, W. S. (ed.), *Psychosomatic obstetrics, gynecology and endocrinology*. Thomas Publishing, Springfield, Ill.

Fisher, Ruth   1964   Severe post-partum reactions. *Pennsylvania Psychiatric Quarterly* 4(2):68–77.

Fried, P. N., A. E. Rakoff, R. R. Schopback, and A. J. Kaplan   1951   Pseudocyesis: A psychosomatic study in gynecology. *Journal of the American Medical Association* 145:1329.

Gill, M. M.   1943   Functional disturbances of menstruation. *Bulletin of the Menninger Clinic* 7:12.

Greaves, D., P. Green, and L. West   1960   Psychodynamics and psychophysiological aspects of pseudocyesis. *Psychosomatic Medicine* 22(1):24–31.

Grimm, Elaine R.   1962   Psychological investigation of habitual abortion. *Psychosomatic Medicine* 24(4):369–378.

Hochstaedt, B.   1960   Emotionally conditioned endocrine disorders. *Acta Psychotherapeutica* 8:31–43.

Jacobson, L., L. Kay, and A. Nilsson   1965   Post-partum mental disorders in an unselected sample: Frequency of symptoms and predisposing factors. *British Medical Journal* 1: 1940.

Javert, C. T.   1957   *Spontaneous and habitual abortion*. McGraw-Hill, New York.

Kelley, K., G. E. Daniels, J. Poe, L. Easser, and R. Monroe   1954   Psychological correlates with secondary amenorrhea. *Psychosomatic Medicine* 16:129.

Kelly, J. V.   1962   Effects of fear upon uterine mobility. *American Journal of Obstetrics and Gynecology* 83(5):576–581.

Kroger, W. S., and S. C. Freed   1951   *Psychosomatic gynecology*. Saunders, Philadelphia.

Loftus, T. A.   1962   Symposium: Psychogenic factors in anovulatory women: III. Behavioral and psychoanalytic aspects of anovulatory amenorrhea. *Fertility and Sterility* 13:20.

Piotrowski, A. A.   1962   Symposium: Psychogenic factors in anovulatory women: II. Psychological evaluation. *Fertility and Sterility* 13:11.

Reifenstein, E. C., Jr.   1946   Psychogenic or hypothalamic amenorrhea. *Medical Clinics of North America* 30:1103.

Weill, R. J., and C. Tupper   1960   Personality, life situation and communcation: A study of habitual abortion. *Psychosomatic Medicine* 22(6):448–455.

CHAPTER 5 DIFFERENCES BETWEEN MALE AND FEMALE BRAINS

Endocrines, Brain Function, and Sex Reversal

August, G. P., M. Tkachuk, and M. M. Grumbach 1969 Plasma testosterone-binding affinity and testosterone in umbilical cord plasma, late pregnancy, prepubertal children, and adults. *Journal of Clinical Endocrinology and Metabolism* 29(7):891–899.

Ford, C. S., and F. A. Beach 1951 *Patterns of sexual behavior.* Harper and Row, New York, pp. 244–247.

Gagnon, J. H. 1965 Sexuality and sexual learning in the child. *Psychiatry* 29:212–228.

Goy, R. W. 1968 Organizing effects of androgen on the behavior of rhesus monkeys. In Michael, R. P. (ed.), *Proceedings of the London conference: Endocrines and human behavior.* (Cited in Valenstein, 1968.)

Goy, R. W., and C. H. Phoenix 1963 Hypothalamic regulation of female sexual behavior; establishment of behavioral oestrus in spayed guinea pigs following hypothalamic lesions. *Journal of Reproduction and Fertility* 5(1):23–40.

Harris, G. W. 1964 Sex hormones, brain development and brain function. *Endocrinology* 75:627–647.

Levine, S. N. 1966 Sex differences in the brain. *Scientific American,* April, pp. 84–90.

Levine, S. N., and R. F. Mullins, Jr. 1966 Hormonal influences on brain organization in infant rats. *Science* 152:1585–1592.

Money, J. 1965 Psychosexual differentiation. In Money, J. (ed.), *Sex research: New developments.* Holt, Rinehart and Winston, Inc., New York, pp. 3–23.

Sheldon, W. H., and S. S. Stevens 1942 *The varieties of temperament.* Harper and Row, New York.

Valenstein, E. S. 1968 Steroid hormones and the neuropsychology of development, in Isaacson, R. L. (ed.), *The neuropsychology of development: A symposium.* Wiley, New York, 1968, pp. 1–39.

Young, W. C., R. W. Goy, and C. H. Phoenix 1964 Hormones and sexual behavior. *Science* 143:212–218.

Young, W. C., R. W. Goy, and C. H. Phoenix 1965 Hormones and sexual behavior. In Money, J. (ed.), *Sex research: New developments.* Holt, Rinehart and Winston, Inc., New York, pp. 176–196.

Infant Differences

Bayley, Nancy 1964 Consistency of maternal and child behaviors in the Berkeley growth study. *Vita Humana* 7:73–95.

Bayley, Nancy, and E. S. Schaefer 1964 Correlations of maternal and child behaviors with the development of mental abilities. *Monographs of the Society for Research in Child Development* 29(6):97.

Bell, R. Q. 1960 Relations between behavior manifestations in the human neonate. *Child Development* 31:463–477.

Bell, R. Q., and Naomi S. Costello 1964 Three tests for sex differences in tactile sensitivity in the newborn. *Biologia Neonatorum,* pp. 335–347.

Bell, R. Q., and Joan F. Darling 1965 The prone head reaction in the human neonate: Relation with sex and tactile sensitivity. *Child Development* 36(4):943–949.

Escalona, Sibylle K., and Grace M. Heider   1959   *Prediction and outcome.* Basic Books, New York.

Garn, S. M.   1957   Roentgenogrammetric determinants of body composition. *Human Biology* 29:337–353.

Garn, S. M.   1958   Fat, body size and growth in the newborn. *Human Biology* 30:265—280.

Harlow, H.   1962   The heterosexual affectional response system in monkeys. *American Psychology* 17(1):1–9.

Jensen, G. D., and Ruth A. Bobbitt   1968   Monkeying with the mother myth. *Psychology Today* 1(12):41.

Kagan, J., and M. Lewis   1965   Studies of attention in the human infant. *Merrill-Palmer Quarterly* 11 (2):95–127.

Kagan, J., and H. A. Moss   1962   From birth to maturity. Wiley, New York.

Knop, C.   1946   The dynamics of newly born babies. *Journal of Pediatrics* 29: 721–728.

Lewis, M., J. Kagan, H. Campbell, and J. Kalafat   1965   The cardiac response as a correlate of attention in infants. Paper read at the American Psychological Association, Chicago.

Lewis, M., J. Kagan, and J. Kalafat   1965   Patterns of fixation in the young infant. Paper read at the Society for Research in Child Development, Minneapolis, Minn.

Lewis, M., J. Kagan, and J. Kalafat   1966   Patterns of fixation in the young infant. *Child Development* 37(2):331–341.

Lewis, M., W. Meyers, J. Kagan, and R. Grossberg   1963   Attention to visual patterns in infants. Paper presented at the Symposium on Studies of Attention in Infants, American Psychological Association, August 1963, Philadelphia.

Lipsitt, L. P., and N. Levy   1959   Electrotactual threshold in the human neonate. *Child Development* 30:547–554.

Macfarlane, J. W., L. Allen, and M. P. Honzik   1954   *A developmental study of the behavior problems of normal children between twenty-one months and fourteen years.* University of California Press, Berkeley, Calif.

Murphy, Lois B., *et al.*   1962   *The widening world of childhood.* Basic Books, New York.

Schaefer, E. S., and Nancy Bayley   1963   Maternal behavior, child behavior, and their intercorrelations from infancy through adolescence. *Monographs of the Society for Research in Child Development* 28(3).

Silverman, J.   Attentional styles and the study of sex differences. In Mostofsky, D. (ed.), *Attention: contemporary studies and analysis.* Appleton, New York, in press.

Terman, L. M., and Leona E. Tyler   1954   Psychological sex differences. In Carmichael, L. (ed.), *A manual of child psychology.* 2nd ed. Wiley, New York, chap. 19.

The Transsexual

Benjamin, H. (ed.)   1966   *The transsexual phenomenon.* Julian Press, Inc., New York.

Green, R. 1966 Transsexualism: mythological, historical and cross-cultural aspects. In Benjamin, H. (ed.), *The transsexual phenomenon.* Julian Press, Inc., New York.

Hamburger, C. 1953 Desire for change of sex as shown by personal letters from 465 men and women. *Acta Endocrinologica* 14:361–375.

Hampson. J. S., and J. G. Hampson 1961 The otogenesis of sexual behavior in man. In Young, W. C. (ed.), *Sex and internal secretions,* vol. 2. Williams and Wilkins, Baltimore, Md., pp. 1401–1432.

Hastings, D. W., and J. A. Blum 1967 A transsexual research project at the University of Minnesota Medical School. *Lancet* 87(7).

Money, J., J. G. Hampson, and J. L. Hampson 1957 Imprinting and the establishment of gender role. *Archives of Neurology and Psychiatry* 77:333–336.

Pauly, L. 1965 Male psychosexual inversion: Transsexualism. *Archives of General Psychiatry* 13(2):172–181.

Stoller, R. J. 1967 Etiological factors in male transsexualism. *Transactions of the New York Academy of Science* 29(4):431–434.

Stoller, R. J. 1964 A contribution to the study of gender identity. *International Journal of Psychoanalysis* 45:220–226.

Stoller, R. J. 1965 Passing and the continuum of gender identity. In Marmor, J. (ed.), *Sexual inversion.* Basic Books, New York, pp. 190–210.

CHAPTER 6 SEX DIFFERENCES IN PERSONALITY AND LEARNING ABILITY

Anastasie, Anne 1958 *Differential psychology: Individual and group differences in behavior.* 3rd ed. Crowell-Collier-Macmillan, New York.

Anastasie, Anne, and J. Foley 1949 *Differential psychology: Individual and group differences in behavior.* 2nd ed. Crowell-Collier-Macmillan, New York.

Bakan, P., and R. Manley 1963 Effects of visual deprivation on auditory vigilance. *British Journal of Psychology* 54:115–119.

Bayley, Nancy 1964 Consistency of maternal and child behaviors in the Berkeley growth study. *Vita Humana* 7:73–95.

Bentzen, Frances 1963 Sex ratios in learning and behavior disorders. *American Journal of Orthopsychiatry* 33(1):92–98.

Bentzen, Frances 1966 Sex ratios in learning and behavior disorders. *The National Elementary Principal* 46(2):13–17.

Bridger, W. H., and Birns, Beverly 1963 Neonates' behavioral and autonomic responses to stress during soothing. In Wortis, J. (ed.), *Recent advances in biological psychiatry* 5:1–6.

Castaneda, A., and B. R. McCandless 1956 The children's form of the manifest anxiety scale. *Child Development* 27:317–326.

Cortes, J. B., and Florence Gatti 1966 Physique and motivation. *Journal of Consulting Psychology* 30(5):408–411.

Dayton, G. O., Margaret H. Jones, P. Aiu, R. A. Rawson, B. Steele, and M. Rose 1964 Developmental study of coordinated eye movements in the human infant: I. Visual acuity in the newborn. *Archives of Ophthalmology* 71:865–870.

Diamond, S. 1957 *Personality and temperament.* Harper and Row, New York.

Erikson, E. H.   1964   Inner and outer space: Reflections on womanhood. *Daedalus* Spring, pp. 582–606.

Erikson, E. H.   1951   Sex differences in the play configurations of preadolescents. *American Journal of Orthopsychiatry* 21:667–692.

Escalona, Sibylle K.   1963   Patterns of infantile experience and the developmental process. In Hoffer, W., *et al.* (eds.), *Psychoanalytic study of the child,* vol. 18. International Universities, New York, pp. 197–243.

Escalona, Sibylle K., and Grace M. Heider   1959   *Prediction and outcome.* Basic Books, New York.

Exline, R. W.   1962   Effects of need for affiliation, sex, and the sight of others upon initial communications in problem-solving groups. *Journal of Personality* 30(4): 541–556.

Exline, R. W.   1957   Group climate as a factor in the relevance and accuracy of social perception. *Journal of Abnormal and Social Psychology* 55:382–388.

Goldstein, M.   1959   The relationship between coping and avoiding behavior and responses to fear arousing propaganda. *Journal of Abnormal and Social Psychology* 58:247–252.

Grinsted, A. D.   1939   Studies in gross bodily movement. Ph.D. dissertation, Louisiana State University, unpublished.

Honzik, Marjorie P., and Jean W. Macfarlane   1963   Prediction of behavior and personality from 21 months to 30 years. Unpublished. Cited in Bayley, Nancy 1964   *Vita Humana* 7:73–95.

Kagan, J.   1965   Developmental studies of reflections and analysis. In Kidd, A. H., and J. L. Rivoire (eds.), *Conceptual development in children.* International Universities, New York.

Kagan, J., and M. Lewis   1965   Studies of attention in the human infant. *Merrill-Palmer Quarterly* 11(2):95–127.

Kagan, J., and H. A. Moss   1962   *Birth to maturity.* Wiley, New York.

Kagan, J., H. A. Moss, and I. Sigel   1963   Psychological significance of styles of conceptualization. *Monographs of the Society for Research in Child Development* 28(2).

Kelly, F. J., and C. S. Berry   1931   Special education: The handicapped and the gifted. White House Conference on Child Health and Protection. Appleton, New York.

Kessen, W., and M. Hershenson   1963   Ocular orientation in the human newborn infant. Paper read at the American Psychological Association, Philadelphia.

Kopel, D., and H. Geerded   1933   A survey of clinical services for poor readers. *Journal of Education and Psychology Monographs* 13:209–224 (Warwick and York, Baltimore, Md.)

L'Abate, L.   1960   Personality correlates of manifest anxiety in children. *Journal of Consulting Psychology* 24:342–348.

Lewis, M., J. Kagan, and J. Kalafat   1965   Patterns of fixation in the young infant. Paper read at the Society for Research in Child Development, Minneapolis, Minn.

Lewis, M., J. Kagan, H. Campbell, and J. Kalafat   1965   The cardiac response as a correlate of attention in infancy. Paper read at the American Psychological Association, Chicago.

Lippitt, R., and M. Gold   1959   Classroom social structures as a mental health problem. *Journal of Social Issues* 15:40–50.

McCall, R., and J. Kagan   1967   Stimulus-schema discrepancy and attention in the infant. *Journal of Experimental Child Psychology* 5(3):381–390.

McCarthy, Dorothea   1930   Language development of the preschool child. *Institute for Child Welfare Monographs* No. 4 (University of Minnesota Press, Minneapolis, Minn.).

McCarthy, Dorothea   1953   Some possible explanations of sex differences in language development and disorders. *Journal of Psychology* 35:155–160.

Maccoby, Eleanor E.   1966   Sex differences in intellectual functioning. In Maccoby, Eleanor E. (ed.), *The development of sex differences*. Stanford University Press, Stanford, Calif.

Maccoby, Eleanor E., Edith M. Dowley, J. W. Hagen, and R. Degerman 1965 Activity level and intellectual functioning in normal preschool children. *Child Development* 36(3):761–770.

Meyer, W. J., and G. G. Thompson   1963   Teacher interactions with boys as contrasted with girls. In Kuhlens, R. G., and G. G. Thompson (eds.), *Psychological studies of human development*. Appleton, New York.

Mills, A. W.   1947   Reports of a speech survey in Mount Holyoke, Massachusetts. *Journal of Speech Disorders* 7:161–167.

Murphy, G.   1958   *Human potentialities*. Basic Books, New York.

Murphy, Lois B.   1962   *The widening world of childhood*, Basic Books, New York.

Pishkin, V., and J. T. Shurley   1965   Auditory dimensions and irrelevant information in concepts identification in males and females. *Perceptual and Motor Skills* 20:673–683.

Rosenblith, Judy F.   1964   Prognostic value of neonatal assessment. Paper read at the American Psychological Association, Los Angeles.

Sarason, S.   1959   *Psychological problems in mental deficiency*. 3rd ed. Harper and Row, New York.

Schachtel, E. G.   1959   *Metamorphosis: On the development of affect, perception, attention and memory*. Basic Books, New York.

Schaefer, E. S., and Nancy Bayley   1963   Maternal behavior, child behavior, and their inter-correlations from infancy through adolescence. *Monographs of the Society for Research in Child Development* 28(3).

Schuell, H.   1947   *Differences which matter: A study of boys and girls*. Von Boeckman-Jones, Austin, Texas.

Sears, Pauline, and D. H. Feldman   1966   Teacher interactions. *The National Elementary Principal* 46(2):30–36.

Sigel, I., P. Jarman, and H. Hanesian   1963   Styles of categorization and their perceptual, intellectual, and personality correlates in young children. Merrill-Palmer Institute, unpublished.

Silverman, J.   Attentional styles and the study of sex differences. In D. Mostofsky (ed.), *Attention: Contemporary studies and analysis*. Appleton-Century-Crofts, New York, in press.

Sontag, L. W., C. T. Baker, and V. L. Nelson   1958   Mental growth and personality development: A longitudinal study. *Monographs of the Society for Social Research in Child Development* 23(2).

Spaulding, R. L.   1963   Achievement, creativity, and self-concept correlates of teacher-pupil transactions in elementary schools. Cooperative Research Project

No. 1352, U.S. Department of Health, Education, and Welfare; Office of Education, Washington, D. C.

Stechler, G.   1965   Attention and arousal in the infant. Paper read at the Society for Research in Child Development, Minneapolis, Minn.

Steinschneider, A., E. L. Lipton, and J. B. Richmond   1965   Stimulus duration and cardiac responsivity in the neonate. Paper read at the Society for Research in Child Development, Minneapolis, Minn.

Terman, L. M., and Leona E. Tyler   1954   Psychological sex differences. In Carmichael, L. (ed.), *A manual of child psychology.* 2nd ed. Wiley, New York, chap. 19.

Torrance, E. P.   1962   *Guiding creative talent.* PrenticeHall, Englewood Cliffs, N. J.

Walker, R. N.   1962   Body build and behavior in young children: I. Body build and nursery school teachers' rating. *Monographs of the Society for Research in Child Development* 27(3).

Witkin, H. A., R. B. Dyk, H. F. Faterson, D. R. Goodenough, and S. A. Karp   1962   *Psychological differentiation.* Wiley, New York.

Witkin, H. A., Helen B. Lewis, M. Herzman, Karen Machover, Pearl B. Meissner, and S. Wapner   1954   *Personality through perception.* Harper and Row, New York.

Witryol, S. L., and W. A. Kaess   1957   Sex differences in social memory tasks. *Journal of Abnormal and Social Psychology* 54:343–346.

CHAPTER 7   DEPENDENCE, PASSIVITY, AND AGGRESSION

Bach, G. R.   1945   Young children's play fantasies. *Psychological Monographs* 59(2).

Buss, A. H.   1963   Physical aggression in relation to different frustrations. *Journal of Abnormal and Social Psychology* 67:1–7.

Buss, A. H. and T. C. Brock   1963   Repression and guilt in relation to agression, *Journal of abnormal and social psychology* 66: 345-350.

Cosentino, F., and A. B. Heilbrun, Jr.   1964   Anxiety correlates of sex-role identity in college students. *Psychological Reprints* 14:729–730.

Dawe, Helen C.   1934   An analysis of 200 quarrels of preschool children. *Child Development* 5:139–156.

Deutsch, Helene   1944   *The psychology of women,* vol. 1. Grune and Stratton, New York.

Douvan, Elizabeth, and J. Adelson   1966   *The adolescent experience.* Wiley, New York.

Erikson, E. H.   1964   Inner and outer space: Reflections on womanhood. *Daedalus* Spring:582–606.

Goodenough, Evelyn W.   1957   Interest in persons as an aspect of sex differences in the early years. *Genetic Psychology Monographs.* 55: 287-323.

Gordon, J. E., and E. Smith   1965   Children's aggression, parental attitudes, and the effects of an affiliation-arousing story. *Journal of Personality and Social Psychology* 1:654–659.

Green, Elise H.   1933   Friendships and quarrels among preschool children. *Child Development* 4:236–252.

Hart, H.   1961   A review of the psychoanalytic literature on passivity. *Psychiatric Quarterly* 35:331–352.

Hattwick, Laberta A.   1937   Sex differences in behavior of nursery school children. *Child Development* 8:343–355.

Heilbrun, A. B.   1964   Social values: social behavior consistency, parental identification and aggression in late adolescence. *Journal of Genetic Psychology* 104: 138–146.

Kagan, J., and H. A. Moss   1962   *Birth to maturity*. Wiley, New York.

Lansky, L. M., V. J. Crandall, J. Kagan, and C. T. Baker   1961   Sex differences in aggression and its correlates in middle-class adolescents. *Child Development* 32:45–58.

McCandless, B. R., C. B. Bilous, and H. L. Bennett   1961   Peer popularity and dependence on adults in preschool age socialization. *Child Development* 32: 511–518.

McKee, J. P., and F. B. Leader   1955   The relationship of socioeconomic status and aggression to the competitive behavior of preschool children. *Child Development* 26:135–142.

Muste, Myra J., and D. F. Sharpe   1947   Some influential factors in the determination of aggressive behavior in preschool children. *Child Development* 18:11–28.

Pintler, Margaret H., Ruth Phillips, and R. R. Sears   1946   Sex differences in the projective doll play of preschool children. *Journal of Psychology* 21: 73–80.

Rapoport, A., and A. M. Chammah   1965   Sex differences in factors contributing to the level of cooperation in the prisoner's dilemma game. *Journal of Personality and Social Psychology* 2(6):831–838.

Sears, Pauline S.   1951   Doll play aggression in normal young children: Influence of sex, age, sibling status, father's absence. *Psychological Monographs* 65(6):iv, 42.

Sears, R. R.   1961   Relation of early socialization experiences to aggression in middle childhood. *Journal of Abnormal and Social Psychology* 63:266–492.

Sears, R. R., Eleanor E. Maccoby, and H. Levin   1957   *Patterns of child rearing*. Row, Peterson and Company, Evanston, Ill.

Sears, R. R., Lucy Rau, and R. Alpert   1965   *Identification and child rearing*. Stanford University Press, Stanford, Calif.

Terman, L. M., and Leona E. Tyler   1954   Psychological sex differences. In Carmichael, L. (ed.), *A manual of child psychology*. 2nd ed. Wiley, New York, chap. 19.

Walters, J., Doris Pearce, and Lucille Dahms   1957   Affectional and aggressive behavior of preschool children. *Child Development* 28:15–26.

Whiting, J., and Beatrice Whiting   1962   Personal communication. Cited by Oetzel, Roberta M., in the Bibliography in Maccoby, Eleanor E. (ed.), *The development of sex differences*. Stanford University Press, Stanford, Calif, 1966.

CHAPTER 8   IDENTIFICATION

Brown, D. G.   1958   Sex role development in a changing culture. *Psychology Bulletin* 55:232–242.

Douvan, Elizabeth   1960   Sex differences in adolescent character processes. *Merrill-Palmer Quarterly* 6:203–211.

Douvan, Elizabeth, and J. Adelson   1966   *The adolescent experience.* Wiley, New York.

Dubin, R., and Elizabeth R. Dubin   1965   Children's social perceptions: A review of research. *Child Development* 36(3):809–838.

Emmerich, W.   1962   Variations in the parent role as a function of the parent's sex and the child's sex and age. *Merrill-Palmer Quarterly* 8:3–11.

Emmerich, W., and F. Smoller   1964   The role patterning of parental norms. *Sociometry* 27:382–390.

Fenichel, O.   1945   *The psychoanalytic theory of the neuroses.* Norton, New York.

Goodenough, E. W.   1957   Interest in persons as an aspect of sex difference in the early years. *Genetic Psychology Monographs* 55:287–323.

Hartley, Ruth E.   1960   Children's concepts of male and female roles. *Merrill-Palmer Quarterly* 6(3):153–163.

Hoffman, Lois W.   1961   Effects of maternal employment on the child. *Child Development* 32:187–197.

Kagan, J.   1958   The concept of identification. *Psychology Review* 65(5):296–305.

Kagan, J., and H. A. Moss   1962   *Birth to maturity.* Wiley, New York.

Kohn, M. L.   1959   Social class and parental values. *American Journal of Sociology* 64:337–351.

Komarovsky, Mirra   1950   Functional analysis of sex roles. *American Sociological Review* 15:508–516.

Lynn, D. B.   1966   The process of learning parental and sex-role identification. *Journal of Marriage and the Family* 28(4):446–470.

Mussen, P., and E. Rutherford   1963   Parent-child relations and parental personality in relation to young children's sex-role preferences. *Child Development* 34(3):589–607.

Parsons, T.   1958   Social structure and the development of personality: Freud's contribution to the integration of psychology and sociology. *Psychiatry* 21:321–340.

Rabban, M.   1950   Sex-role identification in young children in two diverse social groups. *Genetic Psychology Monographs* 42:81–158.

Rosenberg, B. G., and B. Sutton-Smith.   1960   A revised conception of masculine-feminine differences in play activities. *Journal of Genetic Psychology* 95:165–170.

Rothbart, Mary, and Eleanor E. Maccoby   1966   Parents' differential reactions to sons and daughters. *Journal of Personality and Social Psychology* 4(3):237–243.

Sears, R. R., E. E. Maccoby, and H. Levin   1957   *Patterns of child rearing.* Harper & Row, New York.

Seward, Georgene H.   1964   Sex identity and the social order. *Journal of Nervous and Mental Disease* 139(2):126–137.

Slater, P. E.   1955   Psychological factors in role specialization. Ph.D. dissertation, Harvard University, unpublished.

Slater, P. E.   1961   Toward a dualistic theory of identification. *Merrill-Palmer Quarterly* 7(2):113–126.

Slote, Geraldine M.   1962   Feminine character and patterns of interpersonal perception. *Dissertation Abstracts* 23:1081.

CHAPTER 9   THE EGO AND SELF-ESTEEM

Cohen, Mabel B.   1966   Personal identity and sexual identity. *Psychiatry* 29(19):1–14.

Douvan, Elizabeth, and J. Adelson   1966   *The adolescent experience.* Wiley, New York.

Douvan, Elizabeth, and M. Gold   1966   Model patterns in American adolescence. In Hoffman, M. L., and L. W. Hoffman (eds.), *Review of child development research*, vol. 2. Russell Sage Foundation, New York, pp. 469–528.

Gutmann, D. L.   1965   Women and the conception of ego strength. *Merrill-Palmer Quarterly* 11(3):229–240.

Gutmann, D. L.   1968   Female ego styles and generational conflict. Paper presented at the Midwestern Psychological Association, 3 May 1968, Chicago.

McClelland, D. C.   1965   Wanted: A new self-image for women. In Lifton, R. J. (ed.), *The Woman in America.* Houghton Mifflin, New York, pp. 173–192.

Silverman, J.   Attentional Styles and the Study of Sex Differences, in Mostofsky, D. (ed), *Attention: Contemporary Studies and Analysis,* Appleton-Century-Croft, New York, in press.

CHAPTER 10   THE MOTIVE TO ACHIEVE

Atkinson, J. W.   1964   *An introduction to motivation.* Van Nostrand, Princeton, N. J.

Atkinson, J. W. (ed.)   1958   *Motives in fantasy, action and society.* Van Nostrand, Princeton, N. J.

Baruch, Rhoda   1966   *The interruption and resumption of women's careers.* Harvard Studies in Career Development, No. 50. Cambridge, Mass.

Baruch, Rhoda   1967   The achievement motive in women: Implications for career development. *Journal of Personality and Social Psychology* 5(3):260–267.

Bronfenbrenner, U.   1961   The changing American child—a speculative analysis. *Journal of Social Issues* 17:6–18.

Bronfenbrenner, U.   1961   Toward a theoretical model for the analysis of parent-child relationships in a social context. In Glidewell, J. (ed.), *Parent attitudes and child behavior.* Thomas Publishing, Springfield, Ill.

Crandall, Virginia, Rachel Dewey, W. Katowsky, and Anne Preston   1964   Parents' attitudes and behaviors and grade-school children's academic achievements. Journal of Genetic Psychology 104:53–66.

Crandall, Virginia, W. Katkovsky, and Anne Preston   1960   A conceptual formulation of some research on children's achievement development. *Child Development* 31:787–797.

Crandall, Virginia, W. Katkovsky, and Anne Preston 1960 Parent behavior and children's achievement development. Paper read at the American Psychological Association, Chicago.

Crandall, Virginia, W. Katkovsky, and Anne Preston 1962 Motivational and ability determinants of young children's intellectual achievement behaviors. *Child Development* 33:643–661.

Crandall, Virginia, Anne Preston, and Alice Rabson 1960 Maternal reactions and the development of independence and achievement behavior in young children. *Child Development* 31:243–251.

Crandall, Virginia, and Alice Rabson 1960 Children's repetition choices in an intellectual achievement situation following success and failure. *Journal of Genetic Psychology* 97:161–168.

Davis, R., and Virginia Olsen 1965 The career outlook of professionally educated women. *Psychiatry* 28:334–345.

Horner, Matina S. 1968 A psychological barrier to achievement in women—the motive to avoid success. Symposium presentation at the Midwestern Psychological Association, May 1968, Chicago.

Horner, Matina S. 1969 Fail: Bright women. *Psychology Today* 3(6):36.

Isaacson, R. L. 1964 The relationships between N achievement, test anxiety and curricular choices. *Journal of Abnormal and Social Psychology* 68:447–452.

Kagan, J., and H. Moss 1962 Birth to maturity. Wiley, New York.

Lipinski, Beatrice 1966 Sex role conflict and achievement motivation in college women. *Dissertation Abstracts* 26:4077.

McClelland, D. C., J. Atkinson, R. Clark, and E. Lowell 1953 *The achievement motive*. Appleton, New York.

McClelland, D. C. 1958 The importance of early learning in the formation of motives. In Atkinson, J. W. (ed.), Motives in fantasy, action and society. Van Nostrand, Princeton, N. J., pp. 437–452.

McClelland, D. C. 1958 Risk taking in children with high and low need for achievement. In Atkinson, J. W. (ed.), *Motives in fantasy, action and society.* Van Nostrand, Princeton, N. J., pp. 306–321.

McNeil, E. 1967 Memo to members of the executive committee and the graduate committee. The University of Michigan, 23 January 1967.

Mead, Margaret 1949 *Male and female: A study of the sexes in a changing world.* Morrow, New York.

National Manpower Council 1957 *Womanpower.* Columbia University Press, New York.

President's Commission on the Status of Women 1963 *Report of the Committee on Education,* October 1963.

Radcliffe Committee on Graduate Education for Women 1956 *Graduate education for women: The Radcliffe Ph.D.* Harvard University Press, Cambridge, Mass.

Rostow, Edna 1964 Conflict and accommodation. *Daelalus* 93(Spring).

Sanford, N. 1962 *The American college.* Wiley, New York.

Sears, Pauline S., and H. Levin 1957 Level of aspiration in preschool children. *Child Development* 28:317–326.

Sears, Pauline S. 1962 Correlates of need achievement and need affiliation and classroom management, self-concept and creativity. Stanford University, Laboratory of Human Development, unpublished.

Sears, R.   1963   Dependency motivation. In *Nebraska symposium on motivation*, Lincoln, University of Nebraska Press pp. 25–64.

Sontag, L. W., C. T. Baker, and Virginia A. Nelson   1958   Mental growth and personality development: A longitudinal study. *Monographs of the Society for Research in Child Development* 23(68).

Sundheim, Betty   1963   The relationships between *n* achievement, *n* affiliation, sex role concepts, academic grades, and curricular choice. *Dissertation Abstracts* 23:3471.

Taylor, R.   1964   Personality traits and discrepant achievement: A review. *Journal of Counseling Psychology* 11:76–82.

Tyler, F. B., Janet Rafferty, and Bonnie Tyler   1962   Relationships among motivations of parents and their children. *Journal of Genetic Psychology* 101:69–81.

Veroff, J.   1965   Theoretical background for studying the origins of human motivational dispositions. *Merrill-Palmer Quarterly* 11:1–18.

Veroff, J.   1969   Social comparison and the development of achievement motivation. In Smith, C. (ed.), *Achievement related motives in children*. Russell Sage Foundation, New York, pp. 46–101.

CHAPTER 11   CHANGES IN MOTIVES AND ROLES DURING DIFFERENT STAGES IN LIFE

Barron, F.   1955 The disposition toward originality. *Journal of Abnormal and Social Psychology* 51:478–485.

Baruch, Rhoda   1966   *The interruption and resumption of women's careers*. Harvard Studies in Career Development, No. 50. Cambridge, Mass.

Bem, D. J.   1970   *Beliefs, Attitudes, and Human Affairs*. Brooks/Cole, Belmont, Calif.

Cashdan, S., and G. S. Welsh   1966   Personality correlates of creative potential in talented high school students. *Journal of Personality* 34:445–455.

Dawson, Madge   1965   *Graduate and married*. University of Sydney, The Department of Adult Education (Sydney, Australia).

Friedan, Betty   1963   *The feminine mystique*. Norton, New York.

Getzels, J., and M. Csikszentmihalyi   1964   *Creative thinking in art students*. University of Chicago Press, Chicago.

Gurin, G., J. Veroff, and Sheila Feld   1960   *Americans view their mental health*. Basic Books, New York.

Guilford, J. R.   1967   Some theoretical views of creativity. In Helson, H., and W. Bevan, *Contemporary approaches to psychology*. Van Nostrand, Princeton, N. J., pp. 419–455.

Haimowitz, Natalie R., and M. L. Haimowitz   1966   What makes them creative. In Haimowitz, M. L., and Natalie R. Haimowitz (eds.), *Human development: Selected readings*, 2nd ed. Crowell, New York, pp. 34–43.

Hammer, E.   1964   Creativity and feminine ingredients in young male artists. *Perceptual and Motor Skills* 19:414.

Helson, Ravenna   1966   Personality of women with imaginative and artistic interests; the role of masculinity, originality, and other characteristics in their creativity. *Journal of Personality* 34:1–25.

Helson, Ravenna   1966   Narrowness in creative women. *Psychology Reports* 19:618.

Hilgarde, E. R.   1962   *Introduction to psychology.* Harcourt, New York.

McCormack, Thelma   1967   Styles in educated females. *The Nation* 23 (January):117.

Maccoby, Eleanor E.   1963   Woman's intellect. In Farber, S. M., and R. L. Wilson (eds.), *The potential of woman.* McGraw-Hill, New York, pp. 24–39.

Mannes, Marya   1963   The problems of creative women. In Farber, S. M., and R. H. L. Wilson (eds.), *The potential of woman.* McGraw-Hill, New York, pp. 116–130.

Maslow, A.   1954   *Motivation and personality.* Harper and Row, New York.

Parrish, J. B.   1961   Professional womanpower as a national resource. *Quarterly Review of Economics and Business* 1:54–63.

Parrish, J. B.   1962   Top level training of women in the United States, 1900–1960. *NAWDC Journal* 2:67–73.

Sanders, Marion   1965   The new American female: Demi-feminism takes over. *Harper's* July: 37–43.

Smith, Marguerite   1961   Compliance and defiance as it relates to role conflict in women. Ph.D. dissertation, The University of Michigan, unpublished.

United States Department of Labor.   1962   Fifteen years after college; a study of alumnae of the class of 1945. *Women's Bureau Bulletin* 283.

University of Minnesota Newsletter (February)   1963   The Minnesota plan for the continuing education of women.

Women's Bureau   1962   *Handbook on women workers.* Washington, D. C.

INDEX

Academic achievement, among women, 166
Achievement, 19
  behavior, 169
  changes in, 191–193
  motives in, 156–158, 172–176, 177–178
  need for, 168–172
Adolescence, achievement motives in, 177–178
  identification in, 147–153
  and sexual identity, 143
  and sexuality, 49–50
The Adolescent Experience, 147
Affiliation, motives for, 156–158
  need for, 168–172
Aggression, 13–14, 126–134
Allocentric, 164
Ambition, 18–19

Ambivalence, and psychosomatics, 74–75
  and young girls, 48–49
Amenorrhea, 77
Androgens, 22, 40–45, 84
  and neural tissue, 89
Androstenedione, 26
Anxiety, and pregnancy, 79
Autocentric, 164
Autonomic nervous system, 38

de Beauvoir, Simone, 147
Bem, Sandra and Daryl, 195
Biological force, 97
Bisexual identification, 140–142
Body type, and personality, 106–108
Bonepart, Marie, 7
Brain, sex-type of, 87–88
  sexual differentiation of, 84–86
Breast feeding, 80

Career choice, and motivation, 183–187

Castration, 6, 7

Castration anxiety, 16, 18–19

Children, achievement motives in, 172–176

Climacteric, 37–39

Clitoral masturbation, 46

Clitoral tip (glans), 61

Clitoris, 12, 41, 62
  and orgasm, 60–61

Coitus, adult ambivalence toward, 53
  motives for, 54–58
  perception of, 66–67

Conscience, 8

Corpus luteum, 23, 24

Creativity, and women, 202–205

Cultural determinism, 3

Dating, adolescent, 52

Defense mechanisms, 77

Denial, 77

Dependence, 114–123
  aggressive, 119
  emotional, 119, 120, 121
  instrumental, 119

Dependent behavior, 75, 76

Divorce, 213–214

Edema, 60, 61

Ego, 19
  development of, 155–156
  female, 154–155
  idealized, 8
  styles, 163–166

Endocrine glands, 22–26

Enovid, 35

Erikson, Erik, 9–10, 15

Eroticism, 40, 41
  psychological determination of, 66–69

Erotogenic stimuli, 64

Erotogenic zones, 61, 62

Estrogen, 22–24, 27, 35, 37–39, 42, 44

Eunuchs, 41

False pregnancy, 72, 77, 78

Feminine, defined, 100
  identity, 74–78
  pattern, 149–150
  role, 19

The Feminine Mystique, 147

Feminism, 145, 195–202

Feminization, 140

Follicle-stimulating hormone (FSH), 22, 23, 86

Franck, Kate, 15

Freud, Sigmund, 2
  opposition to, 9–13
  psychoanalytic theory of, 5, 6–9

Friedan, Betty, 147, 197–198

FSH, see Follicle-stimulating hormone

Ginzberg, Eli, 202

Gottschalk's Verbal Anxiety Scale, 30, 36

Handbook of Women Workers (1969), 210

Harris, Geoffrey W., 85

Hormones, sex, 22–26
  and sexual arousability, 40–46
  and sexual development, 84–87

Horner, Matina, 178–183

Horney, Karen, 5, 12

Hypothalamus, 22, 87

Identification, in adolescence, 147–153
  among children, 135–140

Identification, bisexual, 140–142
  and daughters, 138
  and sons, 139

Independence, 115, 116

Infant sex differences, 90–92

Inhibition, 52

IQ, and personality, 107

Ivey–Bardwick study, 37

Jealousy, 13

Johnson, Virginia E., 59–63, 65

Labor, and pregnancy, 79

Luteinizing hormone (LH), 23, 24, 86

Luteotropic hormone (LTH), 23, 24

Manifest Anxiety Scale, 79

Marital conflict scale, 79
Marriage, and identity, 210–211
  and trust, 215
Masculine, defined, 100
  role, 19
Masochism, 7–8, 14
Masters, W. H., 59–63, 65
Masturbation, childhood, 92
  clitoral, 6, 8
  genital, 16, 46
  vaginal, 45
Maternity, 15
  role of, 212
Maturity, and sex differences, 104–105
Menopause, 37–39, 78
Menstruation, 18
  cycle of, 22–26
  onset of, 47–50
Middle-class girls, and achievement, 157
Minnesota Multiphasic Personality Inventory (MMPI), 79
Minnesota Plan for Continuing Education of Women, 193
Mores, 53
  and oral contraceptives, 53–54
Motherhood, demands of, 194–195
Motivation, and career choice, 183–187
Motives in Fantasy, Action and Society, 167
Muscular activity, and children, 101–102

Narcissism, 14–15
Natural childbirth, 78
The New American Female, 198–199
Nonfeminine patterns, 150–151

Object choice, 62
Oedipal conflict, 16
Oedipus complex, 6, 8, 9
Oral contraceptives, 35–37
  and mores, 53–54
Orgasm, 8, 45
  clitoral, 11
  female, 58–62
  physical sensations of, 62
  physiology of, 59–62

psychological sensations of, 62
  vaginal, 11
Orgasmic response, levels of, 62–66
Ovarian regression, 37
Ovulation, 23, 24
Ovum, 23–24

Paige, Karen, 36, 37
Passivity, 123–126
  defined, 13
  and women, 7
Penis, 41, 42
  envy, 6, 7, 10
Personality, and IQ, 107
  qualities of, 42
  and sex differences, 99–101
Personality characteristics, of normal women, 73
  of psychosomatic patients, 74
Pfeifer, Carroll A., 85
Phallocentrism, 5
Pituitary gland, 22
Pregnancy, 33, 34
  and anxiety, 79
  and psychosomatic symptoms, 78
Premenstrual tension, 27–31
Professions, and women, 210
Progesterone, 23, 24, 27, 33–35, 44
Prostitution anxiety, 56
Pseudocyesis, 72, 77, 78
Psychosexual fusion, 29
Psychosomatic disorders, 70–71
  and feminine identity, 74–78
Puberty, 49–50
  and narcissism, 50

Reading skills, and sex differences, 109–112
Role behavior, 158–163
  conflict, 3–4
  expectations, 136
  feminine, 19
  masculine, 19

Sanders, Marion, 198
Secondary sex characteristics, 24
The Second Sex, 147
Sensory thresholds, 100

Sex, attitudes about, 52–53
    characteristics, 22
    differences, 3, 6, 16–18, 90–92
    hormones, 22–26, 87
    preoccupation with, 68
    reversal, 84
    role stereotype, 161
Sex Differences in Infancy and Early
    Childhood (table), 93
Sexual activity, 163–164
Sexual arousability, 63
    and hormones, 40–46
Sexual gratification, 62
Sexual identity, 62
    development of, 142–146
    and working mothers, 146–147
Sexuality, adolescent, 48, 49, 51–53
Socialization of Early Sex Differences
    (table), 94
Stuttering, 108
Subidentities, 156
Sublimation, 104, 105
Success, fear of, 178–183
Superego, 8
Survey Research Center, 193

Test anxiety, 180, 181

Testosterone, 22, 25, 26, 42–44, 84, 85
    and brain differentiation (sexual),
        85, 86
Thematic Apperception Test (TAT),
    57, 163, 164
Thompson, Clara, 12
Training the Woman to Know Her
    Place, 195
Transsexuals, 95–98

Uterine activity, 80–82

Vaginal frigidity, 66
Vaginal masturbation, 45
Vasocongestion, 60, 61
Verbal and spatial skills, 108–113
Vocational competition, 171

Wechsler Intelligence Scale for Chil-
    dren (WISC), 107
Women, and creativity, 202–205
    and passivity, 7, 13, 123–126
Work, return to, 190–195
Working mothers, and sexual identity,
    146–147

74 75 76 77 10 9